PERSON-FOCUSED HEALTH CARE MANAGEMENT

Donald L. Zimmerman, PhD, is a professor and program director of health care management at the University of New Orleans. Previously, he was collegiate professor and director of the Health Care Administration Program at the University of Maryland University College and executive director of the Center for Healthcare Management Studies at Fairleigh Dickinson University. He has also served as a visiting associate professor at the Sloan Program in Health Administration, Cornell University.

Before turning to full-time academic work in 1998, Dr. Zimmerman was actively engaged in national and state health policy developments as senior research sociologist at Research Triangle Institute International, senior policy analyst at the National Health Policy Forum at The George Washington University, and executive director of the Pennsylvania Health Care Cost Containment Council. Over his career, he has also provided advisory services to the U.S. Congress, federal and state government agencies, national associations, health care providers, and major health care consulting firms.

Dr. Zimmerman is a frequent speaker and has authored over 100 health care management and policy articles, technical reports, and professional presentations. He currently serves as vice chair of the Board of Directors of the International Commission for Dalit Rights and continues to work with senior clinical and policy leaders on a range of health care and related issues.

He earned his BA with distinction from the University of Washington and his MA and PhD in sociology from the State University of New York at Stony Brook.

Denise G. Osborn-Harrison, JD, MPH, is a health insurance specialist at the U.S. Department of Health and Human Services, Centers for Medicare and Medicaid Services in Baltimore, Maryland, and adjunct professor for George Mason University in Fairfax, Virginia. She is also a California licensed attorney and holds a master's degree in public health. Her specialty areas are corporate compliance for health care, health care reform, patient safety, medical liability reform, Medicaid expansion, and public health. She has provided consulting services to state agencies, federal agencies, nonprofits, and health care providers, both nationwide and abroad.

Dr. Osborn-Harrison began her teaching career more than 20 years ago while living in Los Angeles, California. She taught law classes for the University of California Los Angeles, Mt. San Antonio College, University of West Los Angeles, and Rio Hondo College. Currently, she serves as an adjunct professor for both undergraduate and graduate health care administration programs for George Mason University, University of Maryland University College, and Southern New Hampshire University. As a continuing education provider, she has trained nurses and physicians on how to conduct root cause analysis to support enterprise-wide patient safety and quality initiatives in a hospital setting.

PERSON-FOCUSED HEALTH CARE MANAGEMENT

A FOUNDATIONAL GUIDE FOR HEALTH CARE MANAGERS

Donald L. Zimmerman, PhD

Denise G. Osborn-Harrison, JD, MPH

Editors

SPRINGER PUBLISHING COMPANY
NEW YORK

Springer Publishing Company, LLC
11 West 42nd Street
New York, NY 10036
www.springerpub.com

Acquisitions Editor: Sheri W. Sussman
Compositor: Westchester Publishing Services

ISBN: 9780826194350
e-book ISBN: 9780826194367
Instructor's Manual ISBN: 9780826194534
PowerPoints ISBN: 9780826195593

Instructors' Materials: Qualified instructors may request supplements by e-mailing textbook@springerpub.com

16 17 18 19 20 / 5 4 3 2 1

The author and the publisher of this book have made every effort to use sources believed to be reliable to provide information that is accurate and compatible with the standards generally accepted at the time of publication. The author and publisher shall not be liable for any special, consequential, or exemplary damages resulting, in whole or in part, from the readers' use of, or reliance on, the information contained in this book. The publisher has no responsibility for the persistence or accuracy of URLs for external or third-party Internet websites referred to in this publication and does not guarantee that any content on such websites is, or will remain, accurate or appropriate.

Library of Congress Cataloging-in-Publication Data

Names: Zimmerman, Donald L. (Donald Lee), 1951– editor. | Osborn-Harrison, Denise G., editor.
Title: Person-focused health care management : a foundational guide for health care managers / Donald L. Zimmerman and Denise G. Osborn-Harrison, editors.
Description: New York, NY : Springer Publishing Company, LLC, [2017] | Includes bibliographical references and index.
Identifiers: LCCN 2016037160 (print) | LCCN 2016037901 (ebook) | ISBN 9780826194350 (hardcopy : alk. paper) | ISBN 9780826194367 (e-book) | ISBN 9780826194534 (instructors manual) | ISBN 9780826195593 (PowerPoints)
Subjects: | MESH: Patient-Centered Care—organization & administration | Patient Satisfaction | Professional-Patient Relations | Quality of Health Care—organization & administration | United States
Classification: LCC R727.3 (print) | LCC R727.3 (ebook) | NLM W 84.7 | DDC 610.69/6—dc23
LC record available at https://lccn.loc.gov/2016037160

Printed in the United States of America by Gasch Printing.

CONTENTS

SECTION III: PATIENT (PERSON) MANAGEMENT

CONCLUSION

CONTRIBUTORS

Robert F. Atlas, MBA, President, EBG Advisors, Washington, DC

Rolando R. Croocks, BA, RLLD, CLM, Top Laundry Executive, University of Michigan, Ann Arbor, Michigan

Judy E. Davidson, DNP, RN, FCCM, FAAN, University of California San Diego Health, San Diego, California

Sandy DeWeese, RN, MSN, Regional COO, IU Health, Southern Indiana Physicians, Bloomington, Indiana

Joanne Disch, PhD, RN, FAAN, Professor ad Honorem, University of Minnesota School of Nursing, Minneapolis, Minnesota

Sheldon Greenfield, MD, Donald Bren Professor of Medicine, School of Medicine, and Executive Co-Director, Health Policy Research Institute, University of California, Irvine, California

Martin J. Hatlie, JD, CEO, Project Patient Care, Chicago, Illinois

Richard H. Hughes IV, JD, MPH, Director, Health Policy & Strategy, and Professorial Lecturer, The George Washington University, Washington, DC

Kori Jones, MEd, PFCC Program Manager, Children's, Women's, and Psychiatry Services, University of Michigan Health System, Ann Arbor, Michigan

Sherrie H. Kaplan, PhD, MPH, Professor of Medicine and Anesthesiology & Perioperative Care, Assistant Vice Chancellor, Healthcare Evaluation and Measurement, School of Medicine, and Executive Co-Director, Health Policy Research Institute, University of California, Irvine, California

Barbara Malizzo, Member, MedStar Health Patient and Family Advisory Council for Quality and Safety

Robert Malizzo, Member, MedStar Health Patient and Family Advisory Council for Quality and Safety

Ziva Mann, MA, Patient Engagement Advisor, Cambridge Health Alliance and the Harvard Center for Primary Care, Cambridge, Massachusetts

Kathleen Martinez, MSN, RN, CPN, Clinical Policy Oversight Manager, Children's Hospital Colorado, Aurora, Colorado

Robert N. Mayer, PhD,[†] The Mayer-Rothschild Foundation, Kirtland, Ohio

---

[†] Deceased.

Giora Netzer, MD, MSCE, Associate Professor of Medicine and Epidemiology, University of Maryland School of Medicine, Baltimore, Maryland

Denise G. Osborn-Harrison, JD, MPH, Health Insurance Specialist, U.S. Department of Health and Human Services, Centers for Medicare and Medicaid Services, Baltimore, Maryland

Stacy Palmer, The Beryl Institute, Southlake, Texas

Kathryn E. Phillips, MPH, Former Program Director, Practice Transformation, Qualis Health, Seattle, Washington

Jennifer Reiter, PharmD, Ambulatory Pharmacist, IU Health, Southern Indiana Physicians, Bloomington, Indiana

James B. Rickert, MD, President, The Society for Patient Centered Orthopedics, and Assistant Clinical Professor, Indiana University School of Medicine, Indianapolis, Indiana

Jonathan R. Sugarman, MD, MPH, President and CEO, Qualis Health, Seattle, Washington

Colleen E. Sweeney, RN, BS, CSP, Founder and Owner, Sweeney Healthcare Enterprises, Ruskin, Florida

Ellen Grady Venditti, MS, RN, CPHRM, FASHRM, Risk Management and Patient Safety Consultant, Past-President, American Society for Healthcare Risk Management, Falmouth, Massachusetts

Charles R. Whipple, Esq., MHSA, Executive Vice President and Chief Legal Officer, Hallmark Health System, Inc., Melrose, Massachusetts

Jason A. Wolf, PhD, CPXP, The Beryl Institute, Nashville, Tennessee

Donald L. Zimmerman, PhD, Professor and Program Director of Health Care Management, University of New Orleans, New Orleans, Louisiana

PREFACE

This book reflects a collective effort by health care professionals, scholars, and policy makers to figure out how we can improve the personal experience of people who need and receive health care services.

The need for this volume was first formed not too long ago after I had been discharged from my local hospital after a complication during surgery led to an episode of "septic shock." Although I received excellent clinical care throughout a long and arduous stay in an intensive care unit, it was a dreadful personal experience.

Socrates reportedly said that the only true wisdom is in knowing you know nothing. If this is right, then I will never be wise because I will never forget what my difficult personal encounter with the U.S. health care system taught me from the viewpoint of the patient. And so I began to wonder—is it just me or do others also have such an awful time when they are treated only as patients rather than as people? And if that is the case, how might our system for producing, delivering, and paying for health care be better managed so that the people being treated as patients fare better than they currently do?

As conversations and discussions started about how to answer that question with my colleagues and experts around the country, the process of preparing this book became a very special opportunity to discover and start to understand a much broader and, in many ways, more difficult set of health care issues than I had ever considered before. Not only did each of these discussions bring a deep understanding and expertise about the personal experience of care to the discussion, many gave important and substantive contributions to the book based on their own professional and, in some cases, personal perspective.

So now the book is done and stands as a collective effort to encourage and support ongoing efforts to improve the personal experience of care. Whatever your role and responsibilities as a health care professional, it is hoped that you will not only learn from these pages but also be inspired to help create and support a more person-focused approach to all those in need of care and treatment.

In support of the text, an Instructor's Manual and classroom PowerPoints have also been prepared. **Qualified instructors can request these ancillaries by e-mail: textbook@springerpub.com.**

Finally, in all efforts like this, all errors of omission or other types are unintentional but remain the full responsibility of the lead editor.

Donald L. Zimmerman, PhD

My interest in participating as an editor for this book was personal and professional in nature. From a personal standpoint, my bout with cancer and experience with the medical profession associated with gaining wellness was the primary driver. Secondarily, my professional career as an attorney and health policy consultant has provided me with a good deal of insight that I feel compelled to share. Most importantly, however, is the inspiration that I receive from my health care administration and nursing students when I serve as an adjunct professor for various universities. It is their energy and eagerness to do the right thing that has moved me toward finding my voice and a platform to express myself.

I have become increasingly intrigued with understanding how the physician–patient relationship can be optimized. I continue to research how trust is cultivated and sustained within that relationship. I have a heightened interest in understanding and mastering the art of empathy in both my personal life and professional endeavors.

In a book titled *From Detached Concern to Empathy: Humanizing Medical Practice*, Jodi Halpern, MD, PhD (2001), explains how a person must be attuned to his or her own emotions so that he or she can understand the emotions of other people. She goes on to say that in medicine emotions play a cognitive role in helping patients recover from illness. She describes how empathy can take patients beyond just recovery because it equips them to "imagine a livable future." She also eloquently explains that:

> *Empathy involves learning from trial and error, or more precisely, accurate empathy depends upon a physician's openness to ongoing feedback and correction.* (p. 73)

It is my hope that learners reading this book will be inspired to be leaders in health care who understand the importance of listening and caring about patients as opposed to simply caring for them. This will require more than commonsense approaches. There are world-renowned experts who understand how to sensitize and influence people to move toward positive change. Tools are available to leaders to help them bring out the best people.

There are many difficult questions that many providers are grappling with across the nation pertaining to improving costs, quality of care, and access to care. Leaders in health care are making the connection between empathy and person-focused care to find answers to these questions. By leveraging their interdependence upon one another, patients and clinicians can truly place patients on the path toward a livable future.

Denise G. Osborn-Harrison, JD, MPH

REFERENCE

Halpern, J. (2001). *From detached concern to empathy: Humanizing medical practice.* New York, NY: Oxford University Press.

ACKNOWLEDGMENTS

We cannot express enough thanks to all those who have made this book possible. Starting with the early interest of Sheri W. Sussman of Springer Publishing Company in the still evolving concept of person-focused care, to each of the individual authors who graciously contributed a chapter, we offer a deeply appreciative thank you to each of you.

But as important as each of these people have been in putting this book together, we also wish to acknowledge the privileged weight of responsibility we have felt for all those people, in and out of the medical care system, who have not been properly recognized and treated with the care they deserve.

Finally, and perhaps most importantly, this book is dedicated to our spouses, families, friends, colleagues, and students who provided the unflinching support, ongoing encouragement, and constant hope that not only made surviving survivable and recovery imaginable, but made this book possible.

CHAPTER 1

OVERVIEW AND FRAMEWORK OF PERSON-FOCUSED HEALTH CARE MANAGEMENT

DONALD L. ZIMMERMAN

LEARNING OBJECTIVES

- Describe the distinction between people and patients and explain why it is so important.
- Understand and use a definition of person-focused health care management.
- Describe and use the four core principles of person-focused health care management as practical tools for improving the personal experience of care.

KEY TERMS

Intensive care unit (ICU)

Patient role

People versus patients

Person-focused care

Post–intensive care syndrome

Sepsis

One of the most important jobs one can have is being a health care manager. More than just being engaged in doing "a good job" of health care management, a health care manager is part of the team that is responsible for people's health. Whether the scenario is a new mother seeking care for her sick infant, a parent going in for surgery, or any of us wanting help in living a long and vigorous life, health care managers play a pivotal and trusted role in providing high-quality, easily accessible, and cost-efficient care to all.

A fundamental mistake that many of us in health care management make is confusing the people who need and use health care services with our patients.

1

This may sound a bit strange at first, because it happens so frequently and with such ease—both in class and in practice. As health care professionals, we are trained from the start to think about, analyze, manage, and improve the accessibility, cost, and quality of patient care (Kissick, 1994).

With our constant focus on patients, we are in danger of falling into a pattern of thinking that social philosophers and scientists of an earlier time called *reification* (Berger & Luckmann, 1966). When we reify something, we give an abstract concept a living and real existence and then forget that it is just an idea and not really real. Thus, our reified concept of "patient" does not get sick, get well, live, or die. However, real people who are being treated "as a patient" do all these things—for real.

At first, the difference between patients and people may not seem all that important. But, as I learned the hard way, this distinction underscores a set of critically important issues about the U.S. health care system that is so big and deep that it may force us to rethink how (and why) we should organize and provide health care services in the first place.

> The difference between patients and people may not seem all that important. But it underscores a set of critically important issues about the U.S. health care system that is so big and deep that it may force us to rethink how (and why) we should organize and provide health care services in the first place.

WHY THE DIFFERENCE BETWEEN PATIENTS AND PEOPLE IS SO IMPORTANT

First as a policy researcher and then as a professor and teacher, I have spent my entire professional career thinking about and working in the world of health care management. Thirty-three years. That is a pretty long time to be involved in health care without ever taking notice of the difference between patients and people. This all changed quite suddenly and dramatically about 2 years ago as a consequence of a surgical operation in my local hospital.

I had been admitted after a CT scan identified the need for a preemptive repair of a brewing aortic aneurysm. Although the surgery was somewhat complex, I was expected to be discharged and back at work within 3 weeks or so. As it turns out, it did not work out that way due to something called *septic shock*—a life-threatening organ dysfunction caused by an internal infection. In my case, a small perforation in one of my organs occurred during surgery. The resulting infection poisoned my body and led to the imminent threat that my vital organs would shut down and I would die.

> A CT scan combines a series of x-ray images taken from different angles and uses computer processing to create cross-sectional images, or slices, of the bones, blood vessels, and soft tissues inside your body. CT scan images provide more detailed information than plain x-rays do (Mayo Clinic, 2016).

> An aneurysm is a bulge or "ballooning" in the wall of an artery (MedlinePlus, 2016).

> *Sepsis* is a life-threatening organ dysfunction caused by a dysregulated host response to infection. *Septic shock* is a subset of sepsis in which particularly profound circulatory, cellular, and metabolic abnormalities are associated with a greater risk of mortality than with sepsis alone (Singer et al., 2016).

After spending 43 days in an intensive care unit (ICU) and 17 more days recuperating, I was finally discharged and able to return home. The experience had almost killed me and I was exhausted, frail, and extremely grateful to be alive. I was also living through a deep and crushing psychological trauma caused by my personal journey through this experience.

I had received excellent clinical care throughout my stay and will always be thankful to all involved for saving my life. But it was also true that the entire experience I had actually endured—as a person—is still very hard to describe through words on a page like these. Not because the words are unavailable, but because my experience required me to confront and live through a very real and forbidding world composed of my deepest fears, anguish, pain, and the near-complete collapse of hope. The specifics of my experience traumatized me and are still difficult to discuss with others (Ulman & Brothers, 1988). As another survivor said of her experience in ICU:

> *In reality, the ICU is a torture chamber. If you take away the knowledge that everyone is trying to keep you alive, what is actually happening can be pretty dreadful.* (Andrews, 2016b)

But stays in the ICU like this are not always spent in a state of fear and terror. For me, there were a few unexplainable moments of respite—like looking up through the periscope of a submarine—in which I was briefly able to see above the sea of drugs, tubes, machinery, and disembodied voices of my caregivers (Andrews, 2016a; Sepsis Alliance, 2016). What I saw during those precious moments forced me to look at the U.S. health care system in a very different and very new way.

At the heart of these brief flashes of clarity about what was happening to me was the cold observation that there was an almost complete disconnect between all the clinical things that the "health care system" was doing to me as a "patient" and all the emotions, thoughts, worries, nightmares, dreams, hopes, and fears of what was actually happening to me—inside the body being treated as a patient. Although the health care system was, indeed, doing almost a heroically good clinical job in keeping me alive, it was also very clear to me that no one seemed to care, even a little, that I was having a truly terrible experience as a real person having to endure their efforts to save my life.

At the time, I felt like I was silently screaming about the obvious. Cannot anyone see my pain and suffering? Do you not understand how awful this is down here inside your patient? Does not anyone actually care about me? Those tough and terrible times in what I learned later is called "ICU delirium" caused many extended moments when I felt it could not get any worse, and then it did.

> ICU delirium is "an acute and fluctuating disturbance of consciousness, and cognition is a common manifestation of acute brain dysfunction in critically ill patients, occurring in up to 80% of the sickest intensive care unit (ICU) populations" (Girard, Pandharipande, & Ely, 2008).

As my clinical situation finally hit the tipping point to gradual recovery and the real world started to become more and more distinct from my hallucinations, I began to collect more and more personal evidence about the same glaring gap between the purely clinical care I was receiving and my personal experience of that care. Whether it was during interactions with clinical staff, while receiving specific services, or when speaking with physicians—all who interacted with me seemed to be participating in a separate conversation "about" me rather than "with" me. It was not that all the people involved in taking care of me were not friendly (though there were some who were decidedly not), it was as if almost all our encounters were part of a "reality" show in which everyone but me had already read the script and knew his or her roles.

And as I lay there day after day, I slowly became convinced that the difference between the "official" clinical story of those providing my care and "my" personal story of how this care was actually being experienced was not just an issue related to my particular situation, but reflected a much bigger problem, deeply rooted in the very workings of the health care system itself.

The problem was not so much with the nature of the clinical care that was being provided as with the routine, everyday ways in which the unique and special characteristics of people like me were reduced and marginalized into a reified concept and predefined set of roles that defined a generalized type of "patient" with a given diagnosis and treatment protocol. This reduction of real people into the role of patient not only defined what would happen to a given person while being treated as a patient, but also prevented the personal experience of that care from being incorporated into that patient's clinical progression through a given sequence of treatment. It was not that those taking care of me in the ICU unit were heartless, callous, and mean. It was that all they took care of was an abstract concept of the patient—not me, the real person who was trying to survive inside what they were doing to me as their patient.

> The problem was not so much with the nature of the clinical care as with the routine, everyday ways in which the unique and special characteristics of people like me were reduced and marginalized into a reified concept and predefined set of roles that defined a generalized type of "patient" with a given diagnosis and treatment protocol.

When I was finally able to return home to start my convalescence from my experience in the ICU, I was unable to walk, dangerously frail, had a massive and still open wound in my belly, and was suffering psychologically with what I later learned is called "post–intensive care syndrome" (Huggins, Stollings, Jackson, &

Sevin, 2015). Similar to posttraumatic stress disorder (PTSD), I knew that I had been thoroughly beaten up but I had little understanding and very few painless memories of exactly who or what had done the beating (Wintermann et al., 2015).

But I also knew that the value of answering my questions about what had happened to me was just one example of something that was likely happening to almost everyone who has their "personhood"—their living sense of their own self—systematically reified and "reduced" into the limited role of a "patient" within the U.S. health care system.

And so, I asked the following question:

How might the entire system for producing, delivering, and paying for health care be better managed so that the people being treated as patients fare better than they currently do?

This book has provided the format and platform for bringing together experts from different disciplines of health care management to carefully examine this question and explore different approaches to answering it. But this book is more than a volume of chapters. It is also a map into a territory that is increasingly being explored but remains new to many. This is a territory that we have broadly defined as "person-focused" care.

As a starting point for understanding the perspective of this approach to health care management, the following sections provide a beginning definition and an outline of four of the most important core principles of person-focused health care management.

WHAT IS PERSON-FOCUSED HEALTH CARE MANAGEMENT?

As I slowly started to regain my footing after my terrible experience in the ICU, not only did I start to physically heal, I began to research and meet others with a wide range of professional interests and different projects intended to improve the overall experience of the care. Indeed, as the chapters for this book grew, a broad definition began to evolve that helped to unify these different efforts as examples of something that can be called "person-focused care."

In general, person-focused care starts with the purposeful escalation of the lived experience of the person receiving or needing care into a management priority for all involved in providing that care.

> In general, person-focused care starts with the purposeful escalation of the lived experience of the person receiving or needing care into a management priority for all involved in providing that care.

This means that a person-focused approach can be used in any system of care by anyone willing and able to simply look through the standard socially constructed role and reified use of the "patient" to take account of the underlying subjective experience of the actual person who is receiving that care.

A few words need to be said on the choice of terms before proceeding further. Although many are concerned about many of the same issues as person-focused care, there is also considerable debate and discussion of exactly how to name and define it (Mavis et al., 2014). For example, such terms as *patient activation, patient alliance, patient collaboration,* and *patient engagement* (and *empowerment, involvement,* and *sharing*) are all in common use as a means of increasing the importance of the patient in a clinical care setting (Mavis et al., 2014). Although these different terms suggest important theoretical distinctions in discussions about the importance of the patient, they all can easily hide the real person inside a standard role of patient and deflect our ability to focus on what that person is actually experiencing within that patient role.

"Person-focused" care is precisely intended to break through the standard role of the patient in order to address the real person trapped inside that role when he or she is being treated as a patient.

The same textual limitation can also be found in the notion of "patient-centered care." Since the groundbreaking report of the Institute of Medicine, an emphasis on the patient has been repeatedly linked to better health outcomes, quality of care, and cost savings (Rickert, 2012).

The importance of the patient in health care might seem obvious to some, but in a system that relies on the clinical authority of medical care providers to deliver care through the institutional power of organizations like hospitals, physician offices, and long-term care facilities, the role of the patient—no matter how "centered" in that delivery system—can be lost or obscured in the routine institutional activities required for a highly complex health care system to function.

Although there are a wide range of important initiatives and projects aimed at elevating the importance of the patient to be at the center of care, these efforts do not necessarily exhaust or fully define the primary elements of a person-focused approach to health care management.

While sharing a natural affinity with the clinical delivery model of patient-centered care, person-focused care is a *management perspective—not* an approach for how the clinical practice of care should be organized.

> While sharing a natural affinity with the clinical delivery model of patient-centered care, person-focused care is a *management perspective—not* an approach for how the clinical practice of care should be organized.

Rather, the idea behind person-focused care is to shift the lens and focus of health care management from looking at the patient as the center of care to looking at the real person locked inside that social role by the highly complex and multidimensional institutions that deliver health care—regardless of the model of delivery in use.

FOUR CORE PRINCIPLES OF PERSON-FOCUSED HEALTH CARE MANAGEMENT

There are two goals in outlining the core principles of a person-focused approach to health care management.

First, taken as a whole, the four core principles help to frame a general perspective, or viewpoint, for incorporating the personal experience of care into the everyday management responsibilities of health care professionals. Whether working on the clinical or administrative side of health care, the perspective of person-focused care helps managers throughout a health care organization routinely incorporate awareness into their decision making of how each individual being treated is feeling, thinking, interpreting, and understanding his or her experience as a patient.

Second, each principle is intended to serve as a practical sensitizing tool for escalating the importance of the personal experience of care into a priority for all involved in managing that care. In this sense, each of the four basic principles of person-focused care is introduced as a simple assertion that can also serve as a "slogan" or "motto" that can be used to help remind health care managers about the importance of the personal experience of the patient in a wide variety of circumstances. As such, the core principles are not designed, proposed, or projected to be definitive canons or fixed tenets of a theory or doctrine, but rather as the starting point for further development of a more person-aware approach to health care management.

> Each principle of person-focused care can serve as a practical sensitizing tool for prioritizing the personal experience of care for all involved in managing that care. It can also serve as a "slogan" or "motto" to help remind health care managers about the importance of the personal experience of the patient in a wide variety of circumstances.

Principle One: The Patient Is Not a Person

The power of the label of "patient" to limit our vision of the person receiving treatment has been directly linked to the current era in which economic, philosophical, and technological advances have transformed medicine, doctoring, and the doctor–patient relationship into "providers," "patients," and "customers" (Egnew, 2009).

Originally, the word *patient* meant "one who suffers" (Neuberger, 1999). The meaning of the word has now been inverted so that the focus is no longer the individual experience of suffering but rather one who receives health care services. This inversion changes the directionality of the word *patient*. The person's experience of suffering is no longer at the center of the definition; instead, the core of the definition is the services provided to that person.

The current metaphor externalizes the experience of the patient from what is being experienced inside the life space of the individual to what is being experienced as a series of acts by others that are directed to that person's suffering. It shifts the heart of the story from the personal suffering of the patient to those individuals who provide care to that patient.

Once the patient's suffering has been abstracted away from personal experience into the world of others, the personal experience is transformed into a patient's diagnosis and then treated separately from any direct concern about the personal experience of that care.

This abstraction is of particular importance as health care moves boldly into a newly emerging future of increased use of such technologies as robotic surgery, precision medicine, smartphone apps, and the Internet of Things (Forbes, 2015). Although the promise of such technologies is high, they also portend a future that is less and less connected to human interaction between the internal life of a patient and specific caregivers. This means that as health care professionals, we need to make sure that we do not ever forget that we are providing care to real people having real experiences of the care that we are managing—regardless of the technology being used.

The escalation of the personal experience as a central component in patient care can be accomplished by anyone within any system of care who simply "deflates" the customary connotation of "patient" and allows the actual person living inside that institutionalized role the opportunity to be present within the given clinical system. As referenced earlier, such a deflation of the patient role may occur though such concepts as patient activation, collaboration, engagement, and the like, but this is only the first step in a larger process that fully recognizes that the patient is not a person. The patient is a role that holds, hides, and prevents the real person inside that role from emerging as a central component of the U.S. health care system.

> The escalation of the personal experience as a central component in patient care can be accomplished by anyone within any system of care who simply "deflates" the customary connotation of "patient" and allows the actual person living inside that institutionalized role the opportunity to be present within the given clinical system.

Principle Two: "Caring About" Is a Prerequisite to Managing the "Caring For" Patients

Let's start this section with a very basic question for you to think about:

Why do you want to build a career in health care?

There are many answers to this question, including gaining access to a good job, a solid paycheck, and a long-term career. There is nothing wrong with these answers, but if all a person was interested in was the money, there are many, many other professional opportunities that offer a much easier road to professional success. For example, the field of "wealth management services" offers the promise of a straight-line approach to riches right in its very name.

No, it is not just about the money for health care professionals. There is something else going on underneath the surface that seems to have its own special calling to those who are disposed to hear it.

This common calling to all true health care professionals—whether on the clinical or management side of the equation—is the clear sound of others calling for their help in a time of need.

Whether it is on the front lines of a community emergency, in the conference rooms of executives, or in the supply rooms of a hospital, the importance of caring about those who need medical attention should be self-evident; this belief and ethical commitment links all health care management professionals into a common bond. This common bond of caring is firmly echoed in the most basic ethics of health care management, as codified by the American College of Healthcare Executives (ACHE):

> *The fundamental objectives of the healthcare management profession are to maintain or enhance the overall quality of life, dignity and well-being of every individual needing healthcare service and to create a more equitable, accessible, effective and efficient healthcare system.* (ACHE, 2011)

The health care field provides a wide variety of professional opportunities for all kinds of caring—whether it be for an individual patient, those without access to care, or everyone in one's community, nation, and the world. But with such wide range of possibilities, what does it really mean to care about others?

The kind of caring at the heart of health care management involves more than just "showing" someone that you care, clicking "like" on a Facebook post, tweeting a sympathetic comment, or participating in a fund-raising event for a given cause. Caring, in its most important sense, stands at the center of the health care profession as an active effort to bring relief, hope, and assurance to all those who trust you with their lives and overall well-being.

There are many barriers to breaking through to the person inside the patient role that are "built into" the very fabric of the U.S. health care system. In a more formal sense, these barriers are composed of the matrix of organizationally defining rules, procedures, and routine social interactions that make up the day-to-day activities of our system of care. Our system of care is a "system" precisely because it is able to automatically reduce the natural, presenting complexity of a real person into a "patient" who can then be treated by people, just like you, who have been equally reduced into their system-appropriate roles of doctors, nurses, managers, and patients.

> Our system of care is a "system" precisely because it is able to automatically reduce the natural, presenting complexity of a real person into a "patient" who can then be treated by people, just like you, who have been equally reduced into their system-appropriate roles of doctors, nurses, managers, and patients.

These mutually defining roles of patient and medical provider work together to create specific experiences for the individual people locked into the roles of patient and health care professional and have long been noted by medical sociologists (Mechanic, 1990). Using Goffman's classic analysis of "total institutions" as a starting point (1961), here are some baseline observations about the day-to-day health care operations that have absolutely nothing to do with the actual people delivering or receiving care:

- There is a highly proscribed social distance between the patient and the clinician that is created by rules of clinical professionalism and objectivity and the subservient needs of the patient.

- There is an institutional structure that standardizes care for each individual patient regardless of the individual providing it.

- A series of clinically related, formalized points of communication and modes of personal contact is present between the clinical staff and the patient.

- The rules, protocols, and schedules for delivering care are provided independently of any specific input from the person receiving those services. For example, feeding, sleeping, social schedules, and other routine behavior under control of the individual in everyday life are eliminated and replaced by standardized organizational processes that are independent of the person's choices.

- Admission and intake procedures literally strip the individual of his or her uniqueness during the transition process required to become a patient; for example, the assignment of patient numbers, the use of gowns, and the summation of the individual condition into generalized clinical categories and expectations.

- The creation and use of written reports of the person's condition and progress through the clinical system by clinical staff are carried out without editorial feedback from the person in question.

- The elimination of professional, educational, and familial identities by a single institutional identity defined by the person's clinical status occurs.

- The discharge of patients is based on clinical requirements that are independently established and implemented without the individual input of the person.

- The definition of "good and bad patients" is based on compliance with institutional expectations of behavior—including not complaining, passive acceptance of all clinical protocols—regardless of its actual necessity, and not asking for more services than offered.

- There are many life-threatening events, threats, and little tragedies that are systematically viewed as part of the domain of "public health" and are therefore ignored as urgent and important health care issues by those "inside" the traditional boundaries of the "medical care system."

In making these observations, it is recognized that many involve clinical and organizational behaviors that are absolutely necessary to provide any level of care within the current configuration of the U.S. health care system. Although the role of the patient may be a structural necessity in the current model of care, what is actually being experienced by the person inside that patient role does not need to be so bad, nor must its system of delivery always be so structured.

> The U.S. health care system is daunting in size, complex in operation, and moored in seemingly endless political debate. Are we ready to concede that the current organizational and clinical systems for producing health care in our nation are the best we can do?

Health care professionals are often faced with day-to-day situations involving life, death, pain, and sorrow. Being personally engaged in such highly emotional situations can easily lead to poor judgment, emotional fatigue, and burnout. In response, health care organizations may default to a professional culture that reflects a lack of interest, nonchalance, and disinterest in the patient experience.

But such cold professionalism does not align with the fundamental purpose of health care organizations to provide care to those in their time of need.

Person-focused care posits the central importance of caring about those who need medical and more generalized health care attention as a central belief that links all health care professionals—whether within a medical care system or working on improving the public's health—into a common professional bond.

This commitment to care is at the heart of a "person-focused" approach to health care management.

Principle Three: Quality of Care Is More Than Just a Clinical Outcome

People receiving health care services are not there just to be treated clinically. They are there as an event in their lives. "Clinical" care is simply one episode along the ongoing flow of life for a person who has encountered his or her own issues of morbidity and mortality. Measuring the "quality of care" by clinical outcomes alone fails to account for the much larger personal experience of being sick, treated, discharged, and then left alone to make sense of the whole "being sick" experience.

> "Clinical" care is simply one episode along the ongoing flow of life for a person who has encountered his or her own issues of morbidity and mortality. Measuring the "quality of care" by clinical outcomes alone fails to account for the much larger personal experience of being sick, treated, discharged, and then left alone to make sense of the whole "being sick" experience.

The "outcome of clinical care" is simply a point of external measurement along the ongoing flow of a personal encounter with issues of morbidity and mortality. This means from the very point of a person contacting a health care professional for assistance to, in some cases, the rest of that person's life, the "outcome" of the care actually reviewed will be a meaningful event in that person's life.

Although all health care is focused on the health of others, often times other considerations can get in the way of caring about what is actually going on in the lives of these "others" (Cleary, 2012).

Caring about others can take a wide variety of forms. For example, one can *care about* people who are suffering as a group because of some type of common set of events, circumstances, or personal characteristics that prevent them from fulfilling their full potential as unique and special people. One can care about specific actions that are aimed at improving the underlying conditions that create harm and are unhealthy situations in the first place.

So, for example, if we look at the impact the over $3 trillion paid into the U.S. health care system annually has on people's overall health, we can then start to ask questions about whether or not all Americans are receiving quality health care services in return for spending more than twice the per capita average of the other developed countries (The Commonwealth Fund, 2015).

Let's look at some data about the "quality" of health care people in need of care are actually receiving in and out of the "medical" part of our health care system.

- **Medical errors:** At a minimum, high-quality health care is care that does not harm patients, particularly through medical errors (Van Den Bos et al., 2011). The true number of premature deaths associated with preventable harm to patients is estimated to be as high as 400,000 per year (James, 2013).

- **Preventable deaths:** Nearly one in three deaths in the United States each year is caused by heart disease and stroke. At least 200,000 of these deaths could have been prevented through changes in health habits, such as stopping smoking, more physical activity, and less salt in the diet; community changes to create healthier living spaces, such as safe places to exercise and smoke-free areas; and managing high blood pressure, high cholesterol, and diabetes. More than half of preventable heart disease and stroke deaths happen to people younger than 65 (Centers for Disease Control and Prevention [CDC], 2013).

- **Adverse events:** The concept of "adverse event" describes harm to a patient as a result of medical care. More than one in five Medicare beneficiaries experienced adverse events during their stays in a skilled nursing facility (U.S. Department of Health and Human Services, 2016).

- **Post-discharge PTSD:** PTSD is often thought of as a symptom of warfare, major catastrophes, and assault. It is rarely considered in patients who survive a critical illness and stay in the ICU. One quarter of ICU survivors are estimated to suffer from PTSD (Bienvenu et al., 2015).

- **Infant and maternal mortality:** The United States ranks behind most European countries as well as Japan, Korea, Israel, Australia, and New Zealand in infant mortality (MacDorman, Mathews, Mohangoo, & Zeitlin, 2014). U.S. women are more likely to die during childbirth than women in any other developed country (Save the Children, 2015).

- **Mental health:** Approximately 11.1 million adults aged 18 or older (4.9% of adults) reported an unmet need for mental health care in the past year. The overall suicide rate rose by 24% from 1999 to 2014 (Curtin, Warner, & Hedegaard, 2016).

- **Low health literacy:** About one third of American adults have limited health literacy. However, among many population subgroups, including older adults and some racial/ethnic minorities, the rate exceeds 50%, leading to patient confusion, more hospitalizations, worse health status, and higher health care costs (Weiss, 2014).

- **Adherence:** Nonadherence to medications is estimated to cause 125,000 deaths annually. Statistically, the odds of patient adherence are 2.26 times higher if a physician communicates well. This translates into more than 183 million medical visits that need not take place if strong interpersonal physician/patient communication occurs (Zolnierek & DiMatteo, 2009).

- **Place of death:** Despite the fact that more than 80% of Medicare benefi-ciaries aged 65 and older would want to die at home, in 2013, one third of 1,904,640 deaths among persons aged 65 and older in the United States occurred in the hospital (CDC WONDER, 2015).

And to further the point, here are some additional data from the CDC (2016):

- Each year, more than 2 million illnesses and about 23,000 deaths are caused by antibiotic resistance.
- More than 75 people die every day in the United States from overdosing on prescription drugs.
- More than 1.2 million Americans live with HIV infection, and one in seven is unaware of his or her HIV status.
- One in six children in the United States have one or more developmen-tal disabilities or other developmental delay.
- About 53,000 workers die each year from work-related illnesses.

In reading over this list, it is easy to gloss over many of these facts and fig-ures as just numbers. If we slow down just a bit so we can really think about the lived realities of the real people that these numbers summarize, it is hard to overlook how the U.S. health care system is failing to address millions of little personal tragedies by not providing quality health services to those in desper-ate need of care.

> If we slow down just a bit so we can really think about the lived realities of the real people that these numbers summarize, it is hard to overlook how the U.S. health care system is failing to address millions of little personal tragedies by not providing quality health services to those in desperate need of care.

A person-focused approach to quality forces us to look far beyond the tech-nical consequences of clinical care to the general overall impact our massive financial investment in health care has on people within and without the formal "medical" boundaries of the health care system.

To fully align management with the four principles of person-focused care, health care professionals must ensure that each person in need of care, whether currently in the in health care system or not, receives the right kind of personal attention to fully address his or her needs. This means that person-focused managers are not only sensitive to the personal experience of patients, but also to all those who need care and treatment but are unable to gain access to it.

Principle Four: Every Health Care Professional Has an Impact on the Personal Experience of Care

Over the last decade and more, the delivery of health care services has been increasingly viewed as a complex, interdependent "system of care" (Ferlie & Shortell, 2001). Such a systems approach to health care has contributed greatly to our appreciation of how to make systematic changes to health systems to improve the quality, efficiency, and effectiveness of patient care (Agency for Healthcare Research and Quality [AHRQ], 2015).

Describing the parts, interconnections, and purpose, Roemer (1991) defined a health system as "the combination of resources, organization, financing and management that culminate in the delivery of health services to the population" (p. 31).

The location of many health care management programs in business colleges and schools has likely encouraged such systems-level thinking to be primarily concerned with how health care organizations can best "manage the allocation and flow of human, material, and financial resources and information in support of care teams" (Reid, Compton, Grossman, & Fanjiang, 2005).

But with this increased awareness of the management structure, functions, and connections among each part of the health care system, it can be easy to forget that "systems," no matter how well managed, never, ever actually provide care to people. Real people do that for other real people—regardless of their function, role, or where they may "fit into the system" (Nadler & Tushman, 1982).

> Despite increased awareness, it can be easy to forget that "systems," no matter how well managed, never, ever actually provide care to people. Real people do that for other real people—regardless of their function, role, or where they may "fit into the system."

This means that no matter what "systems-level" task or job an individual may have within a given health care organization, everything that person actually does contributes, either directly or indirectly, to the personal experience of people in need of or receiving care. For example, consider how each of the following classic functions of health care management can have an important consequence on the personal experience of care (Longest, Rakich, & Darr, 2000).

- **Planning:** This function requires the manager to set a direction and determine what needs to be accomplished to best improve the personal experience of care.

- **Organization:** The overall design of a given health care organization, division, unit, or service must ensure that the lived experience of the person receiving care is routinely escalated into a management priority for all involved in providing that care.

- **Staffing:** All members and employees of a given organization should be hired, developed, and rewarded based on their skills, knowledge, and ability to improve the personal experience of care.

- **Controlling:** Clear and present efforts must be in place to ensure that policies and models of practice supporting and enhancing the personal experience of care are in place and appropriate actions can be taken to continually correct and improve such care.

- **Directing:** Effective leadership, motivation, and communication aimed at improving the personal experience of care are needed throughout health care organizations and the larger community.

- **Decision making:** All decision making related to the provision of health care services, regardless of whether it is at the individual, community, national, or global level, should include the consideration of its impact on the personal experience of care.

Translating these key, core functions into a person-focused approach to health care management means that every individual with the responsibility to plan, organize, staff, control, direct, or make decisions regarding the care of others must:

- Understand the impact of management decisions on the personal experience of clinical care.

- Elevate the importance of the personal experience of care into the management of that care.

- Actively work to improve each dimension of his or her management responsibilities to improve the personal experience of care.

- Expand the importance of the personal experience of the patient into a key point of coordination between clinical care delivery and nonclinical managerial decision making in order to improve the people's overall health within and without the medical care system.

CONCLUSION

One of the easiest and most fundamental mistakes a health care manager can make is to confuse the people who use and need health care services with his or her patients. People are people. Patients are people who have been transformed into a specific "role" that separates and transports them from their day-to-day lives into the complex, inner-workings of doctors, nurses, hospitals, health care managers, and all the other elements that make the U.S. health care system do what it does.

As a busy health care professional, it is extremely easy to forget, ignore, or just not think very much about the real people who are locked in the role of patient or are hidden from view outside of medicine in the field of public health.

Without a clear eye on the real people needing and receiving treatment, health care professionals run the risk of making decisions about a "patient" that may be so abstracted from reality that it might be in direct contradiction with the core interests of the actual person who has been put inside that label.

Based on the strength of a horrible personal experience caused by such a confusion of patients and people, this chapter outlined a quest to answer the following, very basic question about the U.S. health care system:

How might the entire system for producing, delivering, and paying for health care be better managed so that the people being treated as patients fare better than they currently do?

Person-focused health care management was introduced as the first step in developing an answer to this question.

At its most basic, a person-focused approach to health care management starts with the purposeful escalation of the lived experience of the person receiving or needing care into a management priority for all involved in providing that care.

The general idea of this approach is to purposefully shift the lens and focus of health care management from looking at the patient as the center of care to looking at the real people who require treatment—whether they are defined as "patients" or, for that matter, as an individual lost in the aggregate data of the unattended needs defining a population's "underlying health status."

Four core principles of person-focused care were identified and discussed as a starting point for incorporating the personal experience of care into the every-day management responsibilities of health care professionals.

At a technical level, a person-focused approach to health care management offers much to debate and discuss. At a personal, day-to-day level, however, it is intended to help health care professionals stop thinking about patients as "just patients" in order to better see and manage the actual, real-life, lived experience of those who have been forced into the very limited and abstract role of "the patient."

The model of person-focused care is an opportunity to let one's "caring feelings" serve as a critically important centering concept in figuring out how to best serve the interests of all those in need of care.

The four core principles of person-focused care are:

- **Principle One: The patient is not a person:** The escalation of the personal experience as a central component in patient care can be accomplished by anyone within any system of care who simply "deflates" the customary connotation of "patient" and allows the actual person living inside that institutionalized role the opportunity to be present within the given clinical system.

- **Principle Two: "Caring about" is a prerequisite to managing the "caring for" patients:** Person-focused care posits the central importance of caring about those who need medical and more generalized health care attention as a central belief that links all health care professionals— whether within a medical care system or working on improving the public's health—into a common professional bond. This commitment to care is at the heart of a "person-focused" approach to health care management.

- **Principle Three: Quality of care is more than just a clinical outcome:** "Clinical" care is simply one episode along the ongoing flow of a person's life who has encountered his or her own issues of morbidity and mortality. A person-focused approach to quality forces us to look far beyond the technical consequences of clinical care to the general overall impact our massive financial investment in health care has on people within and without the formal "medical" boundaries of the health care system.

- **Principle Four: Every health care professional has an impact on the personal experience of care:** This means that no matter what "systems-level" task or job an individual may have within a given health care organization, everything that person actually does contributes, either directly or indirectly, to the personal experience of people in need of or receiving care. No matter what job in health care you have, it can help improve the personal experience of care.

Taken as a whole, these four core principles help to frame a general approach for incorporating the personal experience of care into the everyday management responsibilities of health care professionals. Each of these principles is also intended to serve as a practical slogan or motto that can be used to help remind health care managers about the importance of the personal experience of patients as well as those who remain in need of treatment.

OVERVIEW OF THE BOOK

In order to better convey how to use the principles of person-focused care in practice, the chapters in this book have been organized into three sections. Section I examines person-focused care from the clinical perspective; Section II looks at it from a "system management" perspective; and Section III takes the viewpoint of the person inside the role of patient. These three sections are followed by a summary of the book and some concluding thoughts.

As you read the chapters in each section, keep the following primary learning objectives in mind.

1. Understand the impact of clinical, systems, and patient-level management decisions on the personal experience of care.

2. Understand and analyze certain personal and clinical problems created through the routine delivery and financing of health care services within the current system.

3. Improve your ability to look and see the real person who is living inside the role of the "patient" or is in need outside the boundaries of the traditional medical system.

4. Learn how to expand and elevate the importance of the personal experience of the patient into a key point of coordination between clinical care delivery and nonclinical managerial decision making within a health care organization.

5. Develop a broader approach to health care management that helps decision making throughout a health care organization grow from purely clinical considerations into a series of "caring questions" about how the individual being treated is feeling, thinking, interpreting, and understanding what is going on around him or her during the experience of a given health care system.

CASE STUDY

My name is Kay and my story begins with an all-over bad feeling. Somehow I managed to work in a fog. I last went to work on a Friday, but was freezing and very thirsty at the same time. I went home, got into bed, and the rest is a fog. I woke up in ICU with bilateral pneumonia, leading to respiratory failure.

I was put in an induced coma and placed on a ventilator. I began communicating with people in the past—like stepping over a line. The entire stay was very bizarre, to say the least. Somewhere in the back of my mind I knew I could not last too many days in the condition I was. My body had atrophied to the point where I had no way of moving. My mind was even worse. I was seeing and hearing things that were not even of this world. I made a family member stay with me at night so the demonic things would not be able to kill me.

I was so weak I would just stay in bed. But still, the horrible things would visit me every night. I have really not much memory left of many things.

(continued)

CASE STUDY (*continued*)

I no longer sleep without drugs. I am depressed and angry because I can't really carry on a conversation.

I applied for disability insurance but was denied. I would like someone to explain to me how I am supposed to carry on with my life.

Issues to Consider

1. How do the personal needs of Kay differ from her treatment as a "patient?"

2. What type and level of "caring" did Kay experience as a patient?

3. What could be done to better address Kay's needs after she was discharged back to home?

4. What could have been done by everyone involved in Kay's care to improve her personal experience as a patient?

REFERENCES

Agency for Healthcare Research and Quality. (2015). Health care/system redesign. Retrieved from http://www.ahrq.gov/professionals/prevention-chronic-care/improve/system/index.html

American College of Health Executives. (2011). Code of ethics. Retrieved from https://www.ache.org/abt_ache/code.cfm

Andrews, N. (2016a). After the ICU: Nancy Andrews at TED. Retrieved from http://tedxtalks.ted.com/video/After-the-ICU-Nancy-Andrews-at

Andrews, N. (2016b). Delirious. Retrieved from http://www.nancyandrews.net/delirious.html

Berger, P., & Luckmann, T. (1966). *The social construction of reality: A treatise in the sociology of knowledge*. New York, NY: Anchor/Doubleday.

Bienvenu, O. J., Colantuoni, E., Mendez-Tellez, P. A., Shanholtz, C., Dennison-Himmelfarb, C. R., Pronovost, P. J., & Needham, D. M. (2015). Cooccurrence of and remission from general anxiety, depression, and posttraumatic stress disorder symptoms after acute lung injury: A 2-year longitudinal study. *Critical Care Medicine, 43*(3), 642–653.

Centers for Disease Control and Prevention. (2013). Preventable deaths from heart disease & stroke: Improving care can save more lives. Retrieved from http://www.cdc.gov/vitalsigns/heartdisease-stroke

Centers for Disease Control and Prevention. (2016). Budget request overview: FY 2017 President's budget request. Retrieved from http://www.cdc.gov/budget/documents/fy2017/cdc-overview-factsheet.pdf

Centers for Disease Control and Prevention WONDER. (2015). About multiple causes of death, 1999–2013. Retrieved from http://wonder.cdc.gov/mcd-icd10.html

Cleary, P. D. (2012). Why is patient-centered health care important? Retrieved from https://www.scholarsstrategynetwork.org/sites/default/files/ssn_basic_facts_cleary_on_patient-centered_care_0.pdf

Curtin, S., Warner, M., & Hedegaard, H. (2016). Increase in suicide in the United States, 1999–2014. Retrieved from http://www.cdc.gov/nchs/products/databriefs/db241.htm

Egnew, T. (2009). Suffering, meaning, and healing: Challenges of contemporary medicine. *Annals of Family Medicine, 7*(2), 170–175.

Ferlie, E. B., & Shortell, S. M. (2001). Improving the quality of health care in the United Kingdom and the United States: A framework for change. *Milbank Quarterly, 79*(2), 281–315.

Forbes. (2015). $117 billion market for Internet of things in healthcare by 2020. Retrieved from http://www.forbes.com/sites/tjmccue/2015/04/22/117-billion-market-for-internet-of-things-in-healthcare-by-2020/#61c555e22471

Girard, T., Pandharipande, P., & Ely, E. W. (2008). Delirium in the intensive care unit. *Critical Care, 12*(Suppl. 3), S3.

Goffman, E. (1961). *Asylums: Essays on the social situation of mental patients and other inmates.* New York, NY: Anchor Books.

Huggins, E., Stollings, J. L., Jackson, J. C., & Sevin, C. M. (2015). Models for a post-intensive care syndrome clinic: Targeted goals and barriers. Retrieved from http://www.sccm.org/Communications/Critical-Connections/Archives/Pages/Models-for-a-Post-Intensive-Care-Syndrome-Clinic---Targeted-Goals-and-Barriers.aspx

James, J. T. (2013). A new, evidence-based estimate of patient harms associated with hospital care. *Journal of Patient Safety, 9*(3), 122–128.

Kissick, W. (1994). *Medicine's dilemmas: Infinite needs versus finite resources.* New Haven and New London, CT: Yale University Press.

Longest, B., Rakich, J., & Darr, K. (2000). *Managing health services organizations and systems.* Towson, MD: Health Professions Press.

MacDorman, M. F., Mathews, T. J., Mohangoo, A. D., & Zeitlin, J. (2014). International comparisons of infant mortality and related factors: United States and Europe, 2010. *National Vital Statistics Reports, 63*(5). Retrieved from http://www.cdc.gov/nchs/data/nvsr/nvsr63/nvsr63_05.pdf

Mavis, B., Rovner, M. H., Jorgenson, S., Coffey, J., Anand, N., Bulica, E., . . . Ernst, A. (2014). Patient participation in clinical encounters: A systematic review to identify self-report measures. *Health Expectations, 18*(6). Retrieved from http://onlinelibrary.wiley.com/doi/10.1111/hex.12186/pdf

Mayo Clinic. (2016). *CT scan.* Mayo Foundation for Medical Education and Research. Retrieved from http://www.mayoclinic.org/tests-procedures/ct-scan/basics/definition/prc-20014610

Mechanic, D. (1990). The role of sociology in health affairs. *Health Affairs, 9*(1), 85–97.

Medline Plus. (2016). *Aneurysms.* U.S. National Library of Medicine. Retrieved from https://medlineplus.gov/aneurysms.html

Nadler, D. A., & Tushman, M. L. (1982). *Frameworks for organizational behavior*. Boston, MA: Little, Brown. Retrieved from http://cumc.columbia.edu/dept/pi/ppf/Congruence-Model.pdf

Neuberger, J. (1999). Let's do away with "patients." *British Medical Journal, 318*(7200), 1756–1758.

Reid, P. P., Compton, W. D., Grossman, J. H., & Fanjiang, G. (Eds.). (2005). Building a better delivery system: A new engineering/health care partnership. Washington, DC: National Academies Press. Retrieved from http://national academies.org/onpi/030909643X.pdf

Rickert, J. (2012). Patient-centered care: What it means and how to get there. *Health Affairs*. Retrieved from http://healthaffairs.org/blog/2012/01/24/patient-centered-care-what-it-means-and-how-to-get-there

Roemer, M. I. (1991). *National health systems of the world, Vol. 1: The countries*. New York, NY: Oxford University Press.

Save the Children. (2015). The urban disadvantage. Retrieved from http://www.savethechildren.org/atf/cf/%7B9def2ebe-10ae-432c-9bd0-df91d2eba74a%7D/SOWM_2015.PDF

Sepsis Alliance. (2016). Faces of sepsis. Retrieved from http://www.sepsis.org

Singer, M., Deutschman, S., Seymour, C. W., Shankar-Hari, M., Annane, D., Bauer, M., . . . Angus, D. C. (2016). The third international consensus definitions for sepsis and septic shock (Sepsis-3). *Journal of the American Medical Association, 315*(8), 801–810. Retrieved from http://jamanetwork.com/journals/jama/full article/2492881

The Commonwealth Fund. (2015). US spends more on health care than other high-income nations but has lower life expectancy, worse health. Retrieved from http://www.commonwealthfund.org/publications/press-releases/2015/oct/us-spends-more-on-health-care-than-other-nations

Ulman, R., & Brothers, D. (1988). *The shattered self: A psychoanalytic study of trauma*. Hillsdale, NJ: The Analytic Press.

U.S. Department of Health and Human Services. (2016). Compendium of unimplemented recommendations. Retrieved from http://oig.hhs.gov/reports-and-publications/compendium/files/compendium2016.pdf

Van Den Bos, J., Rustagi, K., Gray, T., Halford, M., Ziemkiewicz, E., & Shreve, J. (2011). The $17.1 billion problem: The annual cost of measurable medical errors. *Health Affairs, 30*, 4596–4603.

Weiss, B. (2014). How to bridge the health literacy gap. Retrieved from http://cukurovaaile.org/wp-content/uploads/2016/01/Makale-Orijinal-Ahmet.pdf

Wintermann, G. B., Brunkhorst, F. M., Petrowski, K., Strauss, B., Oehmichen, F., Pohl, M., & Rosendahl, J. (2015). Stress disorders following prolonged critical illness in survivors of severe sepsis. *Critical Care Medicine, 43*(6), 1213–1222.

Zolnierek, H., & DiMatteo, K. B. (2009). Physician communication and patient adherence to treatment: A meta-analysis. *Medical Care, 47*(8), 826–834.

SECTION I

CLINICAL MANAGEMENT

CHAPTER 2

PERSON-FOCUSED CARE AND THE PHYSICIAN: EMPHASIZING THE HUMAN CONDITION

JAMES B. RICKERT

A crucial step on the journey toward creating person-focused care is the continual effort of physicians, patient advocates, administrators, and payers to make medical care more patient centered. In tandem with this effort have been physicians' changes in focus from a disease-centered model of illness to an understanding of medical care as an enterprise in which we are treating people who happen to have an illness. Although these changes in emphasis might seem intuitively obvious, they are a radical departure from the way in which the U.S. health care system has traditionally functioned. Person-focused care places the individual's desires and needs—not his illness nor the goals of the treating health care team—at the center of care delivery. This chapter explores these related changes further.

BACKGROUND

Until a few years ago, patients accessing health care in the United States received care within a physician-centered system. Major stakeholders, such as hospital administrators, made decisions designed to attract physicians to their institutions or products. By satisfying doctors' concerns, administrators could keep hospital beds and surgical suites full and utilize ancillary services. In addition, pharmaceutical companies or medical device manufacturers focused almost all of their efforts on the prescribing habits of doctors. Furthermore, doctors, themselves, practiced medicine in a manner designed for their convenience and autonomy. To say that the patient-centered care movement has been a revolutionary change in emphasis away from physicians is no overstatement. It is an attempt to place the wishes and concerns of individuals seeking care at the center of medical delivery systems. Although much more reform is needed in moving from physician to patient centrism and, ultimately, to person-focused care, we have begun the process of transformation.

A few examples will demonstrate the physician centeredness of the system from which we are currently struggling to emerge. Consider a doctor's appointment scheduling. Although we have all waited inordinate amounts of time for a short appointment with our doctor—something we would tolerate almost nowhere else in our daily lives—almost no doctor is purposefully keeping his or her patients waiting. Rather, traditional patient scheduling is designed to align with the physician's desires and expectations; patient convenience is an afterthought. I have often heard physician practice consultants and administrators recommend overscheduling patients in order to prevent doctors from having any unreimbursed downtime between patients. These same consultants often suggest that doctors work patients who wish to be seen urgently into their schedules immediately so that these patients do not decide to go elsewhere for care. No consideration is given to the fact that both those patients who have scheduled appointments and those suddenly being worked into the day's schedule will have long and exasperating waits to be seen. The goal is a steady patient flow—for the doctor—that helps him or her move through his or her day as efficiently as possible while maximizing office revenue. I have known surgeons to be called to the hospital to perform unplanned surgery and exit through the backdoor while instructing their staff to not reschedule patients and to tell those waiting that their wait might be just a little longer than usual. These surgeons are not bad people; rather, they have grown up in a system in which patient convenience was simply not a typical medical consideration.

Another physician-oriented aspect of medical practice involves patient–physician communication. When I first started out in private practice in the early 1990s, administrators, nurses, and other doctors all discussed the importance of acquiring an office staff that could "protect" me. At first, I had no idea what was being discussed; the term sounded vaguely reminiscent of some sort of mob-related protection racket. Quickly, I realized that I was being advised to build a defense limiting direct patient access to me. The idea was that a good staff should typically explain a doctor's unavailability and deal with patient problems and concerns, leaving the physician free to follow whatever pursuits are occupying him or her at the time. This notion, although not typically spoken of in those terms, continues to be widely held within the medical community today. There is some rationale for it—no doctor practicing in traditional medical settings can respond to every patient problem, and it is appropriate for nurses and other clinical staff to deal with certain patient concerns appropriate to their experience. The problem lies in the fact that many doctors utilize their office staff as a wall instead of a filter—all or nearly all patient concerns and questions are dealt with by office personnel—regardless of doctor availability, the severity of the concern, or patient preferences. Furthermore, those patients who insist on discussing concerns with their doctor are labeled as "problem" or unreasonable patients. The doctor, in this traditional mode of care, exerts control over all avenues of patient communication, and his or her prerogatives alone determine which patients and which problems he or she will take time to discuss.

Although effectively addressing patient–physician communication and access to care, as discussed earlier, leads to both higher patient satisfaction rates and improved clinical outcomes, physician centrism also raises significant safety concerns for patients. For instance, every year in the United States, approximately 2,000,000 patients suffer hospital-acquired infections (HAIs) resulting in nearly 90,000 patient deaths (Stone, 2009). The single best preventive strategy available to avoid these infections is handwashing. Doctors, unfortunately, are known to wash their hands with less frequency than nurses (World Health Organization, 2009). Furthermore, hospitals have been slow to institute policies that require physician handwashing due to their tendency to avoid conflict with physicians—hospitals' most important customer. Although there is an economic rationale for the hospital's decisions regarding handwashing, ultimately, patients bear the price for physicians' lower incidence of proper hand hygiene. Again, akin to the aforementioned examples, doctors certainly do not want to pass along infectious agents or increase patient suffering; rather, the long-established physician centrism of our system makes it difficult to change the doctor's behavior in order to solve this type of problem.

> See what the Centers for Disease Control and Prevention have reported regarding the prevalence of and prevention of HAI (www.cdc.gov/hai/prevent/prevention.html).

From these examples, it is clear that a physician-centered system yields lower quality care for patients than one that is patient centered and person focused. Patient-centered policies have now been well studied, and they result in higher patient satisfaction with their care, better patient adherence to treatments, and better outcomes of care. Major facets of patient-centered medicine include the following: prompt access to care, high-quality communication between patient and provider, care coordination, physician empathy, and the ability to understand patients' perspective of their illness and the care that they are receiving.

The most fundamental tenet of patient-centered medicine and person-focused care is the understanding that since medical care exists for those individuals seeking our help, effective care must be defined by, or in close consultation with, those persons seeking medical help. This seems self-evident, but it is often not the case. As an example, the Harris Hip Score (HHS) is one of our better and more widely used tools for measuring the results of hip surgery. It was developed by Dr. William Harris in 1969 as a tool to compare the outcomes of surgery (Harris, 1969). Although it has been modified over time, importantly, like many other such instruments, it does not ask whether a person is satisfied with the results of the treatment.

> What is the Harris Hip Score? How is it used? You can find out more online at www.orthopaedicscore.com/scorepages/harris_hip_score.html

A few years ago, I assumed care for a woman who had undergone a hip arthroscopy (surgery in which a viewing camera and small tools are introduced into the hip through small skin incisions) for a condition known as femoroacetabular impingement. In this condition, the hip ball and socket can painfully pinch surrounding soft tissues or each other. Hip arthroscopy has become its standard treatment. The patient was very dissatisfied and discouraged by her surgical results, and her assessment of the arthroscopy could hardly have been more different from that of her surgeon. In his office notes, her surgeon judged her surgery to be a success, mostly due to her good HHS. Although the score was reasonably accurate, it in no way correlated with this person's experience of care. After years of use for hip arthroscopy, finally in 2012, researchers in Cambridge, England, compared HHS results with patient satisfaction with arthroscopy. They found that many satisfied patients scored fair or poor results, whereas some unsatisfied patients scored good or excellent results (Aprato, Jayasekera, & Villar, 2012). As we see, this type of dichotomy between the patients' perceptions of care and those of their providers is now a well-documented phenomenon, and, therefore, we must continually ask patients about their perceptions—how they rate or judge the quality of their health care—in order for us to understand what treatment modalities and modes of care delivery are actually working for them—not just what their doctors think is effective and appropriate care.

The phenomenon of a mismatch between doctor and patient perceptions of care has been identified in almost all practice settings. As a start, people expect a certain level of service or respect when they see their doctor. On the other hand, American doctors often have a hard time recognizing that we do not deliver the care that our patients are seeking. In recent surveys done by the Altaurm Institute's Center for Consumer Choice in Health Care, doctors serving patients in PPOs felt that 76% of their patients were completely satisfied with their care. Actual patient surveys found that only 39% were completely satisfied (Altaurm Institute, 2012a). Additionally, in a similar survey, physicians believe that 80% of patients who leave their practice do so because the patient is moving or because of a change in insurance. However, only 38% of patients report leaving a doctor's practice for these reasons, whereas 58% cite the desire for better treatment or service as the reason for switching doctors (Altaurm Institute, 2012b). Clearly, the patients' perceptions of their care differs from those of their treating physicians, and as providers, we have difficulty viewing that care from the patients' vantage point.

This same difficulty for doctors or other experts in understanding effective care has been explored by Stewart and colleagues in Canada. They asked experts to study audiotaped doctor–patient interactions for patient centrism while patients also rated these same experiences. Although expert opinion was not correlated with better outcomes, patients' perceived patient-centered care was correlated with "better recovery from their discomfort and concern, better emotional health two months later, and fewer diagnostic tests and referrals" (Stewart et al., 2000, p. 796). A separate study evaluating the effectiveness of mental health care asked both therapists and their patients to rate therapists' empathy. There was no significant agreement among patients and therapists when they both used the same scale, and only the patients' ratings of their care correlated significantly with outcomes (Free, Green, Grace, Chernus, & Whitman, 1985).

One final example reveals the chasm between patients' perceptions of their care and that of their doctors. Many studies show that patients report complications at rates many times higher than those reported by their surgeons (Fränneby, Sandblom, Nyrén, Nordin, & Gunnarsson, 2008). However, the full extent of the gulf between patient and surgeon perceptions is apparent in a 2008 study of more than 1,000 spine surgery patients. Although surgeons reported a 2.6% rate of spinal complications and a 2.9% rate of general complications, patients reported an overall complication rate of 29%. Furthermore, patient-reported complications correlated directly with their satisfaction with their surgery; the authors state a "good" global outcome (operation helped or helped a lot) was found in 79.8% of patients who had no patient-reported complication but only 62.4% of those with such complications (Grob & Mannion, 2009).

This difference in perception between surgeons and patients has profound ramifications for patient care. One can easily imagine a person opting for surgery when discussing a procedure with a 2% to 3% complication rate, but declining that same surgery if discussing a procedure with a complication rate of 30%, and—if a complication develops—a 40% chance that the individual's symptoms will not improve or may even be worse. Clearly without obtaining meaningful patient feedback, we cannot give individuals seeking our care the information necessary to help them make those decisions that are best for them.

Importantly, we should realize that it is not that surgeons are necessarily downplaying risks; a follow-up study shows that surgeons and their patients simply view results with different eyes. In 2013, researchers examined more than 2,000 spine surgeries to compare patient and surgeon perspectives on surgical complications, and they found something very unsettling. In this study, both surgeons and their patients individually reported surgical complications and their severity—they both judged the same episodes of care. When patients reported complications, their surgeons also reported one only 29% of the time. Furthermore, 61% of the patients for whom surgeons reported a complication did not report a complication themselves (Mannion et al., 2013). In other words, patients and their surgeons had very poor agreement on the fundamental question of whether the same surgery had resulted in a complication.

Additionally, we are not discussing minor problems from the patients' point of view; just over half of the patient-reported complications, including many that the surgeon did not recognize as a problem, were ranked by patients as very or extremely bothersome. The authors note, "These [patient reported] complications are neither infrequent nor inconsequential as far as the patient is concerned" (Mannion et al., 2013, p. 623).

Thus, a fundamental component of patient-centered or person-focused care is the ability to take the patient perspective. Although we as providers usually believe that we know everything about our patients and the care that we are delivering, the truth is that we do not. There is a foundational and inevitable difference in outlook and judgment between those of us who yield scalpels or administer surgical suites and those subject to their effects. Providers are simply unable to accurately assess our patients' perceptions of their care—what is important to them, how well we are delivering their care, what factors in our care improve patient-reported outcomes—without asking the individuals we are serving. As we shall see later in this chapter, patient-centered medical practices have procedures in place, such as focus groups or regular patient surveys, in order to continually measure the effectiveness of their interactions with patients.

A second fundamental component of patient-centered medicine concerns the relationship between individuals and their health care providers. This is not a new concept. At the dawn of Western medicine, Hippocrates taught that "it's far more important to know what person the disease has than what disease the person has" (Hippocrates, n.d.). Unfortunately, as medical training and care have evolved, we have continually moved away from treating people who happen to be sick and toward a model of care in which doctors and hospitals treat disease; this is appropriately known as the disease model of care. It has become the most prevalent model of health care in the Western world. In this model, management of disease, not care for the patient who happens to be afflicted, is the central task of medicine. This model overlooks the fact that while doctors treat disease, people experience illness: this includes an individual's personal experience of feeling unwell, his or her social situation, his or her personal beliefs regarding sickness, and his or her individual preferences for medical care (Helman, 1980). Rather than helping patients manage their illness, understanding disease characteristics, prognosis, and treatment has become the job of physicians. Therefore, doctors have typically been taught that quality medical care entails very specific and circumscribed actions regarding our patients. For instance, we learn that a correct diagnosis and the subsequent prescription of an appropriate medication or a well-done surgery are proper and effective care—that these are the tasks of health care providers, and, once accomplished, we should then move onto the next patient.

As a medical student and resident, I understood that clinical stars were made by virtuoso technical skill in the operating room or superior diagnostic acumen in uncovering exotic and rare diseases. It was unimportant in this setting that well over 99% of Americans would never benefit from such skills—they would never contract a rare and exotic disease or require such a complicated and delicate surgery that it should only be done by a subspecialty surgeon with years of training beyond residency. In this training environment, the people behind the diseases were unimportant. Rather than emphasizing a regard for understanding patients' experience of illness and the ability to interact with patients as people, a comprehensive understanding of disease—including the most minute and seemingly unimportant facts—was of paramount importance. As a resident, one of the surgeons whom I regarded most highly was an excellent communicator and very empathic. He listened actively, sought out patient questions, and worked to understand the patient perspective. He was also very competent in his diagnostic and surgical skills. However, he was never considered a star in our orthopedic department. More highly trained or specialized surgeons were continually amazed that patients preferentially sought him out for their care. There was a general lack of understanding that technical or diagnostic skills, while critical, are only a part of effective medical care—that technical skills treat disease but something more is needed in managing illness.

In traditional medical practice, if a patient does not follow a recommended course of action, this is unfortunate, but ultimately not a medical concern, per se, because the doctor and the health care system have done their job—given the right advice or administered the correct drugs—and it is then up to the patient to follow through as instructed. Such patients are, therefore, labeled as problem patients, and their poor outcomes or dissatisfaction with care are regarded as of their own making. As an example of the limitations of this viewpoint, a few years ago now, a well-educated young woman asked for my help in treating a painful metastatic lesion in her femur. She was married and had a young family. Her primary malignancy was lung cancer. I am a survivor of recurrent cancer, myself, and we talked often about our experiences. She told me with grief how she had gone to see a pulmonologist when her symptoms had first started. He had done pulmonary function tests, prescribed inhalers, and instructed her to return for follow-up if her symptoms did not resolve. She never went back to see him, eventually following up with her family doctor who diagnosed her lung cancer, by which time it was metastatic and incurable. Although her pulmonologist correctly pointed out that this tragedy might have been prevented if the patient had followed up as instructed, the story was not so simple. The underlying problem was that this doctor never connected with this patient. She felt his questions, examination, and prescriptions were all rote and perfunctory, and he displayed no warmth or empathy toward her. This lady decided, therefore, that visits with this doctor were a very expensive waste of time, and she did not return. Like almost all patients, this woman needed something more from her doctor than solely diagnostic and therapeutic skills, and without that something more, those skills were nearly worthless—they provided no value to this patient.

In reality, effective medical care begins with the recognition that each patient is also a person, and health care is similar to other interactions between people. Medical providers need to understand that people come to the doctor for help with their individual illness, not just for disease management. Patients desire good communication from their providers, a feeling of personal connection with those who are caring for them, and a degree of empathy for their medical problems. Not only are people who receive this sort of care more satisfied patients, individuals who receive this type of care also enjoy improved outcomes when compared to those who do not.

A personal relationship between patients and providers has been shown to yield improved treatment outcomes and greater patient satisfaction. This has been studied in numerous ways. A British study of patients being treated in the general practice setting shows that a patient's feeling of partnership with his or her doctor correlates highly with patient satisfaction with his or her care; in this particular study, partnership was the most predictive factor regarding satisfaction (Little et al., 2001). Researchers, here, included understanding the patient's emotional needs as an aspect of partnership. They warned, "If doctors don't provide a positive, patient-centred approach patients will be less satisfied, less enabled, and may have greater symptom burden and higher rates of referral [away from the practice]" (Little et al., 2001, p. 911). Furthermore, a comprehensive literature review has shown that interpersonal continuity of care—care delivered to patients primarily by the same doctors—resulted in improved care outcomes—such as better preventive care and a reduced rate of hospitalizations (Saultz & Lochner, 2005). These types of improvements not only make people healthier and improve the quality of their lives; they also can result in large cost savings. Furthermore, a study of medically complex patients and their follow-up after hospitalization shows the benefits of care continuity with a doctor with whom the patient has a personal relationship. In this study, patients were both more satisfied with follow-up appointments and more likely to keep their follow-up appointments when they had a general practitioner who regularly cared for them (Yanga, Zwar, Vagholkar, Dennis, & Redmond, 2010). The benefits of a personal relationship between a physician and the people for whom he or she is caring were summed up nicely in a 2014 study of more than 47,000 patients. Researchers followed patients who had recently been diagnosed with hypertension, diabetes, hypercholesterolemia, or their complications. They found that poorer quality continuity of care was associated with higher all-cause and cardiovascular mortality, cardiovascular events, and health care costs; and based on these findings, they concluded: "Health care systems should be designed to support long-term trusting relationships between patients and physicians" (Shin et al., 2014, p. 535).

Beyond a personal relation with caregivers, other factors in this relationship work to make medical care patient centered or person focused. These include provider empathy and good communication skills. Empathy is defined as the ability to understand and share the feelings of another person. Patients who sense that their physician is empathic—can understand their emotional response to their illness and medical journey—are more satisfied, and achieve better outcomes in their medical care. For example, a common outcome measure in patient–physician interactions is the patient's control of his or her diabetes. This can be objectively measured with a blood test for a certain type of hemoglobin called Hgb A1c. This test measures the amount of hemoglobin in the blood that has sugar molecules attached to it. It gives an excellent view of a patient's average blood sugar over the past few months and is our single best test for tissue damage due to diabetes. Researchers in 2011 found that patients of physicians with high patient-evaluated empathy scores enjoyed significantly better control of their diabetes, as measured by Hgb A1c, than did patients of physicians with low empathy scores (Hojat et al., 2011). Interestingly and importantly, no new expensive app or insulin delivery or monitoring system was needed to achieve these results; rather, they were achieved by physicians who could acknowledge the emotional difficulties of the people they were caring for.

Not only can empathy improve treatment results, it also improves patient satisfaction with their care. A large study of 550 patients demonstrated an association between physician empathy and both higher patient satisfaction rates and better patient compliance with treatment. Researchers found that patients' perceived physician empathy correlated with patient perceptions of trust, physician expertise, and improved information exchange. We would expect improved levels of patient trust, but patients also perceive empathic physicians as being more expert, and they also were more satisfied with the care that they received (Kim, Kaplowitz, & Johnston, 2004). Although empathic doctors may or may not be more expert in their treatment of disease than their nonempathic counterparts, this study makes clear that emotionally available providers are more expert or better at helping people manage their illness, including the emotional trauma of sickness.

These findings are confirmed by a 2012 study of physician empathy in cancer care. Higher levels of provider empathy were associated with increased patient satisfaction and lower levels of emotional distress (Lelorain, Bredart, Dolbeault, & Sultan, 2012). I can confirm this finding, myself. I am a survivor of twice recurrent non-Hodgkin's lymphoma. Treatment for the two recurrences has involved the arduous medical procedure of stem cell transplantation. The second was a transplant of my brother's stem cells into my body after a course of chemotherapy. With each recurrence, my chance of survival lessened, my body was diminished, and the treatment grew more difficult and unpleasant. After the transplant from my brother, I was quite sick, and in and out of the intensive care unit (ICU) continually for nearly 2 years. The new graft rejected my body in a process called graft versus host disease, and I was subject to numerous bouts of pneumonia. At one point, I was taking nearly 20 medications per day. Due to my previous treatment failures, I felt that my chances for success were low, and I was fearful of an ugly death. I was also generally exhausted. I am not at all sure I could have stuck with the program without the obvious empathy and the personal relationship I enjoyed with my doctors and nurses. They understood my fears and concerns, spoke with me about them, and made it clear that they felt a personal stake in my treatment's success. This relationship played a vital role in my healing and recovery—they helped push me to not cut corners and carefully follow the treatment path at a time when I was questioning it.

Although the aforementioned study and my personal experience is with cancer, it is likely that similar effects of empathy would also be evident in any groups of patients suffering through long treatment courses marked with emotional ups and downs. Patients with chronic disease, postoperative complications such as failed back syndrome, or people with multiple severe traumatic injuries all undergo similar treatment and disease burdens and experience concomitant emotional distress.

Finally, when discussing the importance of provider empathy, we should remember that empathy is not an inviolable personality trait. This is important to understand for two reasons. First, research has shown that people who believe empathy can be developed are more likely to expand greater empathic effort in challenging settings than will those persons who feel that empathy is a fixed trait (Schumann, Zaki, & Dweck, 2014). This is quite useful for providers to remember when working with emotionally demanding individuals. Second, training courses on displaying empathy are being developed. One group has shown that medical residents display greater patient empathy after a relatively short training course (Riess, Kelley, Bailey, Dunn, & Phillips, 2012). Further efforts to develop provider empathy should be expanded.

As important as provider empathy and a personal relationship are to effective person-focused care, they are incomplete without meaningful patient–provider communication. No aspect of medical care holds such promise for improvement and such importance to patients. According to a recent report from the Institute of Medicine (Alston et al., 2012), more than 80% of patients strongly agree that they want their providers to listen to them and want full information about their medical problems and treatment, regardless of how uncomfortable or unpleasant such knowledge might be. Unfortunately, this same survey found that less than half of all patients feel that their doctor takes the time and asks all the questions necessary to understand their goals and concerns (Alston et al., 2012). Importantly, this report concludes that people whose providers listen to them, elicit their goals and concerns, and fully explain available medical options for care are, among other things, three to five times more satisfied with their doctor and their care.

However, quite a bit more is at stake with good communication than just patient satisfaction. As addressed in the Institute of Medicine report, communication within our health care system continues to be a problem. Another large study of more than 1,000 patient encounters across specialties of medicine found that fully informed consent for treatment occurs in only 9% of interactions (Braddock, Edwards, Hasenberg, Laidley, & Levinson, 1999). This lack of effective communication is all the more disturbing because of the impact good communication has for individuals under our care—including both their view of care and the results we can achieve. For instance, it has been shown that good communication and provider empathy when treating diabetics results in greater diabetes control, greater compliance with the treatment course, and reduced symptoms (Prueksaritanond, Tubtimtes, Asavanich, & Tiewtranon, 2004). Additionally, a study of 750 Americans showed that physicians' failure to have a discussion with patients about their diagnosis and prognosis was the most common cause of unmet patient expectations and resulted in poorer symptom relief and functional outcomes (Jackson & Kroenke, 2001).

Researchers hoping to optimize outpatient encounters have found that individuals whose physicians ascertain the specific reasons for their office visit and then specifically check that their patients' concerns have been addressed experience a reduced symptom burden (Henbest & Stewart, 1990). This should not at all surprise us and touches close to the heart of person-focused care; rather than just addressing problems that the physician feels are important, the doctors in this study reached out to also be sure that problems important to their patients were also addressed. This is not to say that the concerns that physicians have for their patients are not relevant to the people for whom they care. It is just that often physicians are responding to results that, in and of themselves, are not high on patients' lists of worries. Raw lab numbers, results of imaging studies, or metrics such as blood pressure readings often do not correlate with how patients are feeling at that moment. Although it is important that they are discussed and acted upon in some way, patients, like people in all other situations, want their own concerns to be addressed at least equally with those of their physicians.

It is important to understand that this is not due to patient ignorance or apathy. For example, I currently take many medications for the sequelae of my bouts of cancer and my resulting graft versus host disease. I know how important proper management of these diseases is to my long-term health and happiness. Despite this knowledge, the medication I most fret over when I am close to needing a refill is not my immunosuppressant or various pulmonary medicines; it is a medication for my decidedly not life threatening, but very unpleasant, migraine headaches. I have learned to fear uncontrolled migraines so this is the drug that I most closely watch. It is, in other words, the medicine that makes the greatest difference in my current daily life; so, despite the obvious need for all my blood tests, imaging studies, and all my medication renewals when I visit my doctor, I always also chat with them about my migraines and obtain refills for this medicine. I, like diabetics or patients with congestive heart failure or failing kidneys, understand and appreciate my doctors' concerns for me and the importance of their questions, and I want to actively engage with them on these matters, but management of my migraine headaches is equally important to me.

Because of potential communication problems and the different vantage points of patients and their doctors in treating diseases, shared decision making is emerging as an opportunity to ensure that the patient voice is heard and acted upon. With shared decision making, physicians bring clinical expertise to the discussion, whereas patients bring their unique goals, risk tolerance, and personal situation to that same conversation. Shared decision making has been shown to be effective in all sorts of clinical settings—ranging from primary care to cancer treatment to bariatric and orthopedic surgery. We have learned that persons under medical care who engage in this sort of communication and decision-making process feel empowered, suffer from reduced anxiety, and reach what they perceive as better decisions (Stacey et al., 2011). Shared decision making has been studied particularly for management of preference-sensitive conditions, such as total joint replacement for degenerative arthritis. Group Health in Washington State and Idaho has shown that the use of decision-making aids reduced the overall number of hip and knee replacements, whereas secondary analysis suggests that the decision aids encouraged good candidates for the procedure to proceed with it (Arterburn et al., 2012). The use of shared decision-making techniques is still far from commonplace, but it gives individuals seeking care a more formal and identifiable role in medical decision making by encouraging them to both really understand what their goals of treatment are and the likelihood that a suggested treatment can actually achieve their goals. It, furthermore, helps physicians understand what patients will consider a therapeutic success. Sources for obtaining decision aids include nonprofits, such as The Health Foundation in London, UK (The Health Foundation, n.d.) and the Informed Medical Decisions Foundation in Boston, Massachusetts.

Decision aids from The Health Foundation can be found online at www.health .org.uk

Decision aids from the Informed Medical Decisions Foundation are available at www.informedmedicaldecisions.org

---

To end our discussion of person-focused medical care, let us return to the issue of patient versus provider perceptions of care. As discussed, patient perceptions correlate with an individual's satisfaction with care and outcomes, whereas provider perceptions often do not. In order to access these perceptions, we must gather patient feedback. Doctors are quite good at managing disease processes, but, as we have seen, not so good at gauging the emotions or experience of those for whom we are caring. Another way of looking at this is to realize that medicine is a service profession, but providers focus on the technical side of our craft. Therefore, person-focused practitioners regularly gather data from their patients to help them continually measure the patient experience.

Focus groups of individuals under care are sometimes used for this purpose, but, most commonly, providers ranging from health care systems to individual solo practitioners use surveys. Numerous studies have found that patient surveys can predict accurately such important outcomes as hospital readmission rates when the surveys focus on specific aspects of the individual's experience, such as communication with nurses and doctors, rather than trying to capture a patient's general feeling of well-being (Boulding, Glickman, Manary, Schulman, & Staelin, 2011). Patient satisfaction rates also highly correlate with effective elective surgical care; patients are generally happy with surgery that achieves expected goals and unhappy with surgery that fails to do so (Chotai, Sivaganesan, Parker, McGirt, & Devin, 2015). Satisfaction surveys have even been correlated with inpatient mortality rates, suggesting that "patient-centered information can have an important role in the evaluation and management of hospital performance" (Glickman et al., 2010, p. 188).

When using surveys, physicians and administrators should be careful to employ validated instruments that meaningfully capture an individual's experience of care as a patient. The Consumer Assessment of Healthcare Providers and Systems surveys are validated tools that are free to use. These are the most commonly used survey instruments available today.

> What information do we know from the design and results of the Consumer Assessment of Healthcare Providers Systems surveys? See www.ahrq.gov/cahps/index.html

They are an initiative of the Agency for Healthcare Research and Quality (AHRQ), a branch of the U.S. Department of Health and Human Services. Several surveys are available to meet different clinical needs (AHRQ, n.d.).

> What consumer surveys can you find on the AHRQ website for the U.S. Department of Health and Human Services?

Physicians and administrators using these surveys will gain actionable knowledge of how they or their institution are interacting with the individuals whom they are treating. A key focus is quality of communication skills. Although we may all feel that we communicate well, if our patients do not understand our explanations or instructions, then we have work to do. Surveys give us the feedback necessary to improve. Surveys allow us to understand the patient experience and give our patients the care that they need and want. Patients often ask themselves whether their doctors care about them or not. Researchers in Massachusetts addressing this profound question summarized their results as follows: "The most important element of caring may not be the set of behaviors but a set of underlying abilities that include taking the patient's perspective and reflecting on the patient's responses" (Quirk et al., 2008, p. 359). Patient feedback gives us the patient's perspective and allows us the opportunity for such reflection.

TABLE 2.1 – A Comparison of Person-Focused and Traditional Care

	Traditional	Person Focused
Agenda	Doctor sets the agenda for care	Person seeing doctor sets agenda with doctor input
Goals of care	Physician-derived metrics	Person-centered goals that doctors help achieve
Communication	Physician instructions and recommendations Patient questions regarding these instructions and recommendations	A conversation about goals and strategies to achieve them
Treatment	Treatment of the disease or injury that the patient has	Treatment of a person who happens to have an illness or injury
Relationship	Doctor–patient relationship	Doctor and person receiving care have a relationship
Medical profession	A technical profession	A service profession
Medical care	Proper prescribing or surgery	Holistic care of a person, including drug prescribing or procedures
Evaluation of care	Success determined by physicians providing care	Feedback from persons receiving care used in evaluation of success

Person-focused care is the next iteration of patient-centered medicine. It allows us to see the individuals before us seeking our care as whole people who happen to be afflicted with medical problems or disease. An emphasis is placed on understanding the perspective of those for whom we are caring rather than imposing our values and framework on them. Person-focused care seeks to replace our current disease model of illness with one that recognizes that the personal experience of illness is much more than just a labeled diagnosis. It also changes the delivery system from its current focus on provider needs and preferences to one revolving around the goals and preferences of those seeking our care. As such, it is a promising and necessary improvement over traditional medical care delivery.

As a summary, Table 2.1 succinctly describes the differences between person-focused and traditional medical care.

CASE STUDY

A 64-year-old woman comes to your clinic for medical care. She is a native Spanish speaker but can communicate in English. She lives alone in an apartment, but several family members live near enough to visit regularly. She is overweight and has a history of diabetes, hypertension, and has been prescribed medications for these problems. She has left her previous providers and is looking for new care. She tells the staff that she does not always take her medicines—sometimes she does not have the energy to do so. She often feels listless but states that she perks up considerably when her children or grandchildren come to visit. Her most pressing concern is left hip pain, which she describes as intense and limits her ability to interact with her family. Medical records from her previous provider label her as "noncompliant." She wants medication refills and wants a medicine to "make her feel better."

Issues to Consider

1. What steps can the clinic take now that will best serve this person? As this is a concern of hers, should this first visit focus on finding a medicine to "make her feel better?"

2. Should the services of an interpreter be obtained? This person can speak English somewhat and the clinic staff states that working with the interpreter can slow them down; they think that they might be able to adequately communicate.

3. How likely will prescription renewals alone help this person? Upon what do you base this opinion? What other interventions might make management of this person's problems more successful?

4. On this first visit, with so many different problems to discuss, should this woman's hip pain be addressed? Or, would it be better to focus on her medical problems and address that at a later time?

5. What obstacles do you foresee in providing person-centered care to this person?

REFERENCES

Agency for Healthcare Research and Quality. (n.d.). CAHPS®: Surveys and tools to advance patient-centered care. Retrieved from https://cahps.ahrq.gov

Alston, C., Paget, L., Halvorson, G. C., Novelli, B., Guest, J., McCabe, P., . . . Von Kohorn, I. (2012, September 25). Communicating with patients on health care evidence. Discussion Paper, Institute of Medicine, Washington, DC. Retrieved from http://nam.edu/perspectives-2012-communicating-with-patients-on -health-care-evidence

Altaurm Institute. (2012a). Altarum comparison of physician and consumer health care opinions. Retrieved from http://altarum.org/sites/default/files/ uploaded-related-files/CCCHC_Spring_2012_Physician_Consumer_Health _Care_FINAL.pdf

Altaurm Institute. (2012b). Physicians underestimate consumer likelihood to switch doctors. Retrieved from http://altarum.org/sites/default/files/uploaded -related-files/CCCHCResults03_LikelihoodSwitch_0.pdf

Aprato, A., Jayasekera, N., & Villar, R. N. (2012). Does the modified Harris Hip Score reflect patient satisfaction after hip arthroscopy? *American Journal of Sports Medicine, 40*(11), 2557–2560.

Arterburn, D., Wellman, R., Westbrook, E., Rutter, C., Ross, T., McCulloch, D., . . . Jung, C. (2012). Introducing decision aids at Group Health was linked to sharply lower hip and knee surgery rates and costs. *Health Affairs, 31*(9), 2094–2104.

Boulding, W., Glickman, S. W., Manary, M. P., Schulman, K. A., & Staelin, R. (2011). Relationship between patient satisfaction with inpatient care and hospital readmission within 30 days. *American Journal of Managed Care, 7*(1), 41–48.

Braddock, C. H., Edwards, K. A., Hasenberg, N. M., Laidley, T. L., & Levinson, W. (1999). Informed decision making in outpatient practice: Time to get back to basics. *Journal of the American Medical Association, 282*, 2313–2320.

Chotai, S., Sivaganesan, A., Parker, S. L., McGirt, M. J., & Devin, C. J. (2015). Patient-specific factors associated with dissatisfaction after elective surgery for degenerative spine diseases. *Neurosurgery, 77*, 157–163.

Fränneby, U., Sandblom, G., Nyrén, O., Nordin, P., & Gunnarsson, U. (2008). Self-reported adverse events after groin hernia repair: A study based on a national register. *Value Health, 11*(5), 927–932.

Free, N. K., Green, B. L., Grace, M. C., Chernus, L. A., & Whitman, R. M. (1985). Empathy and outcome in brief focal dynamic therapy. *American Journal of Psychiatry, 142*, 917–921.

Glickman, S. W., Boulding, W., Manary, M., Staelin, R., Roe, M. T., Wolosin, R. J., . . . Schulman, K. A. (2010). Patient satisfaction and its relationship with clinical quality and inpatient mortality in acute myocardial infarction. *Circulation: Cardiovascular Quality and Outcomes, 3*, 188–195.

Grob, D., & Mannion, A. F. (2009). The patient's perspective on complications after spine surgery. *European Spine Journal, 18*(Suppl. 3), 380–385.

Harris, W. H. (1969). Traumatic arthritis of the hip after dislocation and acetabular fractures: Treatment by mold arthroplasty. An end-result study using a new method of result evaluation. *Journal of Bone and Joint Surgery, 51*(4), 737–755.

Helman, C. G. (1980). Disease versus illness in general practice. *The Journal of the Royal College of General Practitioners, 31*(230), 548–552.

Henbest, R. J., & Stewart, M. (1990). Patient-centredness in the consultation: 2: Does it really make a difference? *Family Practice, 7*, 28–33.

Hippocrates. (n.d.). It's far more important to know what person the disease has than what disease the person has. Retrieved from http://www.azquotes.com/quote/602910

Hojat, M., Louis, D. Z., Markham, F. W., Wender, R., Rabinowitz, C., & Gonnella, J. S. (2011). Physicians' empathy and clinical outcomes for diabetic patients. *Academic Medicine, 86*, 359–364.

Informed Medical Decisions Foundation. Retrieved from https://www.informedmedicaldecisions.org

Jackson, J. L., & Kroenke, K. (2001). The effect of unmet expectations among adults presenting with physical symptoms. *Annals of Internal Medicine, 134*, 889–897.

Kim, S. S., Kaplowitz, S., & Johnston, M. V. (2004). The effects of physician empathy of patient satisfaction and compliance. *Evaluation and the Health Professions, 27*, 237–251.

Lelorain, S., Bredart, A., Dolbeault, S., & Sultan, S. (2012). A systematic review of the association between empathy measures and patient outcomes in cancer care. *Psychooncology, 21*, 1255–1264.

Little, P., Everitt, H., Williamson, I., Warner, G., Moore, M., Gould, C., . . . Payne, S. (2001). Observational study of effect of patient centredness and positive approach on outcomes of general practice consultations. *British Medical Journal, 323*(7318), 908–911.

Mannion, A. F., Fekete, T. F., O'Riordan, D., Porchet, F., Mutter, U. M., Jeszenszky, D., . . . Kleinstueck, F. S. (2013). The assessment of complications after spine surgery: Time for a paradigm shift? *The Spine Journal, 13*(6), 615–624.

Prueksaritanond, S., Tubtimtes, S., Asavanich, K., & Tiewtranon, V. (2004). Type 2 diabetic patient-centered care. *Journal of the Medical Association of Thailand, 87*, 345–352.

Quirk, M., Mazor, K., Haley, H. L., Philbin, M., Fischer, M., Sullivan, K., & Hatem, D. (2008). How patients perceive a doctor's caring attitude. *Patient Education and Counseling, 72*(3), 359–366.

Riess, H., Kelley, J. M., Bailey, R. W., Dunn, E. J., & Phillips, M. (2012). Empathy training for resident physicians: A randomized controlled trial of a neuroscience-informed curriculum. *Journal of General Internal Medicine, 27*, 1280–1286.

Saultz, J. W., & Lochner, J. (2005). Interpersonal continuity of care and care outcomes: A critical review. *Annals of Family Medicine, 3*(2), 159–166.

Schumann, K., Zaki, J., & Dweck, C. (2014). Addressing the empathy deficit: Beliefs about the malleability of empathy predict effortful responses when empathy is challenging. *Journal of Personality and Social Psychology, 107*, 475–493.

Shin, D. W., Cho, J., Yang, H. K., Park, J. H., Lee, H., Kim, H., . . . Guallar, E. (2014). Impact of continuity of care on mortality and health care costs: A nationwide cohort study in Korea. *Annals of Family Medicine, 12*(6), 534–541.

Stacey, D., Bennett, C. L., Barry, M. J., Col, N. F., Eden, K. B., Holmes-Rovner, M., . . . Thomson, R. (2011). Decision aids for people facing health treatment or screening decisions. *Cochrane Database of Systematic Reviews, 10*, CD001431.

Stewart, M., Brown, J. B., Donner, A., McWhinney, I. R., Oates, J., Weston, W. W., & Jordan, J. (2000). The impact of patient-centered care on outcomes. *The Journal of Family Practice, 49*(9), 796–804.

Stone, P. W. (2009). Economic burden of healthcare-associated infections: An American perspective. *Expert Review of Pharmacoeconomic Outcomes Research, 9*(5), 417–422.

The Health Foundation. (n.d.). Retrieved from http://www.health.org.uk

World Health Organization. (2009). *WHO guidelines on hand hygiene in health care: A summary.* Geneva, Switzerland: Author. Retrieved from http://whqlibdoc.who.int/hq/2009/WHO_IER_PSP_2009.07_eng.pdf

Yanga, S. C., Zwar, N., Vagholkar, S., Dennis, S., & Redmond, H. (2010). Factors influencing general practice follow-up attendances of patients with complex medical problems after hospitalization. *Family Practice, 27*(1), 62–68.

CHAPTER 3

CREATING PATIENT- AND FAMILY-FOCUSED CARE IN THE INTENSIVE CARE UNIT

GIORA NETZER AND JUDY E. DAVIDSON

LEARNING OBJECTIVES

- Research and analyze health care reform for the intensive care unit (ICU) environment.
- Understand opportunities to design a person-focused care ICU.
- Apply a management plan that incorporates person-focused care for the ICU including family involvement.
- Compose a literature review for future reference.

KEY TERMS

Family support zone	Intensive care unit syndrome
ICU delirium	Shared decision making

Intensive care units (ICUs) nationwide generate significant costs within health care. Due to the nature of the environment, clinicians find many opportunities to provide person-focused care in the ICU. Older Americans in particular suffer from critical illnesses that cause them to stay in the ICU. These Americans often require caregivers. The presence and engagement of caregivers has been recognized by some professional associations as the standard of care for a certain population of elderly patients. Providers have learned valuable lessons from family presence in the ICU and have implemented techniques, such as liberal visitation, bedside process to improve care, pastoral support, facilitated sense making, and

Acknowledgment: We thank Deb and Sal Colianni for their contribution of the case study in this chapter.

family coaching. This chapter provides a physician perspective of how the ICU unit can be transformed into a venue for physicians to interact with patients and their families toward positive person-focused outcomes.

BACKGROUND

Approximately 100,000 of the hospital beds in the United States are in ICUs, and the cost of caring for the patients in them is about $82 billion (Halpern & Pastores, 2015). Many of these patients will not be able to make their own decisions (Covinsky et al., 1994). More than 20% of Americans die after receiving care in the ICU (Angus et al., 2004). At the end of life, the majority of decisions are made by a loved one rather than the patient (Smedira et al., 1990). The families of these patients, as their surrogate decision makers, play a crucial role in the care of these patients.

More than 200,000 older Americans are survivors of critical illness (Iwashyna, Cooke, Wunsch, & Kahn, 2012). The care received from families, who become caregivers following discharge, may determine whether the functional limitations incurred by many of these survivors then become disabilities (Iwashyna & Netzer, 2012). In this sense, patient- and family-centered care is a commitment not only to those directly affected by illness, but also to the community itself. Given their presence and engagement in ICU caregiving and post-ICU care, the role of the family as the essential part of the collaborative care team has been recognized by professional critical care organizations and is the current standard of care (Carlet et al., 2004; Truog et al., 2008).

Respecting and supporting patients' families in the ICU is essential not only because it is the right thing to do as health care professionals, but also because a failure to do so has important consequences on resource utilization. Inadequate communication delays the time needed for families to direct care to comfort for their dying loved ones (Majesko, Hong, Weissfeld, & White, 2012). Poor-quality communication results in increased lengths of stay in the ICU, as well as increased hospital costs (Lilly et al., 2000; Teno et al., 2000).

A case study on communication of caring can be found online at theberyl institute.site-ym.com/default.asp?page=CASE0614

Patients in the ICU have the highest acuity of illness and suffer from life-threatening illness. They may suffer both physically and emotionally. While recognizing that stress and fear in the ICU cannot be eliminated, strategies to overcome the impact of the intensive care environment and experience on patients and families can be implemented. A transition from a concept of *visiting hours* to one of a family engagement philosophy is necessary. The same is true with the balance of care activities. Person-centered care is more than allowing presence; it is about adopting a philosophy of encouraging engagement and inclusion. In a true person-centered care model, when we enter the patient room we should feel as if we have entered *their* space. The patient and family own the space. This is their temporary home. We are the visitors. We have entered into their lives as consultants. Families find the traditional power balance of us over them as unsatisfactory (Osborn et al., 2012). Person-centered care requires giving up power and adopting the framework that patients and families are true partners in health care delivery. Their feedback and input regarding values and past experience is equally as important as our medical knowledge.

See the WHO statement on "Including patients and families, consumers and citizens in patient safety work" (www.who.int/patientsafety/patients_for_patient/ statement/en). Why is the approach of including families and patients in the delivery of health care a global issue?

The patient and the family are welcome, as they desire, in all aspects of care. Furthermore, consider that more than half of ICU patients will require caregiving by the family after discharge (Desai, Law, & Needham, 2011; Unroe et al., 2010). Many do not feel comfortable with this role on transfer or discharge ("NICHE Geriatric Resource Nurse," 2011). Most would have liked more information on how to participate in care ("NICHE Geriatric Resource Nurse," 2011). Any effort we take to assimilate to the caregiving role will help prepare them for transfer out of the ICU and also in the home environment. Family integrity is threatened during critical illness because of role disruption (Harbaugh, Tomlinson, & Kirschbaum, 2004; Van Horn & Tesh, 2000; Youngblut et al., 2000). Families expect us to help them through this transition (Harbaugh, Tomlinson, & Kirschbaum, 2004; Meyer, Ritholz, Burns, & Truog, 2006). Qualitative research suggests that family members assist nurses by helping them get to know the patient through the family, and by their direct contributions to care (Williams, 2005). Indeed, family members consider themselves historians, as well as facilitators and protectors of their loved ones (McAdam, Arai, & Puntillo, 2008). Our role, then, includes the responsibility to engage in activities that preserve family integrity through this family crisis.

Resources to explain key points regarding creating patient- and family-focused care in the ICU:

- The Institute of Medicine (IMO), in its *Quality Chasm* series, addresses the importance of patient-centered care and the need to engage family members in the process, particularly in the ICU (see IOM, 2001)

- The Society of Critical Care Medicine's ICU Patient Communicator App can be found at www.sccm.org/News/Pages/ICU-Patient -Communicator-App.aspx

- Critical practice guidelines for support of the family in the patient- centered intensive care unit: American College of Critical Care Medicine Task Force 2004–2005 are available from www.learnicu .org/Docs/Guidelines/Patient-CenteredIntensive.pdf

- Home Office: The Power of Person-Centeredness in Long-Term Care: A View Across the Continuum can be found at www.vetterhealth services.com/home-office-power-person-centeredness-long-term -care-view-across-continuum

- For more on patient-centered care, go to ajcc.aacnjournals.org/content/ 23/4/325.full.pdf+html

(continued)

(continued)

> Who are the main stakeholders? Patients, families, hospitals, physicians, nurses, or hospital staff.
>
> What can be done to address the issue? According to the *American Journal of Critical Care* (ajcc.aacnjournals.org/content/23/4/325.full):
>
> - Work with the clinical nurse specialist to design a brief survey for your unit staff, including physicians, on attitudes about and barriers to patient-centered care.
>
> - Review the data to determine common areas of concern to be addressed with all staff.
>
> - Develop a common unit understanding of reasonable limitations to family presence that can be described by all staff.
>
> - Ask the clinical nurse specialist for articles and references suitable for a journal club to discuss the needs of families *and* of staff members.
>
> - Consider facilitated discussions led by your social worker or clinical nurse specialist to establish some unit-based communication styles for your patient/family population.
>
> - Establish systems to recognize and address moral distress and burnout among intraprofessional staff, especially when dealing with long-term patients/families.

THE EFFECTS OF ACUTE, CRITICAL ILLNESS MAY LINGER

The effects of critical illness can persist long after hospital discharge. Although the physical and psychological morbidity persisting after critical illness is well characterized, it is infrequently discussed with patients and their families prior to discharge (Govindan, Iwashyna, Watson, Hyzy, & Miller, 2014). This constellation is recognized as the post–intensive care unit syndrome (PICS; Needham et al., 2012).

> For more on post–intensive care syndrome, see www.americannursetoday.com/?s=PICS+Davidson+Harvey

More than half of ICU survivors may experience persistent deficits in cognition, which may be as severe as those with moderate traumatic brain injury or mild dementia (Girard et al., 2010; Pandharipande et al., 2013). Longitudinal study finds that those surviving sepsis not only have developed new cognitive impairment, but have new functional impairments as well (Iwashyna, Ely, Smith, & Langa, 2010; Jackson et al., 2007). Psychological impairments are also common after ICU hospitalization, with depression and anxiety found commonly (Jackson et al., 2007; Mikkelsen et al., 2012). More than one in five will suffer significant posttraumatic stress disorder (PTSD; Parker et al., 2015).

In addition to the cognitive and psychological sequelae, survivors may also have resultant deficits in physical function. To describe the constellation of neurological and muscular deficits that drive this, the term *ICU-acquired weakness* is used (Schweickert & Hall, 2007). This weakness is common; while it may improve after hospital discharge, it can result in functional deficit and reduced quality of life for years afterward (De Jonghe et al., 2002; Fan et al., 2014; Herridge et al., 2011). Persistent deficits in lung function can also be found (Orme et al., 2003). Chronic pain is also common among survivors of critical illness (Battle, Lovett, & Hutchings, 2013).

The ICU is a difficult clinical setting that inflicts significant morbidity upon family members. Family members suffer high levels of stress and anxiety (Delva, Vanoost, Bijttebier, Lauwers, & Wilmer, 2002; Pochard et al., 2005; Sullivan et al., 2012). The majority of family members develop clinically significant depression (Choi et al., 2012). For these families, the symptoms of PTSD may begin even when their loved ones are still in the ICU (Paparrigopoulos et al., 2006).

> "What is posttraumatic stress disorder?" See www.adaa.org/understanding-anxiety/posttraumatic-stress-disorder-ptsd

The experience also takes a physical toll on family members. Sleep deprivation has been noted to be common among families in the ICU (McAdam, Dracup, White, Fontaine, & Puntillo, 2010; Novaes et al., 1999). When quantified, decreased sleep-associated functional outcomes are found among ICU families, with more than half being excessively sleepy, cognitively blunted to the point of intoxication, or both (Verceles et al., 2014).

A significant proportion—at least half—of family members are affected by anxiety both at and after discharge (Gries et al., 2010; Jones et al., 2004; McAdam et al., 2010). Depression and PTSD are also common among families (Anderson, Arnold, Angus, & Bryce, 2008; Jones et al., 2004; Paparrigopoulos et al., 2006). The duration of all these symptoms is unknown but is at least 6 months (Anderson et al., 2008; Azoulay et al., 2005; Delva et al., 2002; Gries et al., 2010; Jones et al., 2004; Paparrigopoulos et al., 2006; Pochard et al., 2005). This constellation of symptoms is known as the post–intensive care syndrome–family (PICS-F) response to critical illness (Davidson, Jones, & Bienvenu, 2012).

> What does the Society of Critical Care Medicine say about PICS-F? See www.sccm.org/News/Pages/New-Resources-Highlight-Post-Intensive-Care-Syndrome.aspx and www.myicucare.org/Thrive/Pages/Post-intensive-Care-Syndrome.aspx

Given the functional limitations incurred by many survivors of critical illness, this morbidity among their families is particularly worrisome. In other settings, caregivers can reduce limitations and prevent transfer to a nursing home (Hebert, Dubois, Wolfson, Chambers, & Cohen, 2001; Holt-Lunstad, Smith, & Layton, 2010). In this respect, the families of critical illness survivors play a crucial role in their relative functional independence or disability after hospitalization (Iwashyna & Netzer, 2012), as is seen in other clinical settings (Perez-San-Gregorio, Martin-Rodriguez, & Perez-Bernal, 2008).

POLICIES AND PHYSICAL ENVIRONMENT CAN BOTH IMPROVE OUTCOMES AND SUPPORT FAMILIES

Visitation Policies

Family members wish to both protect and provide reassurance and support for their loved ones in the ICU (Burr, 1998). Historically, ICU staff has viewed open visitation with concern that their presence would either impede care or cause direct injury to the patient (Marco et al., 2006). The data suggest otherwise. In patients with neurological injury, the presence of visitors did not increase intracranial pressure or result in deterioration of vital signs; while in the cardiac care unit, the presence of visitors is associated with decreased cardiovascular complications with no increase in infection (Fumagalli et al., 2006; Hepworth, Hendrickson, & Lopez, 1994). Although current guidelines recommend unrestricted visitation (Davidson et al., 2007), 90% of American ICUs have limitations on visitation (Liu, Read, Scruth, & Cheng, 2013).

> What do critical care nurses do? How many critical care nurses are there in the United States? What is the future of critical care nursing? See www.aacn.org/wd/publishing/content/pressroom/aboutcriticalcarenursing.pcms?menu

Families welcome open visitation, and their implementation increases family satisfaction (Roland, Russell, Richards, & Sullivan, 2001; Schnell et al., 2013; Whitcomb, Roy, & Blackman, 2010). In fact, open visitation reduces anxiety (Garrouste-Orgeas et al., 2008; Simon, Phillips, Badalamenti, Ohlert, & Krumberger, 1997; Whitcomb et al., 2010). Families also find that unlimited visitation allows them more time to get to know their loved ones' physicians and nurses (Garrouste-Orgeas et al., 2008), and improves communication (Henneman, McKenzie, & Dewa, 1992).

The physical environment created plays an important interaction with families. Dedicated meeting rooms reduce anxiety in family members (Pochard et al., 2001). Current guidelines also advocate a "family support zone" (Thompson et al., 2012). This should include fold-out furniture for sleep, as many family members in the ICU are severely sleep deprived (Netzer & Sullivan, 2014). Family members are often afraid to leave their loved ones' rooms to eat. Food should be easily accessible to the ICU, for example, vending machines. For many families in the ICU, they are far from home and may also need a place for bathing or washing clothes. Laundry facilities are available in many children's hospitals but often are lacking in facilities for critically ill adults.

Staffing

Physician staffing models in the ICU may impact care. In collaboration with high-intensity organization, 24-hour physician staffing may reduce mortality and length of mechanical ventilation (Goh, Lum, & Abdel-Latif, 2001; Netzer et al., 2011), though data are conflicting (Kerlin et al., 2013; Wallace, Angus, Barnato, Kramer, & Kahn, 2012). What is apparent is that nighttime intensive care physician staffing can increase patient centeredness during these hours. Overnight attending physician staffing is associated with increased patient/family satisfaction

(Gajic et al., 2008). The in-house attending during these night hours also can discuss end-of-life care and reduce the time needed to transition care to comfort when appropriate (Kerlin, Harhay, Kahn, & Halpern, 2015; Kerlin et al., 2013; Reineck, Wallace, Barnato, & Kahn, 2013).

Bedside Processes to Improve Care: Family-Centered Rounds

The inclusion of families on health care team rounds has been part of the pediatric critical care culture for some time, with a large body of literature supporting the practice. Providers should be aware that these inclusive rounds are recommended by the American College of Critical Care Medicine/Society of Critical Care Medicine guidelines. Multiple benefits are derived from families joining rounds, including increased family satisfaction, decreased family stress, and increased presence and job satisfaction among nurses (Davidson, 2013; Jacobowski, Girard, Mulder, & Ely, 2010).

> What evidence has been discovered to support the effectiveness of family-centered rounds for the ICU? According to the Nursing Alliance for Quality Care (www.naqc.org), this topic area carries much weight. For more detail on the topic, see www.naqc.org/Main/Resources/FamilyParticipation-Rounds.pdf

Concerns that family-centered rounds will curtail education among trainees are not supported by evidence (Mittal, 2014; Rappaport, Cellucci, & Leffler, 2010). Including families on daily rounds honors their role as stakeholders and should be implemented by ICU teams (Anderson et al., 2015; Netzer & Siegel, 2015). Communication is enhanced through structured approaches during rounds, while providing care and through routine summative conferences. Team members, particularly nurses, can coach the family member on what to expect during rounds and have them prepare questions in advance. The nurse can review the questions and provide answers to the simpler ones prior to rounds. Additionally, family inclusion provides an opportunity to teach house staff and new employees how to provide person-centered care. Although family-centered, inclusive rounds may increase time by 1–2 minutes per patient, this time is offset by a decreased need to answer phone calls or questions later in the day (Aronson, Yau, Helfaer, & Morrison, 2009; Kleiber, Davenport, & Freyenberger, 2006; Phipps et al., 2007; Rosen, Stenger, Bochkoris, Hannon, & Kwoh, 2009). Designating a quality monitor for family involvement in care may provide not only an assessment of whether or not family were present during rounds, but also whether they were actively included in the discussion, whether the team made eye contact with the family, and whether their suggestions or comments were recognized as valuable input.

Pastoral Care and Support of Spirituality

To best support families in the ICU, administrators should be aware that an interdisciplinary approach that includes specialists outside of the ICU may help to provide best care and, subsequently, best support for end-of-life decision making (Nelson, Mulkerin, Adams, & Pronovost, 2006). This is more likely to be successful when utilizing an interdisciplinary approach, with the enlistment of institution-specific, local champions (Black et al., 2013). One of these disciplines is social work (McCormick, Engelberg, & Curtis, 2007). As part of interdisciplinary bundles designed to improve palliative care, social workers act to reduce conflict and increase family comfort (McCormick, Curtis, Stowell-Weiss, Toms, & Engelberg, 2010). Another is pastoral care (McCormick et al., 2007). Spirituality is an important value for many families in the ICU. Frequently, these spiritual values guide both their perception of prognosis and their decision making (Boyd et al., 2010; Robinson et al., 2006; Siegel & Prigerson, 2010). Although these family decision makers often voice these considerations with the health care team, their loved ones' providers rarely pursue or clarify these needs (Ernecoff, Curlin, Buddadhumaruk, & White, 2015). Chaplains are especially active and important in end-of-life care (Choi, Curlin, & Cox, 2015).

> What purpose can spirituality serve in person-focused care? For more on the critical role of spirituality in patient experience, see www.theberylinstitute.org/store/download.asp?id=C043C5EC-15E3-40D3-A2D3-744C4343CF21

Patient/Family Engagement

Families can assist with the best process of care, improving patient outcomes. For example, data support early mobilization of ICU patients, for example, early rehabilitation, sitting in chairs, standing, and walking. This mobilization improves outcomes in the hospital—by reducing length of stay and length of time on mechanical ventilation, and reducing delirium—and also increases the likelihood that patients will be discharged without functional limitations (Schweickert et al., 2009). By enlisting family members to participate in early mobilization, the amount of this therapy is increased (Rukstele & Gagnon, 2013). Delirium is common in the ICU (McNicoll et al., 2003), and is associated with greater cognitive deficit after critical illness (Pandharipande et al., 2013). Family members can be engaged at the bedside to deploy cognitive activities with the patient, reducing rates of delirium, particularly among older patients (Chatham, 1978; Inouye et al., 1999). Educating families about delirium may help them better understand their loved ones' experience in the ICU. Additionally, this may help them provide caregiver support, as memories of frightening experiences in the ICU are a risk factor for PTSD (Parker et al., 2015). Activities contributing to these goals can be incorporated into family members' involvement in facilitated sense making, as described next.

> Practical guidance for evidence-based ICU family conferences is available online at www.ncbi.nlm.nih.gov/pmc/articles/PMC2628462
>   How does shared decision making add value to the process of including families in the ICU?

Facilitated Sense Making

Facilitated sense making is a mid-range theory that is prescriptive in nature, outlining exact steps staff may take to optimize the family portion of person-centered care. It is understood that the patient and family experience the crisis of critical illness, then adjust given the care received, and have consequences (e.g., PICS or PICS-F) at the end of the process. Interventions are focused on those that help make sense out of the environment and the role of the caregiver, foster a shared decision-making approach, improve communication, enhance presence and engagement, and develop caring relationships. It is proposed that through this approach staff may minimize the fear, horror and helplessness experienced by families, thereby reducing the stress response and resultant disorders that may linger following discharge (Davidson, 2010; Davidson, Daly, Agan, Brady, & Higgins, 2010).

Coaching the Family

Outside of the ICU, coaching is necessary for success and integration into the workplace or service. According to the facilitated sense making model, clinicians can coach families to make sense of their new role as a caregiver and also to make sense of what has happened. Met and unmet family needs are proactively assessed. Families are provided with a list of resources, such as spiritual support, social service, and where to find financial counseling. This list is used to identify resources helpful to them along the way. During testing of this intervention in a faith-based hospital, one family actually responded that they did not know spiritual support was available or that the hospital had a chapel, even though she had walked by a 10-foot tall statue of Jesus at the front door of the chapel every day. Asking the question, "Is there anything I can do to make this day as good as possible given what you are going through?" is good, but will not produce the same result as the provision of a list and asking, "Would any of these resources be helpful to you or your family at this time?" (Davidson et al., 2010).

Decoding the Environment

The ICU environment needs to be explained to patients and families repeatedly in terms they can understand (Engstrom & Soderberg, 2004). The function of each piece of equipment is explained. Audible alarms cause anxiety in family members, and their use and meaning should be explained to them. One approach is to make the analogy of clothes in the dryer, a cake in the oven, and a fire in the house (Davidson et al., 2010). Explain the following:

> When the clothes are done an alarm goes off, but nothing bad will happen if they wait a while. The worst case scenario would be that the clothes would wrinkle. If a cake is overcooked by a minute or two, nothing bad will happen and it will likely be fine, but if you leave it longer it will be crispy around the edges. If you don't answer the smoke alarm you could lose the house. All alarms have unique sounds. The staff can tell the difference between the ones that are like the clothes in the dryer vs. the ones that signify an emergency like your smoke alarm.

Another priority for patients and families is to explain the equipment and then the numbers on the monitors. While family members may not remember all of this, the explanation will reassure them that knowledgeable people are caring for their loved ones. Families also need to be provided the context that the values seen on monitors fluctuate constantly. Nurses generally provide this type of detailed information while providing care at the bedside. With experience, the explanations can be built into care and do not take extra time. Getting into the habit of talking out loud while providing care, creating a running dialogue of what you are doing and why, can help families adjust to the environment. Once they understand what is happening around them, they will be better equipped to participate in care.

DECISION MAKING

Because navigating through critical illness is foreign to most people, guidance is necessary to assure engagement. Each family member may desire a different level of involvement, so both caregiving and shared decision-making preferences need to be assessed. This process starts with the surrogate decision maker or designated family spokesperson. The concept of shared decision making is not inherently understood. The process needs to be explained and the surrogate's role in decision making is outlined (Cox et al., 2012). Then, the family is assessed for their desired level of participation in the process. This may range all the way from allowing the medical team to make all of the decisions, to equal partnership in decision making. Cultural norms for lineage and decision making are honored (Davidson et al., 2007). This discussion is generally handled by the patient's primary physician.

The designated patient surrogate helps the team identify those friends or family members who might be appropriate to participate in care and/or discussions during rounds if the patient cannot speak for himself or herself. Peripherally involved family members deserve to feel welcomed in the environment and given the benefit of basic information and instructions on how they can help. The patient drives these discussions and decisions when conscious and communicative.

COMMUNICATION
Reflective Inquiry

Reflective inquiry is performed daily with families (Davidson, 2010; Davidson et al., 2010). It is an iterative process that filters out misconceptions and serves to develop the situational awareness and factual narrative of what is happening as time goes on. Before the family goes home, or the day shift nurse ends the shift, or at the end of night rounds, the family is asked to think back on the day. The question to ask is, "If you were going to explain today to the rest of the family, how would you describe your husband's progress?" This open-ended reflection helps to sort out the events that were priorities and put in perspective whether or not there has been progress. Often, these moments of reflection reveal mistruths or false assumptions that can be corrected before becoming cemented in the brain by the family as fact. Reviewing the day together also provides the team with a moment to praise the family for their presence and involvement. Articulate that their presence helps to calm the patient by bringing in familiar voices and discussion. For instance, state aloud that their encouragement as a mobility coach has surely helped to move him to the next level of activity. Assure them that their role is important and appreciated. This role clarification and encouragement further endorses engagement, decreases the sensation of helplessness, and forms caring relationships that bolster the tenor of the healing environment. *Saying it out loud* for them with verbal expressions of praise creates as positive as possible of a reality for family members to form memories from. Without hearing it, they will wonder if they are doing everything they could or should, and whether they indeed have a valuable role in this experience. Your affirmations will soothe and cultivate a healing environment.

Diary

Maintenance of a diary has been found to decrease stress disorders in patients and families (Jones, Backman, & Griffiths, 2012; Jones et al., 2010). Diaries have been deployed in a variety of ways. Usually the clinicians make daily entries to explain major points of progress or change, explain noxious stimuli like restraints that may cause nightmares in the future, and also enter caring statements into the journal. These caring statements may reflect empathy, support, praise, or hope.

Messages of prayer may be included when spiritual assessment indicates this would be acceptable. Pictures of ICU technology may be included with an explanation of purpose. Families may also enter notes or words of prayer, hopes, or notes to reflect upon later. Either at the time of transfer, discharge, or follow-up meeting, family members are debriefed in a 1:1 appointment by reviewing the diary together with a designated member of the team. The family can then explain the diary to the patient when he or she is well enough to absorb the information or the team can debrief the patient at a future appointment. Debriefing the patient often comes at a later date due to the timeline of cognitive recovery. The purpose of the debriefing is to clarify misconceptions and help provide a constructive and factual narrative to explain what happened over time. Debriefing provides a point in time when unresolved questions can be answered about why or how different events occurred. The debriefing is also an opportunity for service recovery if there are any concerns expressed by the patient or family regarding the delivery of care.

> One method of implementing a diary program can be found online at www .icudiary.org

Written Communication

Written or electronic information is provided to support verbal communication. These materials may be helpful because families overwhelmed in the moment may forget the detail of instructions; in combination with patient conferencing, this has been shown to decrease stress disorders at 3 months following discharge (Lautrette et al., 2007). Written and electronic information are intended to be supplemental and not replace discussions. It is best if printouts are highlighted together at the time of education as to which portions of the material on the page are most pertinent to this patient. Learning occurs best when the materials are reviewed together, individualized to the patient, and targeted questions are asked to evaluate understanding. The teach-back method of instruction is advocated. This includes giving small chunks of information at a time, and asking reflective open-ended questions to assure that the information was understood (*Always Use Teach-Back!*, 2015; Fidyk, Ventura, & Green, 2014).

> Pamphlets created for the purpose of ICU patient/family education can be found on a variety of topics through www.sccm.org and key wording the topic of interest.

Family Conferences

Family conferences are associated with increased family satisfaction (Kodali et al., 2014). Family conferences are indicated when the patient may not survive the event, at least every 7 days, when conflict exists, to clarify goals of care, or to clarify the treatment plan when multiple consultants are involved on the case

(Davidson et al., 2007). An initial meeting should occur within 72 hours of admission, as this is associated with reduced ICU length of stay and higher scores on quality of death and dying metrics by families (Curtis & White, 2008). Nursing should be present along with the physician of record. The nurse often reclarifies the discussion with family members following the conference and must be present to prevent fractured or disjointed communication later. Other disciplines are invited to participate in the conference as indicated by involvement in the case. If consultants cannot be present, a status summary is secured with them prior to the meeting and presented by a member of the team. Spiritual advisors are welcome if desired by the family. The surrogate or family spokesperson invites appropriate members of the family to be present.

The method for conferencing should include communication strategies that include exploring patient values and family concerns through active listening, provision of empathic statements, and provision of statements to reflect nonabandonment when goals of care change. This approach has been found to decrease stress disorders in family members (Lautrette et al., 2007). A record of the discussion and any decisions made as a result of the conference are noted in the record.

Role coaching, teaching bedside activities, decoding the environment, provision of written materials, reflective inquiry, participation in rounds, provision of summative conferences, and maintenance of a diary all impart knowledge. Knowledge decreases fear of the unknown, which stimulates the limbic system to activate the fight versus flight response and is a precursor to the development of stress disorders. Communication, then, is more than satisfaction. It is part of the algorithm of care that promotes a healing environment and prevents harm in the form of PICS or PICS-F.

FOSTERING CARING RELATIONSHIPS

Families of ICU patients are treated in a manner that promotes the development of caring relationships. This includes acknowledging their input in an authentic positive manner, providing empathic and active listening, assessing values and preferences, and advocating for families when their needs are not met. Setting a welcome tone and atmosphere of respect, comradery, and teamwork also demonstrates caring. Families should feel "I am welcome here" instead of "May I visit?" Anticipating family needs and taking the time to provide explanations are also acts of caring. Calling family members by name demonstrates greater caring than saying "wife of bed 4." Getting to know the patient can start as simply as "tell me about your dad." Integrating the patient's favorite music or discussions about his favorite topics into bedside activities demonstrates respect and caring for the person as an individual. Talking to the patient whether or not it is felt he or she can hear or understand demonstrates respect. In one self-biographical report of an ICU experience, the patient describes how the physicians conducted rounds over her bed, assuming she could not hear, and discussed daily her high likelihood of death. Following rounds, the nurses would try to send the family home to rest. Both the patient and her mother lived in fear that when separated the patient would die, alone in her bed, with no one in the room. The fear was traumatic in nature, requiring counseling for both the patient and her mother for many years (Davidson, Harvey, Schuller, & Black, 2013). Keeping the patient clean and covered without visible blood or fluid stains also maintains a calmer, more respectful environment for the family. When a caring relationship has been established, it would be hard to leave the shift for home without saying good-bye. Furthermore, showing emotion was once frowned upon in health care. Our experiences in the ICU suggest that families interpret emotional expressions following setbacks or death as caring. Families will often express, in writing and through thank you letters, that they appreciate those clinicians that shed a tear with them during their loss or trying times.

PRESENCE AND ENGAGEMENT
Role Model Caregiving Behaviors

Clinicians role-model caring behaviors during bedside care. Families learn from us by watching how we provide care. They learn how they can touch or communicate with patients who are in an altered physical or cognitive state (Harbaugh et al., 2004). Presence is encouraged instead of "allowed," yet individual desires for caregiving preference are assessed and honored. Respite is offered but not enforced or dictated. Bedside activities are taught and encouraged. These can be as simple as application of lip balm, hand or foot rubs, passive or active range of motion, and coaching through mobility exercises. Cognitive exercises such as reading to the patient, provision of music, provision of prayer, playing word puzzles, number puzzles, simple card games, or dominoes can help with "brain strengthening" as patients are able. Word puzzles can be reduced in complexity to finding the letter "A" on the page, whereas card games can be simplified to "pointing to the Jack." Engagement in activities provides families with purpose during crisis, which may help to minimize the fear associated with the unknown and ameliorate the development of stress disorders. Being able to look back and quantify how they were helpful, despite a negative outcome, is thought to be protective in the long term.

Privacy: A Potential Obstacle to Person-Centered Care

Clinicians often express concerns about privacy and inclusion (Bramwell & Weindling, 2005; Duncan, Vigen, Richards, & Garros, 2005). Privacy regulations state that information may be shared in the best interest of the patient (www.pbgc.gov/about/policies/pg/summary-of-privacy-act.html). When asked, families value the presence on rounds and information received during rounds higher than the risk of breach of privacy (Phipps et al., 2007). Privacy should not be regarded as an excuse to exclude families from participating in care or exclude the designated surrogate decision maker from inclusion in decision making or rounds.

- Families need incremental and repeated information to minimize stress reaction to the unknown and foreign experience of critical illness.
- Families who participate in rounds may impart information that is necessary for formation of an accurate treatment plan based on patient values and past experience.
- Family involvement in decision making assures patient values are met.
- Family involvement in bedside activities provides a sense of purpose that may decrease helplessness and improve caring capacity.

What is the scope and impact of visitation in the ICU? The American Association of Critical-Care Nurses (AACN) addresses this at www.aacn.org/wd/practice/content/practicealerts/family-visitation-icu-practice-alert.pcms?menu=practice

CONCLUSION

In summary, the healing environment can be optimized through the development of caring relationships, coaching to the role of caregiver, and encouragement of engagement in care. It is hoped that these efforts will decrease fear, horror, and helplessness that are precursors to stress disorders. By decreasing stress in the environment and providing families with purpose through crisis, family integrity may be strengthened while increasing the capacity for caregiving.

CASE STUDY

DC was a young, healthy woman who developed community-acquired pneumonia, which progressed to acute respiratory distress syndrome and multi-organ failure, including the need for dialysis. Transferred from a community hospital to a tertiary care, academic facility, she spent 21 days on mechanical ventilation.

SC [my spouse] felt that the inclusion of our family on a daily basis along with the physicians involved during their rounds, every day 14–20 physicians and staff, in my room was a significant factor in his understanding of what was occurring. He felt as though he knew what path/direction things would be going and could not have gotten through it without that process. The fear of the unknown as we all know is tormenting, so the honest interaction on a daily basis with such amazing individuals was so important. . . . Keep in mind that they had been told the possibility of my leaving the hospital was not in my favor so every word was important. I think that this is a crucial issue in assisting the family in understanding what is occurring. We depend on health care professionals as we do not know what is happening.

Policies prompting family-centered rounds provide an important opportunity for communication between the health care team and patients' families, as well as an opportunity to build trust between providers and the loved ones of their patients. DC's spouse was included on a daily basis during the physician rounds. Every day 14 to 20 physicians and staff were in DC's room. SC felt as though he knew what path/direction things were going and could not have gotten through the experience without that process. The physicians actively built trust with DC and SC by communicating with them during rounds without being rushed or distracted. The fear of the unknown was tormenting, so the honest interaction on a daily basis with physicians was important to SC.

I cannot fully explain to you what occurred in the ICU and how I was so confused. I was reduced to a paranoid scared person thinking I was being held against my will. This was only my interpretation; it had nothing to do with staff. My mind became something I cannot, to this day, explain. It is important that every time a staff member enters that room to go over with the patient, why they are here, what has occurred,

(continued)

CASE STUDY *(continued)*

what is happening, that they are there to help them, that they want them to return to their regular environment, etc.

Delirium is common in the ICU and can result in frightening memories for patients. Family-centered care acknowledges this, and provides family members with an opportunity to participate in care, potentially reducing delirium. Acknowledging patients and families as individuals may be reassuring.

Hospital policies can dictate that every time a staff member enters the room he or she should review with patients and their families why they are in the ICU, what has occurred, and what is happening. Staff can help patients return to their regular environment as soon as possible. These policies need to be correctly socialized and embedded into the culture. Nurse managers can ask patients and their families how they feel about this policy to make sure that it was consistently utilized.

The one thing that I am very concerned with is when someone is discharged from the ICU/CCU, I truly believe there should be an intermediate care plan. My discharge to "the general population" was so welcome as I just wanted so badly to come home. But, the staffing was not able to handle what I needed. I was not ready to wait for 10 or 15 minutes to go to the bathroom so that resulted in several accidents [of] which I was so terribly embarrassed. When my food tray was brought to me, I could not open a simple carton of milk, so most times I did not eat because it was too difficult and the staff was so busy and I knew that they had multiple patients and surely could not expect them to do everything for me. There should have, perhaps, been intermediate care that was sort of in the middle until I could do things on my own. At that point, I still could not get out of bed without assistance to use a commode, which was right next to my bed. It was very hard for me to accept that.

Most ICU teams do not inform patients and their families regarding the sequelae of critical illness. It is important for ICU providers to work within an interdisciplinary team aware of ICU-acquired weakness and other effects of critical illness. Family members need to be included in this discussion, because they will be important determinants of patients' trajectories after discharge. An interdisciplinary team can work together to both educate patients and create a care plan that extends past the ICU. Both the team and the pathways for this need to be delineated by carefully created policies.

Issues to Consider

1. Give one example of how this case study illustrates how managerial decision making positively impacted patient care in the ICU. How did those decisions positively affect the personal experience of patient care? What other managerial options were available that would have enhanced the positive impact?

2. Give one example of how this case study illustrates managerial decisions that negatively impacted patient care in the ICU. How did those decisions negatively affect the personal experience of patient care? What other managerial options were available that would have mitigated the negative impact?

REFERENCES

Always use teach-back! (2015). Cambridge, MA: Institute for Healthcare Improvement.

Anderson, W. G., Arnold, R. M., Angus, D. C., & Bryce, C. L. (2008). Posttraumatic stress and complicated grief in family members of patients in the intensive care unit. *Journal of General Internal Medicine, 23*(11), 1871–1876.

Anderson, W. G., Cimino, J. W., Ernecoff, N. C., Ungar, A., Shotsberger, K. J., Pollice, L. A., . . . White, D. B. (2015). A multicenter study of key stakeholders' perspectives on communicating with surrogates about prognosis in intensive care units. *Annals of the American Thoracic Society, 12*(2), 142–152.

Angus, D. C., Barnato, A. E., Linde-Zwirble, W. T., Weissfeld, L. A., Watson, R. S., Rickert, T., . . . Robert Wood Johnson Foundation ICU End-Of-Life Peer Group. (2004). Use of intensive care at the end of life in the United States: An epidemiologic study. *Critical Care Medicine, 32*(3), 638–643.

Aronson, P. L., Yau, J., Helfaer, M. A., & Morrison, W. (2009). Impact of family presence during pediatric intensive care unit rounds on the family and medical team. *Pediatrics, 124*(4), 1119–1125.

Azoulay, E., Pochard, F., Kentish-Barnes, N., Chevret, S., Aboab, J., Adrie, C., . . . FAMIREA Study Group. (2005). Risk of post-traumatic stress symptoms in family members of intensive care unit patients. *American Journal of Respiratory and Critical Care Medicine, 171*(9), 987–994.

Battle, C. E., Lovett, S., & Hutchings, H. (2013). Chronic pain in survivors of critical illness: A retrospective analysis of incidence and risk factors. *Critical Care, 17*(3), R101.

Black, M. D., Vigorito, M. C., Curtis, J. R., Phillips, G. S., Martin, E. W., McNicoll, L., . . . Levy, M. M. (2013). A multifaceted intervention to improve compliance with process measures for ICU clinician communication with ICU patients and families. *Critical Care Medicine, 41*(10), 2275–2283.

Boyd, E. A., Lo, B., Evans, L. R., Malvar, G., Apatira, L., Luce, J. M., & White, D. B. (2010). "It's not just what the doctor tells me": Factors that influence surrogate decision-makers' perceptions of prognosis. *Critical Care Medicine, 38*(5), 1270–1275.

Bramwell, R., & Weindling, M. (2005). Families' views on ward rounds in neonatal units. *Archives of Disease in Childhood-Fetal and Neonatal Edition, 90*(5), F429–F431.

Burr, G. (1998). Contextualizing critical care family needs through triangulation: An Australian study. *Intensive & Critical Care Nursing: The Official Journal of the British Association of Critical Care Nurses, 14*(4), 161–169.

Carlet, J., Thijs, L. G., Antonelli, M., Cassell, J., Cox, P., Hill, N., . . . Thompson, B. T. (2004). Challenges in end-of-life care in the ICU. Statement of the 5th International Consensus Conference in Critical Care, Brussels, Belgium, April 2003. *Intensive Care Medicine, 30*(5), 770–784.

Chatham, M. A. (1978). The effect of family involvement on patients' manifestations of postcardiotomy psychosis. *Heart & Lung: The Journal of Critical Care, 7*(6), 995–999.

Choi, J., Sherwood, P. R., Schulz, R., Ren, D., Donahoe, M. P., Given, B., . . . Hoffman, L. A. (2012). Patterns of depressive symptoms in caregivers of mechanically ventilated critically ill adults from intensive care unit admission to 2 months post-intensive care unit discharge: A pilot study. *Critical Care Medicine, 40*(5), 1546–1553.

Choi, P. J., Curlin, F. A., & Cox, C. E. (2015). "The patient is dying, please call the chaplain": The activities of chaplains in one medical center's intensive care units. *Journal of Pain and Symptom Management, 50*(4), 501–506.

Covinsky, K. E., Goldman, L., Cook, E. F., Oye, R., Desbiens, N., Reding, D., . . . Phillips, R. S. (1994). The impact of serious illness on patients' families. SUPPORT Investigators. Study to Understand Prognoses and Preferences for Outcomes and Risks of Treatment. *Journal of the American Medical Association, 272*(23), 1839–1844.

Cox, C. E., Lewis, C. L., Hanson, L. C., Hough, C. L., Kahn, J. M., White, D. B., . . . Carson, S. S. (2012). Development and pilot testing of a decision aid for surrogates of patients with prolonged mechanical ventilation. *Critical Care Medicine, 40*(8), 2327–2234.

Curtis, J. R., & White, D. B. (2008). Practical guidance for evidence-based ICU family conferences. *Chest, 134*(4), 835–843.

Davidson, J. E. (2010). Facilitated sensemaking: A strategy and new middle-range theory to support families of intensive care unit patients. *Critical Care Nurse, 30*(6), 28–39.

Davidson, J. E. (2013). Family presence on rounds in neonatal, pediatric, and adult intensive care units. *Annals of the American Thoracic Society, 10*(2), 152–156.

Davidson, J. E., Daly, B. J., Agan, D., Brady, N. R., & Higgins, P. A. (2010). Facilitated sensemaking: A feasibility study for the provision of a family support program in the intensive care unit. *Critical Care Nursing Quarterly, 33*(2), 177–189.

Davidson, J. E., Harvey, M. A., Schuller, J., & Black, G. (2013). Post-intensive care syndrome: What to do and how to prevent it. *American Nurse Today: American Nurses Association*, 32–38.

Davidson, J. E., Jones, C., & Bienvenu, O. J. (2012). Family response to critical illness: Postintensive care syndrome-family. *Critical Care Medicine, 40*(2), 618–624.

Davidson, J. E., Powers, K., Hedayat, K. M., Tieszen, M., Kon, A. A., Shepard, E., . . . American College of Critical Care Medicine Task Force 2004-2005, Society of Critical Care Medicine. (2007). Clinical practice guidelines for support of the family in the patient-centered intensive care unit: American College of Critical Care Medicine Task Force 2004–2005. *Critical Care Medicine, 35*(2), 605–622.

De Jonghe, B., Sharshar, T., Lefaucheur, J. P., Authier, F. J., Durand-Zaleski, I., Boussarsar, M., . . . Groupe de Réflexion et d'Etude des Neuromyopathies en Réanimation. (2002). Paresis acquired in the intensive care unit: A prospective multicenter study. *Journal of the American Medical Association, 288*(22), 2859–2867.

Delva, D., Vanoost, S., Bijttebier, P., Lauwers, P., & Wilmer, A. (2002). Needs and feelings of anxiety of relatives of patients hospitalized in intensive care units: Implications for social work. *Social Work in Health Care, 35*(4), 21–40.

Desai, S. V., Law, T. J., & Needham, D. M. (2011). Long-term complications of critical care. *Critical Care Medicine, 39*(2), 371–379.

Duncan, S. M., Vigen, K., Richards, S., & Garros, D. (2005). The attitudes and perceptions of healthcare professionals towards family presence during rounds: 202-M. *Critical Care Medicine, 33*(12), A107.

Engstrom, A., & Soderberg, S. (2004). The experiences of partners of critically ill persons in an intensive care unit. *Intensive and Critical Care Nursing, 20*(5), 299–308; quiz 9–10.

Ernecoff, N. C., Curlin, F. A., Buddadhumaruk, P., & White, D. B. (2015). Health care professionals' responses to religious or spiritual statements by surrogate decision makers during goals-of-care discussions. *Journal of the American Medical Association, 175*(10), 1662–1669.

Fan, E., Dowdy, D. W., Colantuoni, E., Mendez-Tellez, P. A., Sevransky, J. E., Shanholtz, C., . . . Needham, D. M. (2014). Physical complications in acute lung injury survivors: A two-year longitudinal prospective study. *Critical Care Medicine, 42*(4), 849–859.

Fidyk, L., Ventura, K., & Green, K. (2014). Teaching nurses how to teach: Strategies to enhance the quality of patient education. *Journal for Nurses in Professional Development, 30*(5), 248–253.

Fumagalli, S., Boncinelli, L., Lo Nostro, A., Valoti, P., Baldereschi, G., Di Bari, M., . . . Marchionni, N. (2006). Reduced cardiocirculatory complications with unrestrictive visiting policy in an intensive care unit: Results from a pilot, randomized trial. *Circulation, 113*(7), 946–952.

Gajic, O., Afessa, B., Hanson, A. C., Krpata, T., Yilmaz, M., Mohamed, S. F., . . . Wylam, M. E. (2008). Effect of 24-hour mandatory versus on-demand critical care specialist presence on quality of care and family and provider satisfaction in the intensive care unit of a teaching hospital. *Critical Care Medicine, 36*(1), 36–44.

Garrouste-Orgeas, M., Philippart, F., Timsit, J. F., Diaw, F., Willems, V., Tabah, A., . . . Carlet, J. (2008). Perceptions of a 24-hour visiting policy in the intensive care unit. *Critical Care Medicine, 36*(1), 30–35.

Girard, T. D., Jackson, J. C., Pandharipande, P. P., Pun, B. T., Thompson, J. L., Shintani, A. K., . . . Ely, E. W. (2010). Delirium as a predictor of long-term cognitive impairment in survivors of critical illness. *Critical Care Medicine, 38*(7), 1513–1520.

Goh, A. Y., Lum, L. C., & Abdel-Latif, M. E. (2001). Impact of 24-hour critical care physician staffing on case-mix adjusted mortality in paediatric intensive care. *The Lancet, 357*(9254), 445–446.

Govindan, S., Iwashyna, T. J., Watson, S. R., Hyzy, R. C., & Miller, M. A. (2014). Issues of survivorship are rarely addressed during intensive care unit stays. Baseline results from a statewide quality improvement collaborative. *Annals of the American Thoracic Society, 11*(4), 587–591.

Gries, C. J., Engelberg, R. A., Kross, E. K., Zatzick, D., Nielsen, E. L., Downey, L., . . . Curtis, J. R. (2010). Predictors of symptoms of posttraumatic stress and depression in family members after patient death in the ICU. *Chest, 137*(2), 280–287.

Halpern, N. A., & Pastores, S. M. (2015). Critical care medicine beds, use, occupancy, and costs in the United States: A methodological review. *Critical Care Medicine, 43*(11), 2452–2459.

Harbaugh, B. L., Tomlinson, P. S., & Kirschbaum, M. (2004). Parents' perceptions of nurses' caregiving behaviors in the pediatric intensive care unit. *Issues in Comprehensive Pediatric Nursing, 27*(3), 163–178.

Hebert, R., Dubois, M. F., Wolfson, C., Chambers, L., & Cohen, C. (2001). Factors associated with long-term institutionalization of older people with dementia: Data from the Canadian Study of Health and Aging. *The Journals of Gerontology: Series A, Biological Sciences and Medical Sciences, 56*(11), M693–M699.

Henneman, E. A., McKenzie, J. B., & Dewa, C. S. (1992). An evaluation of interventions for meeting the information needs of families of critically ill patients. *American Journal of Critical Care, 1*(3), 85–93.

Hepworth, J. T., Hendrickson, S. G., & Lopez, J. (1994). Time series analysis of physiological response during ICU visitation. *Western Journal of Nursing Research, 16*(6), 704–717.

Herridge, M. S., Tansey, C. M., Matte, A., Tomlinson, G., Diaz-Granados, N., Cooper, A., . . . Canadian Critical Care Trials Group. (2011). Functional disability 5 years after acute respiratory distress syndrome. *The New England Journal of Medicine, 364*(14), 1293–1304.

Holt-Lunstad, J., Smith, T. B., & Layton, J. B. (2010). Social relationships and mortality risk: A meta-analytic review. *PLOS Medicine, 7*(7), e1000316.

Inouye, S. K., Bogardus, S. T., Jr., Charpentier, P. A., Leo-Summers, L., Acampora, D., Holford, T. R., & Cooney, L. M., Jr. (1999). A multicomponent intervention to prevent delirium in hospitalized older patients. *The New England Journal of Medicine, 340*(9), 669–676.

Institute of Medicine. (2001). *Crossing the quality chasm: A new health system for the 21st century.* Washington, DC: National Academies Press.

Iwashyna, T. J., Cooke, C. R., Wunsch, H., & Kahn, J. M. (2012). Population burden of long-term survivorship after severe sepsis in older Americans. *Journal of the American Geriatrics Society, 60*(6), 1070–1077.

Iwashyna, T. J., Ely, E. W., Smith, D. M., & Langa, K. M. (2010). Long-term cognitive impairment and functional disability among survivors of severe sepsis. *Journal of the American Medical Association, 304*(16), 1787–1794.

Iwashyna, T. J., & Netzer, G. (2012). The burdens of survivorship: An approach to thinking about long-term outcomes after critical illness. *Seminars in Respiratory and Critical Care Medicine, 33*(4), 327–338.

Jackson, J. C., Obremskey, W., Bauer, R., Greevy, R., Cotton, B. A., Anderson, V., . . . Ely, E. W. (2007). Long-term cognitive, emotional, and functional outcomes in trauma intensive care unit survivors without intracranial hemorrhage. *The Journal of Trauma, 62*(1), 80–88.

Jacobowski, N. L., Girard, T. D., Mulder, J. A., & Ely, E. W. (2010). Communication in critical care: Family rounds in the intensive care unit. *American Journal of Critical Care, 19*(5), 421–430.

Jones, C., Backman, C., Capuzzo, M., Egerod, I., Flaatten, H., Granja, C., . . . RACHEL Group. (2010). Intensive care diaries reduce new onset post traumatic stress disorder following critical illness: A randomised, controlled trial. *Critical Care, 14*(5), R168.

Jones, C., Backman, C., & Griffiths, R. D. (2012). Intensive care diaries and relatives' symptoms of posttraumatic stress disorder after critical illness: A pilot study. *American Journal of Critical Care, 21*(3), 172–176.

Jones, C., Skirrow, P., Griffiths, R. D., Humphris, G., Ingleby, S., Eddleston, J., . . . Gager, M. (2004). Post-traumatic stress disorder-related symptoms in relatives of patients following intensive care. *Intensive Care Medicine, 30*(3), 456–460.

Kerlin, M. P., Harhay, M. O., Kahn, J. M., & Halpern, S. D. (2015). Nighttime intensivist staffing, mortality, and limits on life support: A retrospective cohort study. *Chest, 147*(4), 951–958.

Kerlin, M. P., Small, D. S., Cooney, E., Fuchs, B. D., Bellini, L. M., Mikkelsen, M. E., . . . Halpern, S. D. (2013). A randomized trial of nighttime physician staffing in an intensive care unit. *The New England Journal of Medicine, 368*(23), 2201–2209.

Kleiber, C., Davenport, T., & Freyenberger, B. (2006). Open bedside rounds for families with children in pediatric intensive care units. *American Journal of Critical Care, 15*(5), 492–496.

Kodali, S., Stametz, R. A., Bengier, A. C., Clarke, D. N., Layon, A. J., & Darer, J. D. (2014). Family experience with intensive care unit care: Association of self-reported family conferences and family satisfaction. *Journal of Critical Care, 29*(4), 641–644.

Lautrette, A., Darmon, M., Megarbane, B., Joly, L. M., Chevret, S., Adrie, C., . . . Azoulay, E. (2007). A communication strategy and brochure for relatives of patients dying in the ICU. *The New England Journal of Medicine, 356*(5), 469–478.

Lilly, C. M., De Meo, D. L., Sonna, L. A., Haley, K. J., Massaro, A. F., Wallace, R. F., & Cody, S. (2000). An intensive communication intervention for the critically ill. *American Journal of Medicine, 109*(6), 469–475.

Liu, V., Read, J. L., Scruth, E., & Cheng, E. (2013). Visitation policies and practices in US ICUs. *Critical Care, 17*(2), R71.

Majesko, A., Hong, S. Y., Weissfeld, L., & White, D. B. (2012). Identifying family members who may struggle in the role of surrogate decision maker. *Critical Care Medicine, 40*(8), 2281–2286.

Marco, L., Bermejillo, I., Garayalde, N., Sarrate, I., Margall, M. A., & Asiain, M. C. (2006). Intensive care nurses' beliefs and attitudes towards the effect of open visiting on patients, family and nurses. *Nursing in Critical Care, 11*(1), 33–41.

McAdam, J. L., Arai, S., & Puntillo, K. A. (2008). Unrecognized contributions of families in the intensive care unit. *Intensive Care Medicine, 34*(6), 1097–1101.

McAdam, J. L., Dracup, K. A., White, D. B., Fontaine, D. K., & Puntillo, K. A. (2010). Symptom experiences of family members of intensive care unit patients at high risk for dying. *Critical Care Medicine, 38*(4), 1078–1085.

McCormick, A. J., Curtis, J. R., Stowell-Weiss, P., Toms, C., & Engelberg, R. (2010). Improving social work in intensive care unit palliative care: Results of a quality improvement intervention. *Journal of Palliative Medicine, 13*(3), 297–304.

McCormick, A. J., Engelberg, R., & Curtis, J. R. (2007). Social workers in palliative care: Assessing activities and barriers in the intensive care unit. *Journal of Palliative Medicine, 10*(4), 929–937.

McNicoll, L., Pisani, M. A., Zhang, Y., Ely, E. W., Siegel, M. D., & Inouye, S. K. (2003). Delirium in the intensive care unit: Occurrence and clinical course in older patients. *Journal of the American Geriatrics Society, 51*(5), 591–598.

Meyer, E. C., Ritholz, M. D., Burns, J. P., & Truog, R. D. (2006). Improving the quality of end-of-life care in the pediatric intensive care unit: Parents' priorities and recommendations. *Pediatrics, 117*(3), 649–657.

Mikkelsen, M. E., Christie, J. D., Lanken, P. N., Biester, R. C., Thompson, B. T., Bellamy, S. L., . . . Angus, D. C. (2012). The adult respiratory distress syndrome cognitive outcomes study: Long-term neuropsychological function in survivors of acute lung injury. *American Journal of Respiratory and Critical Care Medicine, 185*(12), 1307–1315.

Mittal, V. (2014). Family-centered rounds. *Pediatric Clinics of North America, 61*(4), 663–670.

Needham, D. M., Davidson, J., Cohen, H., Hopkins, R. O., Weinert, C., Wunsch, H., . . . Harvey, M. A. (2012). Improving long-term outcomes after discharge from intensive care unit: Report from a stakeholders' conference. *Critical Care Medicine, 40*(2), 502–509.

Nelson, J. E., Mulkerin, C. M., Adams, L. L., & Pronovost, P. J. (2006). Improving comfort and communication in the ICU: A practical new tool for palliative care performance measurement and feedback. *Quality & Safety in Health Care, 15*(4), 264–271.

Netzer, G., Liu, X., Shanholtz, C., Harris, A., Verceles, A., & Iwashyna, T. J. (2011). Decreased mortality resulting from a multicomponent intervention in a tertiary care medical intensive care unit. *Critical Care Medicine, 39*(2), 284–293.

Netzer, G., & Siegel, M. D. (2015). Guiding the guiders. Recognizing surrogates' needs and advancing communication in the intensive care unit. *Annals of the American Thoracic Society, 12*(2), 237–238.

Netzer, G., & Sullivan, D. R. (2014). Recognizing, naming, and measuring a family intensive care unit syndrome. *Annals of the American Thoracic Society, 11*(3), 435–441.

NICHE Geriatric Resource Nurse: Family Caregiving. (2011). New York, NY: Hartford Institute for Geriatric Nursing, New York University College of Nursing.

Novaes, M. A., Knobel, E., Bork, A. M., Pavao, O. F., Nogueira-Martins, L. A., & Ferraz, M. B. (1999). Stressors in ICU: Perception of the patient, relatives and health care team. *Intensive Care Medicine, 25*(12), 1421–1426.

Orme, J., Jr., Romney, J. S., Hopkins, R. O., Pope, D., Chan, K. J., Thomsen, G., . . . Weaver, L. K. (2003). Pulmonary function and health-related quality of life in survivors of acute respiratory distress syndrome. *American Journal of Respiratory and Critical Care Medicine, 167*(5), 690–694.

Osborn, T. R., Curtis, J. R., Nielsen, E. L., Back, A. L., Shannon, S. E., & Engelberg, R. A. (2012). Identifying elements of ICU care that families report as important but unsatisfactory: Decision-making, control, and ICU atmosphere. *Chest, 142*(5), 1185–1192.

Pandharipande, P. P., Girard, T. D., Jackson, J. C., Morandi, A., Thompson, J. L., Pun, B. T., . . . BRAIN-ICU Study Investigators. (2013). Long-term cognitive impairment after critical illness. *The New England Journal of Medicine, 369*(14), 1306–1316.

Paparrigopoulos, T., Melissaki, A., Efthymiou, A., Tsekou, H., Vadala, C., Kribeni, G., . . . Soldatos, C. (2006). Short-term psychological impact on family members of intensive care unit patients. *Journal of Psychosomatic Research, 61*(5), 719–722.

Parker, A. M., Sricharoenchai, T., Raparla, S., Schneck, K. W., Bienvenu, O. J., & Needham, D. M. (2015). Posttraumatic stress disorder in critical illness survivors: A metaanalysis. *Critical Care Medicine, 43*(5), 1121–1129.

Perez-San-Gregorio, M. A., Martin-Rodriguez, A., & Perez-Bernal, J. (2008). Influence of the psychological state of relatives on the quality of life of patients at 1 year after transplantation. *Transplantation Proceedings, 40*(9), 3109–3111.

Phipps, L. M., Bartke, C. N., Spear, D. A., Jones, L. F., Foerster, C. P., Killian, M. E., . . . Thomas, N. J. (2007). Assessment of parental presence during bedside pediatric intensive care unit rounds: Effect on duration, teaching, and privacy. *Pediatric Critical Care Medicine, 8*(3), 220–224.

Pochard, F., Azoulay, E., Chevret, S., Lemaire, F., Hubert, P., Canoui, P., . . . French FAMIREA Study Group. (2001). Symptoms of anxiety and depression in family members of intensive care unit patients: Ethical hypothesis regarding decision-making capacity. *Critical Care Medicine, 29*(10), 1893–1897.

Pochard, F., Darmon, M., Fassier, T., Bollaert, P. E., Cheval, C., Coloigner, M., . . . French FAMIREA Study Group. (2005). Symptoms of anxiety and depression in family members of intensive care unit patients before discharge or death: A prospective multicenter study. *Journal of Critical Care, 20*(1), 90–96.

Rappaport, D. I., Cellucci, M. F., & Leffler, M. G. (2010). Implementing family-centered rounds: Pediatric residents' perceptions. *Clinical Pediatrics, 49*(3), 228–234.

Reineck, L. A., Wallace, D. J., Barnato, A. E., & Kahn, J. M. (2013). Nighttime intensivist staffing and the timing of death among ICU decedents: A retrospective cohort study. *Critical Care, 17*(5), R216.

Robinson, M. R., Thiel, M. M., Backus, M. M., & Meyer, E. C. (2006). Matters of spirituality at the end of life in the pediatric intensive care unit. *Pediatrics, 118*(3), e719–e729.

Roland, P., Russell, J., Richards, K. C., & Sullivan, S. C. (2001). Visitation in critical care: Processes and outcomes of a performance improvement initiative. *Journal of Nursing Care Quality, 15*(2), 18–26.

Rosen, P., Stenger, E., Bochkoris, M., Hannon, M. J., & Kwoh, C. K. (2009). Family-centered multidisciplinary rounds enhance the team approach in pediatrics. *Pediatrics, 123*(4), e603–e608.

Rukstele, C. D., & Gagnon, M. M. (2013). Making strides in preventing ICU-acquired weakness: Involving family in early progressive mobility. *Critical Care Nursing Quarterly, 36*(1), 141–147.

Schnell, D., Abadie, S., Toullic, P., Chaize, M., Souppart, V., Poncet, M. C., . . . Azoulay, E. (2013). Open visitation policies in the ICU: Experience from relatives and clinicians. *Intensive Care Medicine, 39*(10), 1873–1874.

Schweickert, W. D., & Hall, J. (2007). ICU-acquired weakness. *Chest, 131*(5), 1541–1549.

Schweickert, W. D., Pohlman, M. C., Pohlman, A. S., Nigos, C., Pawlik, A. J., Esbrook, C. L., . . . Kress, J. P. (2009). Early physical and occupational therapy in mechanically ventilated, critically ill patients: A randomised controlled trial. *The Lancet, 373*(9678), 1874–1882.

Siegel, M. D., & Prigerson, H. G. (2010). The perception gap: Race, religion, and prognosis in the ICU. *Chest, 138*(1), 8–9.

Simon, S. K., Phillips, K., Badalamenti, S., Ohlert, J., & Krumberger, J. (1997). Current practices regarding visitation policies in critical care units. *American Journal of Critical Care, 6*(3), 210–217.

Smedira, N. G., Evans, B. H., Grais, L. S., Cohen, N. H., Lo, B., Cooke, M., . . . Luce, J. M. (1990). Withholding and withdrawal of life support from the critically ill. *The New England Journal of Medicine, 322*(5), 309–315.

Sullivan, D. R., Liu, X., Corwin, D. S., Verceles, A. C., McCurdy, M. T., Pate, D. A., . . . Netzer, G. (2012). Learned helplessness among families and surrogate decision-makers of patients admitted to medical, surgical, and trauma ICUs. *Chest, 142*(6), 1440–1446.

Teno, J. M., Fisher, E., Hamel, M. B., Wu, A. W., Murphy, D. J., Wenger, N. S., . . . Harrell, F. E., Jr. (2000). Decision-making and outcomes of prolonged ICU stays in seriously ill patients. *Journal of the American Geriatrics Society, 48*(Suppl. 5), S70–S74.

Thompson, D. R., Hamilton, D. K., Cadenhead, C. D., Swoboda, S. M., Schwindel, S. M., Anderson, D. C., . . . Petersen, C. (2012). Guidelines for intensive care unit design. *Critical Care Medicine, 40*(5), 1586–1600.

Truog, R. D., Campbell, M. L., Curtis, J. R., Haas, C. E., Luce, J. M., Rubenfeld, G. D., . . . American Academy of Critical Care Medicine. (2008). Recommendations for end-of-life care in the intensive care unit: A consensus statement by the American College [corrected] of Critical Care Medicine. *Critical Care Medicine, 36*(3), 953–963.

Unroe, M., Kahn, J. M., Carson, S. S., Govert, J. A., Martinu, T., Sathy, S. J., . . . Cox, C. E. (2010). One-year trajectories of care and resource utilization for recipients of prolonged mechanical ventilation: A cohort study. *Annals of Internal Medicine, 153*(3), 167–175.

Van Horn, E., & Tesh, A. (2000). The effect of critical care hospitalization on family members: Stress and responses. *Dimensions of Critical Care Nursing, 19*(4), 40–49.

Verceles, A. C., Corwin, D. S., Afshar, M., Friedman, E. B., McCurdy, M. T., Shanholtz, C., . . . Netzer, G. (2014). Half of the family members of critically ill patients experience excessive daytime sleepiness. *Intensive Care Medicine, 40*(8), 1124–1131.

Wallace, D. J., Angus, D. C., Barnato, A. E., Kramer, A. A., & Kahn, J. M. (2012). Nighttime intensivist staffing and mortality among critically ill patients. *The New England Journal of Medicine, 366*(22), 2093–2101.

Whitcomb, J. J., Roy, D., & Blackman, V. S. (2010). Evidence-based practice in a military intensive care unit family visitation. *Nursing Research, 59*(Suppl. 1), S32–S39.

Williams, C. M. (2005). The identification of family members' contribution to patients' care in the intensive care unit: A naturalistic inquiry. *Nursing in Critical Care, 10*(1), 6–14.

Youngblut, J. M., Singer, L. T., Boyer, C., Wheatley, M. A., Cohen, A. R., & Grisoni, E. R. (2000). Effects of pediatric head trauma for children, parents, and families. *Critical Care Nursing Clinics of North America, 12*(2), 227–235.

CHAPTER 4

THE ROLE OF THE HEALTH CARE MANAGER IN DESIGNING AND LEADING A PERSON-CENTERED AMBULATORY CARE PRACTICE

KATHRYN E. PHILLIPS, ZIVA MANN, AND JONATHAN R. SUGARMAN

LEARNING OBJECTIVES

- Identify what a manager needs to do to create a medical environment that aligns with the Institute of Medicine's (IOM) "ten simple rules," with a particular emphasis on person-centered care.
- Compare traditional health care management, which is focused on the needs of the organization, with person-centered management, which places the patient's needs first.
- Understand the benefits of engaging consumers in system changes.
- Explore the promise of the patient-centered medical home (PCMH) and how it can facilitate person-centered care in any clinical setting.

KEY TERMS

Ambulatory care

Crossing the Quality Chasm

IOM's ten simple rules

Patient activation

Patient Activation Measure (PAM)

Patient-centered medical home (PCMH)

Practice transformation

Self-management

Shared decision making

In the late 20th and early 21st centuries, successful managers of ambulatory care practices and facilities focused on assuring positive financial performance, compliance with legal and regulatory requirements, and adherence to generally accepted standards of care associated with quality and patient safety. Although these matters remain core responsibilities of such managers today, the emerging focus on person-centered care requires additional focus and skills. In its landmark *Crossing the Quality Chasm* report, the IOM set forth a vision for 21st-century health care that, if it is to be achieved, requires managers to create environments conducive to the delivery of person-centered care (IOM, 2001). The IOM vision described "ten simple rules" to serve as guiding principles for the design of 21st-century health care systems. The ten rules (shown in Table 4.1)

TABLE 4.1 – Institute of Medicine's Framework for the Enhancement of the Effectiveness of Microsystems, "Ten Simple Rules"

	Current Design Rule	Basic Guiding Principles for Redesign
1	Care is based primarily on visits.	Care is based on continuous healing relationships. Patients should receive care whenever they need it and in many forms, not just face-to-face visits. This rule implies that the health care system should be responsive at all times and that access to care should be provided over the Internet, by telephone, and by other means in addition to face-to-face visits.
2	Professional autonomy drives variability.	Care is customized according to patients' needs and values. The system of care should be designed to meet the most common types of needs, while also having the capacity to respond to individual patients' choices and preferences.
3	Professionals control care.	The patient is the source of control. Patients should be given the necessary information and the opportunity to exercise the degree of control they choose over the decisions that affect them. The health care system should be able to accommodate differences in patients' preferences and encourage shared decision making.
4	Information is a record.	Knowledge is shared freely. Patients should have unfettered access to their own medical information and to clinical knowledge. Clinicians and patients should communicate effectively and share information.
5	Decision making is based on training and experience.	Decision making is based on evidence. Patients should receive care based on the best available scientific knowledge. Care should not vary illogically from clinician to clinician or from place to place.
6	"Do no harm" is an individual responsibility.	Safety is a system property. Patients should be safe from injury caused by the care system. Ensuring safety requires greater attention to systems that help to prevent and mitigate errors.
7	Secrecy is necessary.	Transparency is necessary. The health care system should make information available to patients and their families that allows them to make informed decisions when selecting a health plan, hospital, or clinical practice or when choosing among alternative treatments. This should include information describing the system's performance on safety, evidence-based practice, and patient satisfaction.
8	The system reacts to needs.	Needs are anticipated. The health care system should anticipate patients' needs rather than simply reacting to events.
9	Cost reduction is sought.	Waste is continuously decreased. The health care system should not waste resources or patients' time.
10	Preference is given to professional roles over the system.	Cooperation among clinicians is a priority. Clinicians and institutions should actively collaborate and communicate to ensure an appropriate exchange of information and coordination of care.

Source: Republished with permission of Project HOPE/*Health Affairs* Journal, from Berwick (2002). Permission conveyed through Copyright Clearance Center, Inc.

emphasize the centrality of responding to the needs, wants, and desires of people seeking health care, rather than prioritizing the convenience of health care providers.

This chapter explores how health care managers can cultivate person-centered care in the ambulatory care setting by implementing processes and policies that encourage the active involvement of patients, families, and caregivers (hereafter also called individuals; or, as a collective, consumers) in their own care, and in organizational quality improvement and redesign efforts.

THE IMPORTANCE OF THE PERSONAL EXPERIENCE OF CARE

There is a growing body of evidence demonstrating that individuals who more actively engage in their own care have better health outcomes and care experiences (Greene & Hibbard, 2012); there is also some evidence to suggest they may incur lower health care costs as well (Hibbard & Greene, 2013). Enhancing opportunities for engagement has become a major focus of health care delivery organizations, including ambulatory care practices, eager to capitalize on these potential gains and remain competitive in the rapidly changing health care marketplace.

"Person-centered care" is one approach for enhancing engagement and improving the personal experience of care. What is person-centered care and how is it different from "standard" care? Person-centered care is planned and delivered in partnership with the individual (and his or her family or caregiver) ensuring that care-related decisions reflect the individual's preferences, needs, and values, while also taking into account nonmedical issues that may impact these preferences or outcomes (e.g., living arrangement, financial constraints; Lines, Lepore, & Wiener, 2015). What does this look like? Table 4.2 describes a common situation in an ambulatory care practice and provides both a standard response and a more person-centered response.

The standard response in Table 4.2 does not necessarily reflect poor care, or care that is callous or insensitive to the individual's needs. However, the person-centered response demonstrates a system that is more attentive and more supportive of those needs, and in which health care providers and staff explicitly attempt to engage patients in health care decisions. The person-centered response highlights opportunities for health care managers to develop care delivery processes and approaches that improve the personal experience of care and result in better health outcomes.

ACHIEVING PERSON-CENTERED CARE

Providing person-centered care in the ambulatory care setting requires primary care teams to engage individuals in their own care and in the organization's quality improvement and redesign efforts. Health care managers have the responsibility of creating an environment in which these types of interactions are structurally feasible and culturally valued. In order to fulfill this responsibility, it is critical that managers develop an understanding of what person-centered care is and why it is important, and be able to identify the resources and processes that need to be in place in order for such care to be delivered by staff and experienced by consumers.

TABLE 4.2 – A Person-Centered Response to a Common Health Care Scenario

Situation	Standard Response	Person-Centered Response
Marla works at a day care center. She is 55 years old and overdue for a colonoscopy. Marla believes her uncle had colon cancer, although this was never openly discussed by her family. At Marla's next medical appointment, her primary care provider suggests that she get a colonoscopy. Marla agrees to think it over, but does not schedule an appointment.	The primary care clinic hires a population health manager to help the care team address care gaps like Marla's overdue colonoscopy. The manager calls Marla to introduce the concept of colonoscopy. Unfortunately, he calls during working hours when Marla can't answer her cell phone. Marla decides not to call the population health manager back. "I don't know who this person is," she says to herself.	A medical assistant (MA)—who Marla knows and trusts—calls Marla before her medical visit to give her a "heads up" that colonoscopy will be a topic of discussion at the appointment. Marla's MA understands the topic may be of concern to Marla given her family history, and that it may be difficult for Marla to take a weekday off work for the procedure because of her inflexible schedule. The MA is also able to see in Marla's chart that Marla has previously identified transportation as a challenge. At the visit, the MA reminds Marla about the screening, and asks if she has any questions or concerns to discuss with her care team. The MA shares Marla's responses with the rest of the care team. The provider is able to address Marla's specific questions about the prep process and provide reassurance. The provider and MA then ask Marla: "What *else* would help you complete this screening?" In response, the MA refers Marla to the clinic's patient navigator who helps Marla identify an appointment time, confirm insurance coverage, and identify transportation options.

Health care advocates such as Barbara Balik describe efforts to improve the personal experience of care as moving from a model of health care being done "to" the individual, to care being done "for" the individual, and ultimately, "with" the individual, by engaging with individuals collaboratively, as members of their own health care team (Balik, 2015). For many organizations, engaging individuals in their own care will be the first step toward achieving person-centered care. Hibbard and Greene (2013) identify knowledge, skills, and confidence as key to an individual's ability to take charge of his or her own health and work with his or her medical team. They term this set of attributes *patient activation*, and have studied the way that activation comes as a result of engagement.

Engaging individuals in their own care can be accomplished through shared decision making and self-management support, among other approaches. In shared decision making, the individual, caregiver, and other members of the health care team openly discuss treatment options and how they align with the individual's values, priorities, and resources. Together, they decide on a course of treatment and craft a plan for that individual's health. Staff can use self-management support to build the skills and confidence of the individual and family/caregiver, enabling them to carry out the treatment plan with support from their provider and health care team. For both shared decision making and self-management support, the ultimate goal is to empower the individual to be an active member of his or her health care team.

Providers can assess patient activation through tools such as the Patient Activation Measure (PAM; Hibbard, Stockard, Mahoney, & Tusler, 2004). Such tools often include licensing fees. Similarly, shared decision-making tools such as videos and computerized educational programs often require licensing or purchase. Managers should consider these costs in budget planning. Simple self-assessment forms that build the skills necessary for engagement by inviting the individual to evaluate his or her health and identify key questions or priorities can be found inexpensively or free of charge.

ENGAGING CONSUMERS IN QUALITY IMPROVEMENT AND CARE REDESIGN EFFORTS

In order to be able to improve the personal experience of care, an ambulatory care organization must proactively seek to understand its populations' needs and to improve its care delivery approaches accordingly. Patients, families, and caregivers offer a unique perspective as health care consumers, and as such, they can provide essential information to help identify gaps in service, unmet needs, and other flags that can guide improvement efforts for ambulatory care organizations.

A range of strategies have emerged for engaging health care consumers in practice redesign efforts. Carman et al. (2013) identified a multidimensional framework for understanding patient and family engagement in health and health care through direct care, organizational design and governance, and policy making. The framework defines a continuum of engagement organized by "how much information flows between patient and provider, how active a role the patient has in care decisions, and how involved the patient or patient organization becomes in health organization decisions and in policymaking" (Carman et al., 2013, p. 224; see Table 4.3). At the lower end of the continuum (e.g., consultation) are engagement strategies that position consumers in an advisory role. This could be achieved in the ambulatory setting, for example, by asking consumers to provide feedback on a new scheduling system by way of a survey or focus group. At the other end of the continuum (e.g., partnership and shared leadership) are strategies that position consumers as *full partners* in the redesign process with shared power and responsibility for policies and decisions. This could be achieved in the ambulatory setting, for example, by including consumers as equal members of standing quality improvement councils tasked with identifying and closing gaps in care.

Carman et al.'s framework highlights opportunities to engage consumers in all facets of health and health care including direct care, organizational design and governance, and, ultimately, policy making. Importantly, each level is influenced by factors inherent to the consumer (e.g., health literacy), the health care organization (e.g., culture), and society at large (e.g., social norms, regulations; Carman et al., 2013). Health care managers should be aware of these factors in the context of their own organization and local environment, and identify practical ways to continuously increase opportunities for engagement in each domain.

TABLE 4.3 – Framework for Patient Engagement in Quality Improvement and Practice Redesign

Continuum of Engagement in Improvement Activities[a]	Patients, Caregivers, and Families Are . . .
Consultation	Regularly asked about their experience of care via surveys, focus groups, or targeted interviews.
Involvement	Serve on ad hoc or regular advisory councils and are asked to provide feedback and improvement ideas.
Collaboration	Standing members of clinic-wide and/or system-wide improvement teams, working groups, or taskforces.
Shared Leadership	In a leadership capacity, working to guide organizational priorities and strategies.

[a]The level of engagement increases with each step.
Adapted from Carman et al. (2013).

DESIGNING AND LEADING A PERSON-CENTERED AMBULATORY CARE PRACTICE

In a person-centered ambulatory care practice, the role of the health care manager is to facilitate policies, processes, and systems that encourage all staff to engage and collaborate with consumers at every step of the care redesign process. For the health care manager, this work begins by:

- **Sharing the vision:** Ensure staff at all levels understand person-centered care, and why it is valued by the organization.

- **Setting expectations:** Use job descriptions, policies, and procedures to anchor expectations for a person-centered culture.

- **Making time for the work:** Protect time for the nonclinical work essential for quality improvement and consumer engagement (e.g., team huddles).

- **Investing in systems, tools, and resources:** Encourage investment in systems, tools, and resources that can support person-centered care (e.g., patient portals).

- **Aligning incentives:** Reward activities that enhance the personal experience of care and celebrate progress toward a person-centered culture.

To be effective leaders of person-centered ambulatory care organizations, health care managers will need a new person-centered management mind-set and supporting strategies and techniques. Health care managers are responsible for a broad range of activities (e.g., staff management, financial performance), and there are opportunities in each of the domains described in Table 4.4 to consider and implement solutions that strive to maximize person centeredness.

MANAGEMENT IMPACT IN ACTION: THE SAFETY NET MEDICAL HOME INITIATIVE

The Safety Net Medical Home Initiative, a national demonstration of the patient-centered medical home (PCMH) model of care, illustrates how primary care practices can engage consumers, and how managers can support that engagement.

TABLE 4.4 – Roles and Expectations for the Person-Centered Health Care Manager

Role	Current Expectation	Future Expectation[a]
Staff management	• Recruit, hire, and support qualified staff. • Develop compensation packages.	• Develop teams with the orientation and skills to engage individuals in their own care (e.g., support training for self-management support, motivational interviewing, shared decision making). • Develop policies and procedures that support person-centered processes and decisions (e.g., consider the impact of part-time staff on continuity of care). • Reward performance that enhances person-centered care (e.g., tie consumer experience measures to staff bonuses).
Financial performance	• Maintain positive financial performance. • Steward resources to achieve organizational goals. • Make strategic investments that will allow the organization to remain competitive.	• Invest resources in person-centered care roles (e.g., referral coordinators), tools (e.g., patient portal), and access points (e.g., phone visits, weekend clinic hours). • Invest in resources to facilitate the meaningful involvement of consumers in the care redesign process (e.g., budget stipends for patient and family advisors).
Strategic planning	• Maintain emphasis on organization's mission, values, and vision. • Identify and communicate organizational goals.	• Develop and support a culture of continuous quality improvement. • Set the expectation that the perspectives, values, and preferences of consumers guide both individual care interactions and operational decisions.
Operational oversight	• Manage quality, care delivery, and productivity goals.	• Manage to achieve population health and enhance the personal experience of care.
Regulatory compliance and patient safety	• Comply with local, state, and national regulations; maintain requirements for additional certifications. • Assure privacy and security of patient information. • Design and implement processes that avoid all preventable harm.	• Ensure patients (and others identified by the patient, e.g., caregiver) can access their own medical information. • Create systems that facilitate appropriate health information exchange while adhering to laws such as HIPAA. • Involve consumers in shared decision making so they can decide what risks they are willing to take.

[a]Additional roles required in a person-centered ambulatory care practice.
HIPAA, Health Insurance Portability and Accountability Act.

The Safety Net Medical Home Initiative, launched in 2008, provided technical assistance to 65 primary care safety net sites in five states (Sugarman, Phillips, Wagner, Coleman, & Abrams, 2014). To guide practice transformation efforts, the initiative developed and published an evidence-based change package that included 32 "key changes" or specific ideas for improvement (Wagner et al., 2012). Six of these changes identify specific strategies to engage individuals in their own care and/or to collaborate with consumers on redesign efforts (Wagner et al., 2012):

- Ensure that patients, families, providers, and care team members are involved in quality improvement activities.

- Respect patient and family values and expressed needs.
- Encourage patients to expand their role in decision making, health-related behaviors, and self-management.
- Communicate with their patients in a culturally appropriate manner, in a language and at a level that the patient understands.
- Provide self-management support at every visit through goal setting and action planning.
- Obtain feedback from patients/family about their health care experience and use this information for quality improvement.

The Safety Net Medical Home Initiative developed and tested an assessment tool, the patient-centered medical home assessment (PCMH-A), to help practices monitor their progress over time and identify priority improvement opportunities (Daniel et al., 2013). Staff from participating sites completed the PCMH-A at 6-month intervals throughout the initiative. Although few practices reported meaningful engagement of patients at the beginning of the initiative, by the conclusion in 2013, over half included patients on improvement teams, and all had processes in place to capture patient experience or satisfaction with care through surveys, focus groups, advisory councils, or other means. This progress demonstrates that such transformation is possible even in the challenging, resource-constrained environments that characterized the organizations participating in the initiative: Federally Qualified Healthcare Centers (FQHCs), homeless health centers, rural health centers, critical access hospitals, and urban academic medical centers (Sugarman et al., 2014).

Of note to health care managers, PCMH-A scoring by practice managers and other administrative leaders often reflected a higher level of confidence than expressed by frontline staff and consumers that the key changes were implemented in practice. This suggests that managers should test their assumptions about the extent to which changes are widely implemented in a practice by carefully assessing the perceptions of those closest to care delivery (including patients, families, and caregivers) through interviews, surveys, and other methods.

Experience from the Safety Net Medical Home Initiative also highlights the important role of health care managers in cultivating environments conducive to person-centered care. Organizations that were successful in their practice transformation efforts had health care managers (and other senior administrative and clinical leaders) who were able to (Altman, Philips, & Manning, 2013):

- Provide a clear and compelling vision for why it was important to shift from "traditional care" to more patient- or person-centered approaches
- Allocate time, resources, and tools to implement these new approaches
- Remove barriers that could impede progress

Moreover, maximally effective leaders were able to demonstrate their personal and organizational commitment to person-centered care in bold and visible ways (Stout & Weeg, 2014; Wagner, Gupta, & Coleman, 2014). For example, the executive director of Health West, Inc., in partnership with its board of directors, revised the organization's mission statement to emphasize the new focus on patient-centered care: "Empowering our patients and communities by proactively providing quality, affordable patient-centered healthcare" (Stout & Weeg, 2014, p. S24). The executive director of another health center revised job descriptions for all administrative and clinical roles to directly align with the new expectations of its patient-centered care delivery model. To highlight this change—and signal its importance—the executive director required all staff to reapply for their current positions under the new job descriptions.

CASE STUDY

Family Health Center[1] operates three clinics that serve low-income and other vulnerable populations, including a large community of Haitian-Creole immigrants. One of its clinics recently began offering diabetes care group visits. The intention was to make it easier for individuals to access care by bundling multiple visits (nursing, blood work, nutrition) into one appointment, and to leverage peer support to help individuals learn self-management skills. A nutritionist attends the group visit every other month to provide information on how to read nutrition labels and select healthy foods.

One year into the pilot program, the clinic manager is pleased with attendance; and participants appreciate the convenience of group visits, as reported on patient experience surveys conducted on a quarterly basis. However, blood sugar levels are not improving as expected.

During the final group visit of the year, the nutritionist takes participants to the supermarket to purchase food for an interactive cooking class. She is surprised to see them selecting mostly fresh foods (which do not have nutrition labels) and condiments and sauces from the supermarket's ethnic food aisles. The nutritionist realizes that the recipe book she provided at the beginning of the year did not include these ingredients, or variations on ethnic recipes. She is concerned that the information she provided has not been useful to participants or their families.

Issues to Consider

1. The nutritionist shares her findings at the next all-clinic quality improvement meeting and suggests changing the group visit curriculum for next year to include culturally relevant foods and recipes. The nutritionist says she will need three working days in order to identify new recipes and update the materials on her own. You are the clinic manager. How do you respond?

2. How might you engage members of the current diabetes care group to help improve the next cycle of group visits?

3. Family Health Center is planning to offer prenatal care group visits next year. What can be learned from the diabetes care group visit experience? How will you (as clinic manager) help the care team tasked with planning the prenatal care program better anticipate participants' needs, values, and preferences? What resources, tools, or motivation might be needed?

---

[1] Fictionalized case example based on a composite of experiences. Inspired by Revere Family Health Center, Cambridge Health Alliance (Massachusetts). Used with permission and based on an interview with Somava Stout, MD, MS, former medical director and lead transformation advisor, September 2015.

Disclosures: The authors disclosed receipt of the following financial support for the research, authorship, and/or publication of this article: Funding for this work came from a grant from the Commonwealth Fund (Grant No. 20130308). The Commonwealth Fund is a national, private foundation based in New York City that supports independent research on health care issues and makes grants to improve health care practice and policy.

REFERENCES

Altman, D. D., Philips, K. E., & Manning, C. (2013). Engaged leadership: Strategies for guiding PCMH transformation. In K. E. Phillips & V. Weir (Eds.), *Safety Net Medical Home Initiative implementation guide series* (2nd ed.). Seattle, WA: Qualis Health and The MacColl Center for Health Care Innovation at the Group Health Research Institute.

Balik, B. (2015). *Reflections on learning to–for–with: The journey to understanding partnerships with patients* [Monograph]. Retrieved from www.changefoundation .ca/site/wp-content/uploads/2016/05/To-For-With-Balik.pdf

Berwick, D. (2002). A user's manual for the IOM's "Quality Chasm" report. *Health Affairs, 21*(3), 80–90.

Carman, K. L., Dardess, P., Maurer, M., Sofaer, S., Adams, K., Bechtel, C., & Sweeney, J. (2013). Patient and family engagement: A framework for understanding the elements and developing interventions and policies. *Health Affairs, 32*(2), 223–231.

Daniel, D., Wagner, E. H., Coleman, K., Schaefer, J. K., Austin, B. T., Abrams, M. K., . . . Sugarman, J. R. (2013). Assessing progress towards becoming a patient-centered medical home: An assessment tool for practice transformation. *Health Services Research, 48*(6, Pt. 1), 1879–1897.

Greene, J., & Hibbard, J. H. (2012). Why does patient activation matter? An examination of the relationships between patient activation and health-related outcomes. *Journal of General Internal Medicine, 27*(5), 520–526.

Hibbard, J. H., & Greene, J. (2013). What the evidence shows about patient activation: Better health outcomes and care experiences; fewer data on costs. *Health Affairs, 32*(2), 207–214.

Hibbard, J. H., Stockard, J., Mahoney, E. R., & Tusler, M. (2004). Development of the Patient Activation Measure (PAM): Conceptualizing and measuring activation in patients and consumers. *Health Services Research, 39*(4, Pt. 1), 1005–1026.

Institute of Medicine. (2001). *Crossing the quality chasm: A new health system for the 21st century*. Washington, DC: National Academies Press.

Lines, L. M., Lepore, M., & Wiener, J. M. (2015). Patient-centered, person-centered, and person-directed care: They are not the same. *Medical Care, 53*(7), 561–563.

Stout, S., & Weeg, S. (2014). The practice perspective on transformation: Experience and learning from the frontlines. *Medical Care, 52*, S23–S25.

Sugarman, J. R., Phillips, K. E., Wagner, E. H., Coleman, K., & Abrams, M. K. (2014). The Safety Net Medical Home Initiative: Transforming care for vulnerable populations. *Medical Care, 52*, S1–S10.

Wagner, E. H., Coleman, K., Reid, R. J., Phillips, K. E., Abrams, M. K., & Sugarman, J. R. (2012). The changes involved in patient-centered medical home transformation. *Primary Care, 39*(2), 241–259.

Wagner, E. H., Gupta, R., & Coleman, K. (2014). Practice transformation in the Safety Net Medical Home Initiative: A qualitative look. *Medical Care, 52*, S18–S23.

CHAPTER 5

THE PLACE OF THE MEDICAL OFFICE IN HEALTH CARE

SANDY DeWEESE AND JENNIFER REITER

LEARNING OBJECTIVES

- Explore how the physician–patient relationship affects patient engagement.
- Understand the critical nature of chronic diseases in the United States and the role of case management for individual patients.
- Discover how clinician efforts can positively influence patient behaviors through follow-up care.
- Consider how health outcomes can be improved when physicians' offices make person-centered care a reality.

KEY TERMS

Case management	Patient fears
Chronic disease management	Patient noncompliance
Follow-up care	Person-centric practice
Medication errors	Physician–patient relationship
Patient engagement	

The physician's office provides a unique venue where person-centered care can flourish (Devlin, 2014). The innovative medical office, particularly within a system of care, can reach beyond that system to target people with a propensity for a certain condition, and come together to help provide education to change health outcomes. Case management of chronic diseases includes targeted efforts to assist patients with follow-up protocols and calls for a robust physician–patient relationship that will ultimately lead to better health outcomes (Agency for Healthcare Research and Quality [AHRQ], 2013).

The major focus in health care—in large health care systems, in higher education, in professional development—is the hospital environment (PwC, 2016). Advanced technology, high-cost structure in facilities and operations, external regulations, and more drive this focus. However, the health care consumer is an episodic visitor to this part of the health system. Most people experience this environment only a few times as patients or family members. The birth of a child and an end-of-life experience bookend the hospital experience for many people, with a trip to the emergency department (ED) for a child who fell from the swing and broke an arm or a surgical procedure in between.

The medical office experience, however, can be a consistent long-term place for interaction in the health care setting (Detz, López, & Sarkar, 2013). People talk about and feel ownership of their "doctor," who may be a physician or nurse practitioner. They may seek general primary care services from an internist or a family physician or even an obstetrician/gynecologist. Parents often extend the time with a child's pediatrician as long as possible, because the relationship is established, the procedures and location are familiar, and, most importantly, if the relationship is strong, trust has developed between the patient and the medical practice (Goold & Lipkin, 1999). This is not a relationship that most people look forward to because it is, at the least, disruptive to our daily life or fraught with stress from diagnoses and advice we do not want to hear or may not know how to handle. But if a positive relationship is fostered, the creation of a trusting environment ensues in which people, who are not at their best and worried about themselves or a family member, can seek advice and help with the most intimate details of their lives, their physical health, and their future health outcomes (American Medical Association [AMA], 1993).

With the increased focus on large health care system development, this physician–patient relationship can be viewed from a marketing perspective. Primary care is often the front door to the medical system. Referrals are made to other specialty physicians in the system, resulting in diagnostic testing, procedures, and hospital stays for the system. The system views an investment in the primary care physician as a way to carve out a market that provides downstream revenue for the health care system. As health care systems expand into the insurance industry, this system-wide offering of services furthers the capture of market share.

Based on our experience, a person's relationship with the health care environment is strongly influenced by two major factors: age and state of health. Vaccines, childhood illness, and developmental milestones drive patients to the pediatrician or family physician until their teens. At that point, health care often becomes a convenience commodity. The majority of this young adult age group is relatively healthy; thus, this population will seek episodic care at their convenience from a walk-in clinic, an urgent care setting, or a student health center. With no serious problems, the young adult may need an occasional antibiotic or antiviral agent, but will look at receiving that service with the convenience expected from a drive-through coffee shop. Young families often return to regular health care with the birth of a child and, as women make the bulk of health care decisions, the entire family may be pushed back into the system. These relationships may stay steady until disease or age brings individuals back to more regular interaction with the health care provider.

For patients with chronic disease, such as diabetes, heart disease, hypertension, asthma, or congestive heart failure, the relationship with the physician is more dependent. When people find themselves relying on medication management, the access route to that prescription is the physician office. This relationship may also hold the most promise of medicine's ability to influence patient outcomes through medical management, education, and promotion of healthy lifestyles, to manage disease, or slow the progression of chronic disease (DeBenedette, 2011).

The traditional medical office model has been to provide a service when the patient reaches out requesting an appointment to initiate care. Medical offices often have limited hours, and appointments may be too far in advance for more urgent patient needs. For a medical office to meet the needs of patients, it must possess what one physician has referred to as the important three abilities—medical ability, affability, and accessibility. The drive of consumerism into health care has put pressure on accessibility and has created demands for increased hours, more same-day services, after-hours access, and use of technology to enhance communication both among providers and between providers and patients. The patient as a consumer makes decisions based on practice location, physical access, and electronic access. The relationship, sought by health care providers, can become secondary to the patient seeking service. This convergence of meeting customer needs and demands with evidence-based best medical practice creates a challenge not only for medical office management but also for the entire structure of the health care system.

The health care system has many pressures. Any payment system that promotes the idea of value-based medicine is actually looking at efficiencies to save cost by reducing unnecessary diagnostic testing, shifting cost to the consumer, and reducing unnecessary office and hospital visits. In a traditional primary care practice, the provider might have to refer the patient to one place for laboratory testing, another for x-rays, and maybe additional places for education, therapy, or other services. Increasingly common is the medical model that groups as many outpatient services as reasonable in one location for the patient. The patient can receive lab or simple x-rays in the office setting. In office, education by nurses, community health educators, care managers, dieticians, mental health professionals, pharmacists, and even physical therapy evaluation is increasingly common. This meets the test of improved convenience for the patient but also gives the provider rapid results on which to base their diagnosis and treat as well as more control over services the patient receives. As costs and charging structures are lower in the medical office than in the acute care hospital, this combines that convenience with a more economical service delivery.

Health care leaders have a responsibility to determine what can or should be reasonably offered in the office setting and what value it brings to the patient, the provision of care by the physician, and the financial health of both the medical office and health care system. Care management or case management has grown out of this desire both to help patients navigate the system and to organize the delivery of care. This brings particular focus to patients who have chronic disease and frequently find themselves in the health care environment. If well done, the result can be improved health outcomes for the patient, lower cost of care, and coordination within the system.

PERSON-CENTERED CARE FOR CHRONIC DISEASE MANAGEMENT

After a health care provider visit, patients with chronic problems are often told when necessary follow-up would be. In some cases, the provider will want to see the patient again routinely in 6 months or some other interval; in some cases, where the patient's condition is less stable, more frequent follow-up may be suggested. Depending on when this is to occur, patients may or may not schedule a next appointment at the point of care, before they leave the office setting. Similarly, appointments often get cancelled before they actually occur. Cancellations occur from the office, often due to changes in the provider schedule, or from the patient who may find the scheduled time inconvenient, may have transportation problems, may have financial concerns, or may feel the acuteness of their condition is past and the visit is unnecessary.

This model reinforces the trend to treat patients for "episodic" care instead of chronic care. In order to provide exceptional, person-centered care, patients must be educated on the importance of follow-up. In addition, the practice must consider alternatives to in-person office visits such as phone or electronic follow-up, provide a comfort level with a team of health care professionals as opposed to just the primary care provider, and actively participate with patients to ensure that follow-ups and contacts are made.

A consistent, timely process must be developed to continually pull a patient back into care, rather than putting the responsibility on the patient to decide whether or not and when to return for follow-up. Steps are taken at the point of care and when cancellations and no-show appointments occur to ensure that the practice is contacting patients to guarantee appropriate follow-up is being made. Tailoring follow-up to each patient based on risk of complications and individual need as well as following best practices is essential to good person management.

As part of team-based health care, the patient must be considered part of the team and participate in decision making on treatment and follow-up (Thom, Hall, & Pawlson, 2004). Health care teams consist of many specialists from different disciplines, including (but not limited to) dieticians, nurses, physicians, nurse practitioners, medical assistants, and pharmacists. Patients must feel comfortable interacting with all members of the team. Availability of team members at the point of care is crucial to providing timely education and training on disease states, expectations for follow-up and self-care, and design of the care plan to provide individualized care for each person. A lifelong learning approach to patient education, as opposed to a single classroom experience or hospital discharge teaching, can be centered in the medical office as the patient's health or personal situation changes.

In a medical practice in southern Indiana, a pharmacist-driven disease state management model attempts to encompass these characteristics and provide person-centered care. During routine office visits, a pharmacist is available to provide disease state and medication education while working with providers, nurses, and patients to design care plans. Patients are persistently managed in between provider office visits by either in office, or by telephone or electronic (e-mail, patient web-based portal), communication with continual education and medication modification. Patients are identified based on those at higher risk for diabetic complications through careful and ongoing laboratory testing—defined for diabetics as a hemoglobin A1c (Hgb A1c) level greater than 8%.

As shown in Figure 5.1, an average reduction in Hgb A1c of more than 2% was seen with these interventions, with an average number of contacts outside a provider visit being five.

In-office visits are often held with the entire care team to reinforce the relationship among providers and patients. Patient involvement feedback is welcome at all points of care to further strengthen relationships and continually improve the process.

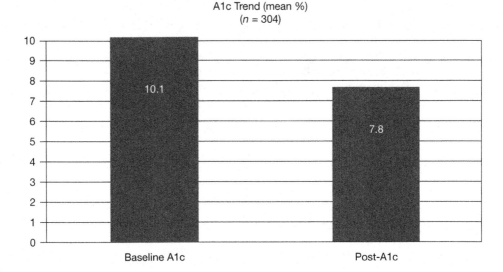

A1c 9.5% = mean blood glucose of 261 mg/dL
A1c 8.5% = mean blood glucose of 225 mg/dL
A1c 7.5% = mean blood glucose of 190 mg/dL

FIGURE 5.1 – Average reduction in hemoglobin A1c.

This case is an example of a leadership model that allows for multidisciplinary input and thinking that challenges the typical office model and requires health care leaders to be open to considering this new model. Integration of disciplines and consistency of message and education delivered conveniently to the patient can improve the overall experience as well as outcome. This shift creates a model of care that does not act upon the patient, giving medical orders for medications and education and then expecting the patient to reach out, but includes the patient and engages him or her in a close and personalized relationship with the caregiving team. The patient knows how and who to call with questions. Both the patient and the caregiver are accountable to one another.

PERSON-CENTERED CARE FOR PREVENTION

The primary care relationship is often one where preventive care is discussed based on medical evidence. The focus is often on behavioral advice on exercise, diet, or smoking, or on age-appropriate vaccines or screening tests for early identification of disease. This includes recommendations on screening mammography, colonoscopy, and lab or other diagnostic work often dictated by family disease history. The innovative medical office, particularly within a system of care, can reach beyond that and target people with a propensity for a certain condition and come together to help provide education to change health outcomes.

This kind of preventive care is not limited to the primary care setting, but can be equally effective from a long medical specialty relationship. Consider the idea of working with patients to prevent kidney stones. Anyone who has had a kidney stone knows it is not something he or she wants to have again; however, once a patient has been diagnosed with kidney stones, he or she is more likely to develop them again in the future. In the traditional model, some education may occur at the time of the initial stone, but that may be a surgical or ED experience clouded by pain and anxiety. An innovative patient-centered approach by a urology practice can focus on the patient outside of the urgency of the kidney stone experience and work to help prevent future occurrence.

Focusing on the individual type of stone, a team, including a physician, dietician, nurse, and pharmacist, can help the patient make long-term lifestyle, diet, and medication changes to prevent future pain and expense of stone development. The focus again is pulling the patient into the system to be an active participant in the care, not waiting for the next medical occurrence. An innovative medical office provides more than a reaction to symptoms.

PERSON-CENTERED CARE FOR SYSTEM NAVIGATION

The idea of electronic medical records creating one system of communication to benefit patient care through the transmission of medical information is a dream in health care that is as yet unrealized. Proprietary electronic systems have difficulty communicating with one another. Patients, particularly the elderly or those with chronic disease, may have different physicians treating different symptoms or body systems. An elderly patient may have a primary care provider, a cardiologist, a podiatrist, a dermatologist, or many other medical or surgical specialists. These practices may be part of a health care system that can communicate information through a shared record, but often one or more of the specialists are outside that system, operating on a different record.

This puts the patient in the position of being his or her own health care historian, sometimes without knowledge of what information might be relevant to each provider, creating the potential for unintentional harm. Medication lists generated from a hospital discharge may not match what the patient had been taking at home. Instructions may be confusing and contradictory among providers who do not have a full view of the care being provided. People who are often supposed to be at the center of their own health care management are confused by who to see for what. Use of different pharmacies can create risk by a pharmacist not seeing the entire medication list and missing out on identification of drug interactions. Even worse is the potential for harm by taking medications prescribed by several different providers, unknown to each other, that may interact with each other, or counter the effects of each other.

Introduce into this equation the patient who may not get the prescription filled, or may not follow up with a diagnostic test or specialist as prescribed, due to financial reasons or because he or she does not understand a compelling case to do so. The patient may not have a good understanding of a commercial or government health plan. He or she may not understand the concept of an insurance network of providers and the financial differences of who is in and out of the network, or of specific drugs that may be on one health plan formulary but not another. They may not understand that hospital rules, corporate relationships, and insurance networks do not mean that care can be provided in any health care setting. We understand this then as a system fraught with opportunity for error.

Consider the example of a patient who has been experiencing new or confusing symptoms. A severe headache, or numbness in an extremity, may convince the patient that he or she needs a trip to the ED on a Saturday night when his or her primary care provider's practice is closed. Rather than bothering the on-call physician, with whom the patient has no personal experience, the patient may decide to head out on his or her own for an assessment at the ED. Unaware of the existence of hospital privileges and rules, the patient may find himself or herself admitted for observation in a hospital not in his or her network, where his or her personal physician has no access to his or her records, no privileges to treat, and may, in fact, never be informed of the admission.

The challenge again is for the patient to have a place in the primary care world that gives him or her a center for his or her care, a touchstone where the patient can go for answers and know that there is a health care advocate who will direct him or her appropriately and may introduce him or her to technologies to manage health. Many primary care providers have developed the role of care manager or case manager to help patients navigate this confusing system. This role is often filled by an RN or social worker with strong communication and team-building skills. Patients and caregivers make specific care plans with all providers involved and sharing information. Although providers often focus on patients with multiple conditions, serious chronic disease, unnecessary ED visits, or other high-cost utilization patterns, the focus is on managing care—the right care at the right time in the right setting—by the development of a strong, long-term health care relationship between patients and primary care providers.

PERSON-CENTRIC PRACTICE MANAGEMENT

Medical office leadership involves implementation of appropriate provider schedules to maximize patient access and care delivery levels. It requires multiple and creative approaches to reach out to patients and to streamline appointment scheduling. Effective medical office/outpatient management requires the ability to develop systems to provide telephone and electronic medical advice and information, patient education, test result reporting, and patient triage according to the complexity or acuity of illness.

Office visit and procedural billing and coding, insurance contract management, and revenue cycle management are key competencies. The art and business of recruiting physicians and advanced practice providers, physician compensation strategies and options, and development of professional relationships and referral patterns are important skills.

Human resource functions such as staff selection and management, timekeeping, payroll, and benefit management may be organized at the practice level or at a corporate level in larger systems. Budgeting cost controls, supply chain, and inventory management skills are essential in the creation of a sustainable business model. An understanding of the competitive environment and available resources will help practice leaders develop a strategic plan for practice success (Kabene, Orchard, Howard, Soriano, & Leduc, 2006).

However, most importantly, outside of typical leadership and business functions, the skilled health care manager can have a direct influence on the culture of the care environment by establishing the patient as the center and focusing on priorities for continuous improvement of patient care. Nowhere in health care is the partnership between leadership, physicians, and other health care professionals more important than in a well-managed medical office environment. Understanding the patient experience in the system can lead to the development of a trusting and rewarding partnership between the patient and the health care provider. This requires an active relationship with our patients and a step outside of the traditional medical model to the creation of a team of essential caregivers designed around a person's needs. Creativity and challenging the norm, as well as gathering and acting on data and feedback from health care consumers, will be factors in this partnership. The use of health care technology to benefit the patient's understanding and experience is still in its infancy and collaboration will be necessary, but the rewards can be great.

Patients approach the health care system with fear and confusion. Insurance benefits are hard to understand, regulations require a great deal of bureaucracy, and a patient's experience is often episodic and poorly coordinated. The medical office is a place where a long-term relationship can be developed and an advocacy forged to improve health for patients with a complex or chronic disease. This is a place where patient care can be managed—through transitions in other parts of the health care system, through appropriate use of all health care disciplines, through education, but most significantly through the relationship formed between the provider and the patients who trust them with their personal care.

CASE STUDY

Your area practice administrator is a family medicine practice in a mid-sized city. Health services in this city attract both city residents and people from the more rural surrounding county. The busiest physician in your practice sees 25 to 28 patients per day. She starts each day with her schedule full, but during the course of the day, four or five patients miss appointments. The physician has asked you to help reduce the no-show rate to improve her efficiency. You are concerned about keeping her schedule full but also concerned about the patients who are not receiving care. The traditional model would be for you to send warning letters to patients notifying them that if they miss a certain number of visits within a specified time period they will be released from the practice. Your concern is that releasing medically fragile patients leaves them with even fewer resources and you would like to identify barriers within your practice model that make access to care difficult. You believe that if you understand the barriers you can remove them and achieve improved efficiency for the physician and improved access for the patients.

Issues to Consider

1. What are some common reasons that might cause patients to miss appointments?
2. How would you collect data on reasons for the broken appointments?
3. How could things like age or economic status affect access to medical care?
4. What are some possible solutions to each of the barriers you identify?

REFERENCES

Agency for Healthcare Research and Quality. (2013). *Outpatient case management for adults with medical illness and complex care needs* (Comparative Effectiveness Review, No. 99; Report No. 13-EHC031-EF). Rockville, MD: Author.

American Medical Association. (1993). Fundamental elements of the patient-physician relationship. *Journal of the American Medical Association, 262*(3), 33.

DeBenedette, V. (2011). Doctor-patient relationship influences patient engagement. *Health Services Research.* Retrieved from http://www.cfah.org/hbns/2011/doctor-patient-relationship-influences-patient-engagement

Detz, A., López, A. I., & Sarkar, U. (2013). Long-term doctor-patient relationships: Patient perspective from online reviews. *Journal of Medical Internet Research, 15*(7), e131.

Devlin, A. S. (2014). *Transforming the doctor's office: Principles from evidence-based design.* New York, NY: Routledge.

Goold, S. D., & Lipkin, M. (1999). The doctor–patient relationship challenges, opportunities, and strategies. *Journal of General Internal Medicine, 14*(Suppl. 1), S26–S33.

Kabene, S. M., Orchard, C., Howard, J. M., Soriano, M. A., & Leduc, R. (2006). The importance of human resources management in health care: A global context. *Human Resource Health, 4,* 20.

PwC. (2016). Medical cost trend: Behind the numbers 2017 (Chart pack). Retrieved from http://www.pwc.com/us/en/health-industries/health-research-institute/publications/assets/pwc-hri-behind-numbers-chartpack.pdf

Thom, D. H., Hall, M. A., & Pawlson, L. G. (2004). Measuring patients' trust in physicians when assessing quality of care. *Health Affairs, 23*(4), 124–132.

CHAPTER 6

EXPLORING PERSON CENTEREDNESS IN LONG-TERM CARE

JASON A. WOLF, STACY PALMER, AND ROBERT N. MAYER[†]

LEARNING OBJECTIVES

- Understand the patient, resident, and family experience in long-term care.
- Describe key practices to support person centeredness in long-term care facilities.
- Recognize opportunities and roadblocks to creating person-centered experiences.

KEY TERMS

Acuity-centric silos

Continuum of care

Nursing home care

Patient experience

Person centeredness

Nursing home quality is a serious issue, with more than one third of nursing homes receiving low government quality ratings (Boccuti, Caslillas, & Neuman, 2015). This is of special note because significant cognitive and functional impairment is common among nursing home residents. In addition, many residents report being in pain, more than one third are severely incontinent, more than 5% have pressure ulcers of stage 2 or greater, and one in four residents (24.2%) receive an antipsychotic medication (Centers for Medicare and Medicaid Services [CMS], 2013).

[†] We author this chapter with and in honor and memory of our friend and colleague Robert N. Mayer. Rob was founder and president of the Hulda B. and Maurice L. Rothschild Foundation and spent his career as a thought leader in elder care reform. He was and will forever be remembered as an unwavering champion for bringing person-centered approaches to the long-term care industry.

New perspectives about long-term care have emerged over the last decade that represent a fundamental shift in thinking about nursing homes (Koren, 2010). Facilities are viewed not as health care institutions, but as person-centered homes offering long-term care services.

In recent years, perceptions of performance and quality of health care organizations have begun to move beyond examining the provision of excellent clinical care, alone, and to consider and embrace the patient experience as an important indicator (Wolf, Brown, Weiner, & Wolterman, 2015; Wolf, Niederhauser, Marshburn, & LaVela, 2014; Wolf & Palmer, 2015).

Yet, in practice and research, the concept of patient experience has had varied uses and is often discussed with little more explanation than the term itself.

In an effort to expand the overall discussion on experience, this chapter explores the perspectives and practices of the patient, resident, and family experience in long-term care. Although there are clear and distinct differences at various points in the care continuum, there is also a much stronger connection than one might expect when we consider the efforts and concepts driving person centeredness in this environment.

It is important to address the use of language and acknowledge the words used for the purpose of this discussion. As the conversation of experience expands more significantly across the continuum, we recognize the breadth of language that is emerging—from "patients" to "customers" to "consumers"; from "residents" to "elders"—and an understanding that *family* as a term represents a comprehensive collection of individuals who are not just directly related, but include loved ones, friends, and support networks. We, too, chose person centeredness to include such ideas as person-directed care and variations of engagement—all of which we see encompassed in the broader construct of experience.

Through engaging with the voices of practice from six leading organizations committed to excellence in long-term care—Beatitudes Campus (Missouri), Breckenridge Village (Ohio), Carolinas HealthCare System (North Carolina), Commonwealth Care of Roanoke (Virginia), Jewish Home Lifecare (New York), and Vetter Health Services (Nebraska)—we seek, in this chapter, to identify key motivations, practices, support, and roadblocks, as well as the impact a focus on experience has in the long-term care setting overall. We also return to the powerful connections across the broader continuum of care and provide some overall reflections and recommendations as organizations move to action on this key health care priority.

The experience conversation is not isolated to certain segments of health care as the idea of person centeredness is not restricted in how it can influence the delivery of care and the outcomes it helps to achieve. By taking a cross-continuum perspective, grounded in the voices of real experiences in long-term care, we hope to provide not only insights, but also inspiration for actions that can have a positive and lasting effect on those receiving care in all segments of the care continuum.

We started our inquiry with participating organizations by asking why person centeredness was a critical focus at all.

PRACTICES TO SUPPORT PERSON CENTEREDNESS

It is clear from the participating organizations that person centeredness is a philosophy ingrained in an organization's nature and overall culture and not something that can be replicated by merely implementing a series of tactics. That said, there are a number of practices these organizations have identified that support their overall efforts to personalize the experience, help residents feel comfortable in their care, and allow people to enjoy a better quality of life.

Comfort Matters

Beatitudes Campus developed Comfort Matters, a research-based program that promotes living better with dementia by focusing on a person's day-to-day comfort. The goal is to make the experience as comfortable as possible, regardless of whether the person is in the mild stage of the illness or in the advanced stage. Key concepts include:

- Comfort care
- Anticipation of needs
- Know the person
- Person-directed practice
- Staff empowerment

"We learned that people with dementia are experts on their own comfort. They know when they are comfortable. They know when something makes sense to them and when it doesn't," said Tena Alonzo of Beatitudes Campus. "How do humans like to live? They like to be comfortable, so the focus is on how we change our personal practices to help people become comfortable and how we change our systems to support people who have trouble thinking."

By focusing on comfort, Beatitudes Campus was able to drastically reduce dementia-related behaviors, such as calling out, rejecting care, and trying to run away—some of the things very problematic for people with the illness. It also noted very good results with identifying and treating undetected physical pain.

Though initially developed to address the significant challenges common to advanced stages of Alzheimer's disease and other dementias, Comfort Matters' education and research can be applied throughout the continuum of care and has been shared with hundreds of interdisciplinary teams from long-term care, assisted living, and dementia care facilities.

Dining as a Social Event

Dining practices emerged as a significant theme with all of our participating organizations. "Meal times are a social event. People don't like going to dinner alone but also don't want a large setting where it is noisy and not very personable," said Dr. Angela Orsky, Assistant Vice President, Continuing Care, Carolinas HealthCare System. "They love dining with a small group (less than 20 people) who can share and learn personal things about each other, about their family members, who is having grandbabies, who has an illness in the family; it becomes more than just a meal. It becomes the highlight of the resident's day."

Audrey Weiner, President and CEO of The New Jewish Home shared how The New Jewish Home's adoption of the Green House project supports that notion. The Green House model fosters the same feeling and experience you get from living in a real home, typically with 10 to 12 residents with individual bedrooms and bathrooms sharing common spaces. Weiner described a visit to The New Jewish Home's first Small House (operating with the Green House standards of practice) that exemplified the experience:

It was 8 o'clock in the morning and there were four elders around the kitchen table and there was a house person (called an Adir, Hebrew for noble) in the kitchen and there were pots and water boiling and all kinds of activity. And I said to the Adir, "Can I help you?" And she said, "Oh no. I have this all under control." And she says to me that the first gentleman . . . she tells me his name . . . every morning he has cornflakes with a banana cut in quarters. The second woman, next to him, every morning she has scrambled eggs and two pieces of toast . . . and the third woman has something different every morning so "I'm going to ask her what she wants and the fourth woman has two eggs over easy." And she goes on to say, "I know that in nursing homes I'm not supposed to have eggs that are runny because of the health concerns but I make them just a tiny bit runny so that she'll enjoy them every morning. And there it was." She took the time to know each of these individuals, what it was that gave them pleasure every morning and what time they wanted their breakfast.

Other organizations cited the need for varied dining menus. Vetter Health Services found younger residents prefer more of a bistro dining experience, whereas older generations prefer hearty foods, such as meat and potatoes, casseroles, and so forth. Their staffs accommodate these preferences along with differences in when people prefer to eat.

Respecting Sleep Preferences

Another common theme among participating organizations was respect of residents' sleep preferences. The New Jewish Home's Green House–modeled residences offer private rooms so elders are able to go to sleep and wake up as they choose. Carolinas HealthCare Systems facilities have certain hallways for residents who prefer to sleep in. "We segmented our medication passage, the delivery of our meals and how we are staggering those hallways so residents have an opportunity to sleep in," said Angela Orsky. "That has become extremely important to those not wanting to be up at 6:00 in the morning."

Embracing Technology

Many organizations use technology to personalize the care experience. Adaptive technology allows family members and caregivers to customize technology interfaces for residents by sharing photos and stories, adjusting settings to meet individual preferences, and creating connection opportunities to family and friends. Use of video technologies connects residents with family members. "We've used Skype for residents to watch grandkids open presents on Christmas morning but we also have the opportunity to have family members 'Skype in' to say goodbye to someone in the final stages of life when they aren't able to get there in time," shared Miekka Milliken, Social Services Coordinator, Vetter Health Services. "Those are things that you just don't get a second chance at."

Accommodating Individual Interests and Hobbies

Social activities in the long-term care setting have evolved in recent years, partially driven by the emergence of baby boomers into the mix with different expectations. Although there are still group activities, those group activities have evolved from bingo nights and board games to more popular things, such as wine and cheese events with live entertainment. Many organizations also bring in massage therapists and nail technicians to provide spa services. The staff at Vetter Health Services works with each individual on what his or her particular interests and desires are. "We've had residents set up sewing machines in their rooms to make gifts or items to sell at the facility-hosted boutique, and we help them with those individual activities—or woodworking, or whatever their social history included that they would like to continue to do," said Miekka Milliken. "We really work hard to meet those needs and to work with them to set up the very best situation for each person."

Milliken shared the story of a resident with Parkinson's disease who wanted to go swimming:

> She really wished she could go to the swimming pool. The team said, "Well why couldn't we do this? Why can't we figure this out?" So together the interdisciplinary team—the memory support coordinator, the life enrichment coordinator and the maintenance director—led the charge. They called home office and asked what they would need to do to make this happen for residents who want to swim. The home office life enrichment coordinator and nursing team worked together to make a checklist of what the team would need to do to ensure safety before they could take residents to the public pool for an open swim night for adults. Then they went around and asked who wanted to go. They even had residents in the late stages of Alzheimer's disease, and most were wheelchair-bound. They took eleven individuals the first time, went back for a second adult swim night, and are planning for several trips in the coming year. It was a public pool with zero depth entry. They wheeled people in and let them slowly float out of their chairs. Each resident had at least one support person with them. They were safe and protected with life vests and it was a fabulous experience. It was all because a resident said "Gee I haven't been swimming in a long time. I'd really like to go." There are unlimited possibilities for what we can do if we put our heads together and listen to what the residents are requesting of us. And the word has gotten out! New inquiries have included questions about swimming. One gentleman said he can't wait; he hasn't been swimming in years!

Community Involvement

Long-term care organizations traditionally enjoy strong ties with the communities they reside in. Churches, schools, and other organizations become active participants with residents. Breckenridge has a "grand letters" program with third graders at the school next door. Students interact through a series of letters and correspondence with residents. The program culminates with a luncheon where the residents and students meet. "This is one of the things we try to nurture," said David Schell, Executive Director, Breckenridge Village. "It really gets to a deeper relationship and understanding."

While volunteers play a vital role in supporting long-term care residents, Schell shared a story about a resident who found a way to give back to the community:

> One of the fears in aging is reaching a point where you feel you are no longer contributing to society; you are no longer helping. One of our earliest residents had the idea to start the "Care Cards" program by recycling old greeting cards and selling them three for $1.00 with the proceeds going to what we call our Life Care Commitment that ensures no one is asked to leave the facility because of inability to pay. Since Care Cards started in 1984, they have donated over $160,000 to the Life Care Commitment. The residents give back. Staff and people all over the community buy these care cards. They

are doing meaningful work. They are socializing when they do it. They are recycling and raising money. They are giving back. It is the ultimate activity in a way.

Staff Training/Support

Building and sustaining a person-centered organization requires participation from everyone on the staff. As Schell stated, "It does take a team. If you're going to do the kind of engagement that is individualized for every person, everyone who comes in contact with that person has to be charged with engaging them."

Staff training and overall culture are key elements of success in person-centered care across all settings. Each organization we spoke with reinforced the importance of staff training to help people understand how important their jobs are and how to nurture relationships with residents. Overall, communication skills are essential. "We provide training (for new employees) that goes into detail in regards to service excellence and our culture," said Regina Mabe, Human Resources Director, Commonwealth Care of Roanoke. "A Service Excellence culture is how we treat each other, each and every day. It's how we interact with each other as well as provide quality care for our residents and patients."

Ivan Hilton, Director of Business Development, Beatitudes Campus, shared a story illustrating the value in teaching all staff members to look at what residents are communicating verbally and through behaviors:

A director was on the unit speaking to a housekeeper about a resident on her floor who she said was just not acting like herself. The director said, "Well, I just saw her. She looks like she is just perfect. I didn't see anything wrong with her." And the housekeeper said, "Every time I go into her room she sings in the morning, and this morning she wasn't singing to me. There is something not right." They looked into it a little further, and the resident had a urinary tract infection. The housekeeper was the one who actually discovered it because of a change in the behavior. I think those are the things we were doing, I think the educational component that we do with all aspects of the people who interact with our residents and with the people who come to us for care is invaluable. They are taught to look for those things.

Carolinas HealthCare Systems started a video training program in which teammates are videotaped interacting with residents. The videos are used as virtual training opportunities for shared feedback and residents enjoy being part of the education of the teammates so they can help teach better communication strategies that impact their care.

Vetter Health Services is creating staff training modules on things such as benefits of massage therapy so that team members can learn basic massage techniques to increase resident comfort. They are also developing a module on sexuality in long-term care, a topic that has been taboo with some generations but is changing as the newer generation enters the care facilities.

Beyond training, it is also important to help staff acknowledge and deal with the emotions that are inherent in long-term care. "In our service and profession, we encounter death of our residents. Many reside with us for a long period of time and become a part of the family of our teammates," said Angela Orsky. "So that becomes a loss that is real to our teammates in addition to the family members that we support." Carolinas HealthCare Systems offers annual memorial services, led by a chaplain, in memory of residents who died while in the facility over the year. The service is a time of reflection when teammates and the family members can share particular moments, stories, and memories. "This is an opportunity for our facilities to embrace our family members that we serve. They come together, and our teammates find this to be such a healing experience for everyone."

This powerful set of exemplary practices provides a taste of what is and can be done to ensure a person-centered focus in the long-term care environment. As you can see in these examples, these are not always significant investments of time or money but rather a shift in awareness, a simple consideration, and a focus on listening, all of which can make a big difference. As we look to decisions made in how to create the best experience for those in our care, it is both understanding what practices we can consider and imagining which we can create that can make a significant difference. The only remaining choice is to take action and, as we can see, these actions have moving impact and outcomes.

SUPPORTS AND ROADBLOCKS TO CREATING PERSON-CENTERED EXPERIENCES

Each participating organization was asked to reflect on what propels their efforts to create person-centered experiences and what gets in the way. Though they represent organizations of varying sizes, in different locations and with unique populations and histories, several key themes emerged.

Supporting Factors

Having *leadership support* and an *organizational philosophy* that supports and drives person centeredness was identified as the top driving force by each organization. "What is supporting our efforts is a board and a senior leadership team that articulate and demonstrate a commitment to put 'patients first always'," said Connie Bonebrake, Senior Vice President, Chief Patient Experience Officer, Carolinas HealthCare System. "Having a senior leader that is responsible for the organization's patient experience strategy is also important."

Leadership/organizational support creates cohesiveness and clarity for staff at all levels and an overall engagement and commitment to doing what is right for residents and families. Participants cited that engagement results in lower turnover and higher employee satisfaction, which leads to better overall care.

Organizations also acknowledge the *support from each other.* Whether it is with sister facilities or industry colleagues, the industry is coming together to share best practices and create momentum for improvement. "There is a lot of opportunity in terms of reexamining the way things are constructed to encourage others along this movement," said Tena Alonzo.

This concept of support also reinforced the value in *maintaining a systemic perspective.* Jane Dawson, AVP, Patient Experience, Carolinas HealthCare System, addressed the power of the cross-continuum support they are able to provide throughout Carolinas HealthCare Systems. She shared, "I am amazed as we think about care transitions and continuity of care, by the availability and access that our nursing home residents have to other parts of the continuum. A resident may need an appointment with a specialist in the community, or they may need to be seen [right] there in their own facility environment. Being part of a system makes obtaining appointments and referrals in house more doable. I think we have something to be thankful for in our system to be able to connect those dots and [provide] the ease of access."

In this light, Commonwealth Care of Roanoke, created a Hub council made up of senior leaders across the company who each act as a service excellence mentor for one of the 12 centers across Virginia. The Hub council meets in person monthly to share challenges and improve communications. "Each of the mentors presents an update of initiatives and activities going on in their individual centers and any challenges or barriers they're facing," said Regina Mabe. "We have that dialogue and establish best practices to address these because some issues/concerns that may be going on in my center are probably the same in others."

With this broad perspective comes the underlying recognition that *everyone can and must play a role.* Michelle Just, President and CEO, Beatitudes Campus, spoke about what drives overall success in an effort focused on person centeredness. She offered, "We do not just work to take care of the person and the family but [we must] also make the experience better for the people who provide that care every day. I think that's important to note; that to make something like this successful, you have to have the buy-in from the housekeeper that is going in and out of the room throughout the day all the way up to the Board of Directors."

Roadblocks

Financial challenges surfaced as the biggest roadblock, from regulatory issues impacting reimbursements to the extraordinary costs of creating ideal care environments.

"In the skilled nursing facility side of long-term care, reimbursement is an issue," said Tena Alonzo. "The systems are set-up for people to get better, but we know that with older adults at some point all chronic conditions become fatal, and dementia is a terminal condition from the beginning. There are aspects to what we do which are not achievable and they (the regulatory goals and guidelines) are unrealistic."

Participating organizations also cited frustration in the *current environment with Medicare and Medicaid resources* being eliminated for many of the social programs and the education and communication needs to support the plethora of regulations around surveys. Those surveys typically follow a medical model, which can create challenges in long-term care. Carolinas HealthCare Systems shared the example of residents having personal refrigerators in their rooms. Medical guidelines require food and beverages to be dated and labeled, which may not be necessary in the long-term care environment. She also mentioned challenges such as transforming the traditional kitchen from a medical model to provide a family-like meal service in long-term care. "We have been very fortunate that our surveyors want to work and collaborate with us, but it does take some creative thinking and management along the way until we can get fully engaged across all of our survey processes to create patient-centered tools and less of a medical survey," said Angela Orsky.

Many are also challenged by an old *mind-set.* "Long-term care has looked somewhat the same for a long time. We say here a lot that we are going to change the view of long-term care and we really believe that we are, but it's a fast paced business for frontline team members," said Miekka Milliken. "They're balancing a lot of tasks. There are new challenges, requests and demands and there can be some inflexibility that goes along with that. It's a process and we are just on the journey."

IMPACTS AND OUTCOMES OF PERSON CENTEREDNESS

In exploring the impact and outcomes of a focus on person centeredness, there was great alignment and clarity about what our participant organizations were experiencing. Although each was at various stages of outcomes or still analyzing overall impact, there were clear common themes that came to light. These ideas were focused on the power of *personal choice* and its influence on cost; more importantly, it involved a reigniting of individuality, the *opportunity for market differentiation* in a highly competitive and potentially crowded marketplace, the *acknowledgment of voice* and the impact giving broader control and input can have, and the *creation of engagement* and buy-in and the sense of ownership and purpose it creates or reignites for all engaged.

The interesting dynamic these concepts offer is that in putting these ideas in place, they also are outcomes that are realized; in providing for voice or choice, you create new opportunities for these ideas to impact the organization overall. These have far-reaching implications from clinical outcomes to financial impact.

Personal Choice

The elevation of opportunities for choices has driven real tangible outcomes. First and most clearly, our participants noted that when providing choice for people and giving them a sense of power again, they saw a two-pronged impact. The first was responsiveness and involvement of the residents/elders in their care. By providing choice in eating, a major suggested practice, healthier eating patterns emerged, and the clinical and practical associated issues also diminished. This included people's overall functioning in many cases from reducing incontinence issues to combating unnecessary weight loss. This impacts the needs for supplies, such as diapers, food supplements, and other items, providing a second outcome for these organizations in cost savings due to a reduction in some product needs and time savings due to greater involvement of patients previously requiring extra personal attention and clinical care.

Audrey Weiner offered this direct impact of providing choice in person centeredness, "Things you would expect like depression and weight loss have been significantly reduced." The ripple effects of these outcomes had a far-reaching and positive impact on the organization overall.

Tena Alonzo concurred, sharing, "When you really change the system to support the person, the individuality of the person, so they can sleep when they want, wake when they want, eat when they want, is no small feat, but it makes sense, its dignified and in the end we are finding it's actually less work for the staff. It is a win-win-win!"

Angela Orsky added that providing choice, specifically with an open approach to dining, has led to great outcomes. She offered, "We have seen very positive overall quality outcomes in focusing on patient-centered care and become more personally related to that resident, acknowledging their preferences and their healthcare needs."

Market Differentiation

There was a consistent understanding across our participants of the consumer choices people have in the long-term care space as well. In creating a positive experience for residents/elders, family members, and staff, facilities can distinguish themselves not only in the outcomes they report, but also in the stories that are shared and the conversations about their organizations in the communities they serve. This is not to diminish the value of the care they provide but rather to reinforce a desire to be quality providers in their respective geographies. As noted earlier, if the consumer mind-set is gripping health care across the continuum, long-term care is perhaps the area with the greatest opportunity just due to the amount of choices and the volume of potential customers.

There may be nothing more critical than caring for our elders; the key is to do it with dignity and respect. This is a message and an experience each organization identified as key to why patient centeredness was important. Although not all organizations could quantify directly the market impact on their efforts or were still early in their data collection, it was evident that they each believed the potential outcome of their focus would be unique position in the market.

Audrey Weiner said of organizations focused on person centeredness, "I do believe that as families come and tour that they can probably feel the difference and I think this takes it to the next level." She and others pointed out you can feel it in the way the staff engages, you can feel it in the built environment, and you can see it in the faces and actions of residents and families in a facility. It is a tangible force that has great influence on the very viability of these organizations.

Nancy Waters, Service Excellence Officer, Commonwealth Care of Roanoke, addressed this as well in offering, "Our owners feel that excellence in service is the one thing that can differentiate us in our community. We really believe that being average is simply not good enough. Therefore, we must always strive to be the leader in customer care and service. Our commitment is to assure person-centered care is central to all aspects of our patient (and resident) experience. This is reflected in our company logo: Committed, Caring and Responsive."

As health care overall continues to expand its focus on centeredness and experience, the impact on the organizations people choose for themselves or their loved ones will also be great. Differentiation will matter both as a focus and as a driver of the best possible outcomes.

Voice and Engagement

Although discrete concepts, these ideas are closely linked. In fact, much of the work at the heart of person centeredness focuses on the importance of choice noted earlier and then providing opportunities for voices to be heard and engagement to be fostered. Simply framed opportunities for voice are about giving people a chance to have a say in what and how things are done. This leads to engagement across individuals and roles. A focus on person centeredness according to many of our participants leads to just that. It has reignited the spirit of all involved, engaged them to new levels of intent, and impacted the range of potential outcomes they look to achieve in the long-term care environment.

Miekka Milliken shared in providing opportunities for voice, "We see more engaged individuals in our communities. We see them believing that their voices make a difference and using their voices more to let us know what they need.

That's one of the indications that we're doing a good job, that we take the time to hear our resident voices and that they matter." Milliken continued to explain how this person-centered approach is changing the nature and perceptions of long-term care overall. "I think there has been a fear in long-term care for a long time, because they're vulnerable adults that if they speak up, someone might retaliate against them. Unfortunately we all know of places where this has happened."

In contrast to the fear, she continued by conveying what providing the opportunity for voice has impacted, "in our communities, our residents feel very comfortable voicing their needs and are confident we will do what we can to meet those and our satisfaction surveys reflect this." David Schell reinforced this point regarding a clear focus on patient centeredness, offering, "I think that the two major outcomes are, one, that people and staff buy into the process and believe in what they are doing and two, that their life and their work has meaningful purpose and they make it as much a life's avocation as opposed to just a job."

This speaks to a powerful outcome not often talked about when implementing positive experience efforts or focusing on person centeredness; the impact these efforts have in enlivening, enriching, and reinvigorating the people providing care themselves. In doing so, you are building a vibrant, focused, and purposeful workforce that can lead to the best in outcomes for all in the care process, namely residents, families, and peers.

The Impact of Person Centeredness

In looking at the ideas shared by our participants, it is easy to point to clinical or financial outcomes as critical measures of progress in this effort, but Tana Alonzo reminded us of one other critical component that at times may not be seen as a measure of success in these efforts. She shared that she saw this work as a "win-win-win," and the third win she noted was for the families in the long-term care experience.

She shared, "An impact of this focus is that families win because they get their person back. I wish I had a dollar for every time I had a family member say, 'You've given me my mother back, You've given me my husband back.'" As she spoke, it reinforced a critical point on what can happen when focusing on person centeredness—"giving a person back." They are given back their own personal dignity and power and, in focusing on what is important to them, you see the impact as well on how they engage with and experience their family, their fellow residents, and their staff. As Tena Alonzo shared, "These are outcomes that are truly tangible to staff and family."

In ensuring a focus on person centeredness, we create opportunities for people to thrive. Perhaps in long-term care, this is the most important outcome of all.

EXPLORING CONNECTIONS ACROSS THE CONTINUUM OF CARE: REFLECTIONS AND RECOMMENDATIONS

Although the intent of this chapter has been to explore the focus on and impact of person centeredness in long-term care, we also gained greater insight in the broader context of the patient/resident experience overall. In our conversations with these committed leaders, core ideas that have been central to much of what we have seen in the roots of the patient experience movement were identified as well. This raises an important point and reinforces a critical understanding about the efforts to address experience in health care today.

In the focus to provide a person-centered experience, core fundamental ideas emerge beyond tactics, or even strict processes or protocols on which the medical field was built. In exploring experience, we touch on the humanity of health care instead, which opens the conversation to that of how organizations are operated, the cultures they support, and how people are treated and engaged across status in the health care system or role they play. It comes back to the construct found at the start of the definition of patient experience—*interactions*. As we have seen in our efforts to explore experience and again in the words and experiences of our participants here—at its core, experience, person centeredness, and the outcomes and impact that they have happen primarily at the contact point between people. This above all else may be the heart of this conversation at all points across the continuum.

We would be remiss though if we did not also highlight what we see as subtle yet important distinctions at play exploring person centeredness and experience in long-term care. The unique nature of long-term care stems from the concept itself. As a "long-term" experience, it connotes something more than having to run cyclical patterns of behaviors to address the next person to occupy room 204. This is not to diminish the acute experience in contrast, but rather to highlight the very nature that long-term care relies even more heavily on a relational mind-set. In this environment, people will be spending more time with one another, with the chance to come to know, understand, and even care deeply for those they care for, live with, and so forth.

This relational aspect is deepened as the opportunity at this stage in the continuum is not necessarily about healing, in so much as it is about enlivenment, the enrichment of life, the reinvigoration of interests or passion, and in creating moments of dignity rather than reminders of the potentially limited time ahead. This relational nature and opportunity is also much more strongly tied to the engagement and involvement of families and support networks—interestingly enough much in the same way, but with longer time frames—that we see in the pediatric world.

We are not suggesting that the idea of relationships is unique to the long-term care environment. Rather, the nature of those relationships, what they mean, and the implications they have on the health care encounter are significant. And with this subtle distinction, the core ideas that drive the best in experience seem to be reinforced as well.

The consistencies are found in the ideas we explored earlier, but they lead us back to some critical and central concepts:

- Acknowledging the individuality of all those receiving and delivering care.

- Reinforcing the importance of choice in both how care is provided and received, giving power back to those in our care.

- Giving voice to all those in the care process regardless of role and, in doing so, engage and provide them with a sense of control all too often lost in care experiences.

- Recognizing the value of team focus and effort. Health care is not, nor will it ever be, an individual sport; when we work better together, we get better together.

- Maintaining a systemic perspective, in that all parts of the process of the organization and the system rely on one another in order to achieve the greatest level of success.

- Focusing on the critical role of leadership at all levels, from board and executives to the front line of care, where people make decisions that affect the organization and outcomes every day.

- Establishing and sustaining a positive, strong, healthy, and vibrant organization culture committed to the support and engagement of all in its midst.

- Continuing to focus on the simple notion that the work to ensure positive and unparalleled experience is not an initiative, but rather a continuous action requiring relentless intention.

In looking at these consistencies, we also begin to shape a recipe for success in creating a focus on person centeredness and the best in experience for all engaged in the care process. As we look to the meaningful and noble work of those in long-term care, we can see there is much that can be learned; yet, we also learn that there is much we all have in common. This gives us great power and provides great opportunity for all we look to accomplish in driving the best outcomes for all.

CONCLUSION

There are many common opportunities and challenges facing health care communities in creating more person-centered cultures and built environments across the health care continuum. Yet, the worlds of acute care and chronic care, of hospitals and nursing homes, have each developed in an entirely separate universe. They have their own industry membership associations, advocacy groups, professional associations, regulations, and so forth. Over time, they also have each developed their own definitions and sense of the centrality of the experience of the patient, resident, and family and its relationship to more positive outcomes. However, we recognize that health care today is no longer a series of balkanized interventions defined by the level of acuity. Rather, it needs to be more of a continuum of care where the person requiring care at differing levels of acuity often receives that care without changing care communities and sometimes even at home, based upon the needs.

In order to understand how the experience of those receiving care can best be enhanced and enriched as they move through that care continuum, we need to begin to break down some of our acuity-centric silos. We need to find ways to share our philosophies, experience, and research between the fields of short- and long-term care, for there is a great deal that we might learn from each other. Of course, there will continue to be a number of significant differences, but we have far more in common with respect to our common goal of placing residents, patients, and families at the center of the care delivery system no matter what the acuity or length of stay.

CASE STUDY

You are a manager in a long-term care facility. There have been several residents who have fallen and broken their hip over the past 6 months. There have been a number of complaints from family members of residents stating that the needs of their loved ones are not being met. There have also been a number of changes in staffing with a very high rate of turnover for approximately 6 months. The director left and there is an interim director serving until the facility finds another director. You are a consultant and have been hired to help the director create change on an enterprise level. Your first priority is to conduct a survey of family members to obtain patient satisfaction data.

Issues to Consider

1. What questions can you include that address meeting basic needs?
2. How can you obtain evidence that demonstrates that the nurses are kind and respectful toward the residents?
3. In what ways can families comment on staffing, care of belongings, and cleanliness of the long-term care facility?
4. How can you create a rating system that will analyze the data obtained in the preceding questions?

REFERENCES

Boccuti, C., Caslillas, G., & Neuman, T. (2015). Reading the stars: Nursing home quality star ratings nationally and by state. Retrieved from http://kff.org/report-section/reading-the-stars-nursing-home-quality-star-ratings-nationally-and-by-state-executive-summary

Centers for Medicare and Medicaid Services. (2013). Nursing home data compendium. Retrieved from https://www.cms.gov/Medicare/Provider-Enrollment-and-Certification/CertificationandComplianc/downloads/nursinghomedatacompendium_508.pdf

Koren, M. J. (2010). Person-centered care for nursing home residents: The culture-change movement. *Health Affairs, 29*(2), 312–317. http://dx.doi.org/10.1377/hlthaff.2009.0966

Wolf, J., Brown, L., Weiner, A., & Wolterman, D. (2015). *A dialogue on improving patient experience throughout continuum of care.* Bedford, TX: The Beryl Institute.

Wolf, J., Niederhauser, V., Marshburn, D., & LaVela, S. L. (2014). *Defining patient experience: A critical decision for healthcare organizations.* Bedford, TX: The Beryl Institute.

Wolf, J., & Palmer, S. (2015). *The power of person-centeredness in long-term care: A view across the continuum.* Bedford, TX: The Beryl Institute.

SECTION II

SYSTEMS MANAGEMENT

CHAPTER 7

PAYING FOR PERSON-CENTERED CARE: THE ROLE OF HEALTH CARE PAYMENT AND QUALITY POLICY

RICHARD H. HUGHES IV AND ROBERT F. ATLAS

When one considers our national dialogue following enactment of the Affordable Care Act (ACA) in 2010, the most common point of reference was the number (in millions) of newly insured Americans. This is a strong indicator that much of U.S. health care policy is population oriented (macro), rather than focused on the individual person (micro).

The Institute of Medicine (IOM) defines *patient-centered care* as "Providing care that is respectful of and responsive to individual patient preferences, needs, and values, and ensuring that patient values guide all clinical decisions" (IOM, 2001). This chapter reviews the major health care payment and quality policy developments intended to accomplish these aims, including those enacted as part of the ACA. Ultimately, we hope to help you, the reader, gain an understanding and critical view of how these policies impact the delivery of care in a manner that is responsive to the needs of the individual person.

AMERICAN HEALTH POLICY'S POPULATION ORIENTATION

After centuries of infectious disease epidemics, public health interventions stemmed millions of preventable deaths. Thanks to the pioneering efforts of men like Edward Jenner and John Snow in the 18th and 19th centuries, English and American health officials learned to identify public health problems and solve them with broad-based interventions. The solutions, whether separating sewage from drinking water, isolating an infected group of people, or vaccinating the masses, proved effective at eliminating much death and disease, measured in millions of lives.

By the latter half of the 20th century, the successes of reducing infectious disease gave way to new leading causes of death—the chronic diseases of cancer, diabetes, and heart disease—many caused by people's lifestyles and genetic makeup. Policy makers continue to address these problems with broad-based approaches, such as antismoking laws and nutrition standards, which are designed to promote healthier individual behavior on a population scale. As illustrated in Figure 7.1, interventions such as these, when deployed at various and correct intervals, hopefully lessen affliction and death for the population.

Of course, chronic disease can be prevented and managed to an extent on a population level. However, complex or multiple chronic conditions cannot be managed only on a population level. Figure 7.1 also maps the experience of an individual as he or she navigates a world in which the person encounters the risk of disease, and a system of prevention and care purportedly designed to protect his or her health. This figure illustrates that there are many factors that affect a patient's experience within our health care system, for example:

- What obstacles to access of health care did the patient have to overcome?
- Did the patient receive timely attention to his or her health needs?
- Was the treatment received effective?
- Did the health care system make the patient healthier or sicker?

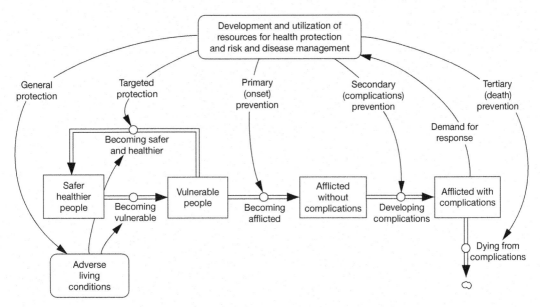

FIGURE 7.1 – A broad view of population health and the spectrum of possible responses.

Note: Rectangles indicate the stock of people; thick arrows with circles and possible clouds represent the flow of people; thinner arrows show causal influence; rounded rectangles manifest multidimensional concepts.

Source: Homer and Hirsch (2006).

20TH-CENTURY DEVELOPMENTS IN HEALTH COVERAGE AND PAYMENT

The earliest models of health insurance did little to ensure that the care provided met the needs of patients. In the late 19th and early 20th centuries, Americans predominantly viewed health insurance as a financial protection. The early model of "sickness insurance" was intended to provide sick pay to employees, although the coverage of health services was an afterthought.

During this same period, the American Medical Association (AMA), seriously concerned about interference with the practice of medicine, opposed national solutions that would provide Americans medical benefit coverage. In the 1930s, Blue Cross and Blue Shield plans emerged as not-for-profit, provider-driven health insurance, with Blue Cross offering hospital benefits and Blue Shield covering physician services. During this time, a number of prepaid group health plans also emerged out of community and employer initiatives, most notably Kaiser Permanente.

After World War II, a wage freeze and the Supreme Court's affirmation of union bargaining power over employee benefits led to a dramatic increase in employer-offered comprehensive health insurance benefits. A series of Congressional attempts to provide the elderly and poor with hospital and physician benefits ultimately led to the passage of Medicare and Medicaid in 1965. Millions of Americans gained coverage as a result of these collective developments.

With these successes came challenges that still confront our health care system today. Perhaps the most notable challenge has been the lack of alignment between provider incentives and the patient experience desired by consumers of health services. The misalignment has at various times resulted in enormous financial costs, poor health outcomes, and consumer dissatisfaction.

Through the 1980s, most payers, including the federal government, paid hospitals on the basis of their costs and health care practitioners what is known as "usual, customary, and reasonable" (UCR) charges. That is, "the amount paid for a medical service in a geographic area based on what providers in the area usually charge for the same or similar medical service" (Schroeder, 2011). Recognizing that this payment structure often overpaid providers for some services, while underpaying for others, Medicare adopted so-called prospective payment for inpatient hospital services in 1983 and then a "resource-based relative value scale" fee schedule for physicians in 1989. The latter scores services on the basis of relative value units (RVUs), taking into account the physician's time and effort, as well as the practice costs and malpractice insurance premiums associated with a particular service.

Both the UCR- and RVU-based approaches entail paying physicians on a fee-for-service (FFS) basis. FFS remains in widespread use today under Medicare, Medicaid, and commercial health insurance, though health care payment is evolving to include many other models, as shown in Figure 7.2. The primary criticism of FFS is that the incentive for providers is to grow the volume and intensity of services rendered, which has the potential to result in unnecessary care being rendered.

The advent of third-party coverage, which gave many consumers better access to health care, combined with payment schemes that rewarded providers for doing more, spurred massive growth in health spending. States and the federal government reacted with a series of actions to curb health cost growth. Many states tried to control health care supply by enacting certificate of need laws intended to scale the capacity of our health care system to its demands. Congress passed and President Nixon signed the Health Maintenance Organization Act of

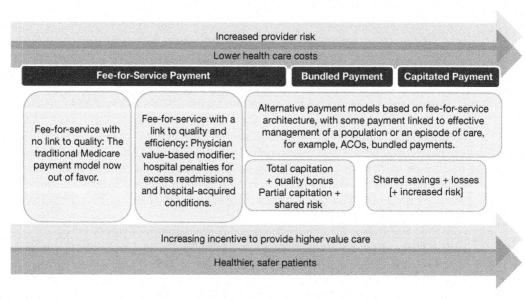

FIGURE 7.2 – Shifting health care payment, quality incentives.
ACOs, accountable care organization.
Sources: Atlas (2015); Rajkumar, Conway, and Tavenner (2014).

1973, delivering a combination of financial aid and mandates that boosted the prepaid group health plan model, newly renamed as health maintenance organizations (HMOs). The HMO led to a proliferation of other payment models bearing its central concept—managed care.

Managed care entails a range of approaches to contain the cost of care and maximize value. This includes a traditional FFS arrangement combined with utilization management—oversight by a health plan to ensure that services rendered are covered and medically necessary. Other managed care arrangements entail bundled or capitated payment. Under a bundled payment arrangement, a provider is paid a fixed sum for an episode requiring care. For example, a provider is paid an agreed-to fee to perform a total knee replacement and must absorb all costs for any follow-up care or associated complications. Similarly, under a capitated arrangement, a provider or practice group is paid a fixed amount to provide complete care for an individual over a long span of time.

As shown in Figure 7.2, a provider assumes increasing risk under bundled and capitated arrangements. These arrangements moderate the problematic FFS incentive to generate volume. Capitated payment has its own unique challenge, however, in that a provider may be incentivized to skimp on the care provided. Consequently, health care payment has become a balancing act—ensuring patients receive the care they need, but no more than that. Thus, payment plays a critical role in achieving the right balance and ensuring that individuals exit their interaction with our health care system less afflicted than they entered.

PATIENT EXPERIENCES LEAD TO FOCUS ON SAFETY, MEASURING, AND PAYING FOR QUALITY

The realities of a system that rewards volume over delivery of high-value care to patients have reached the point of public reckoning. During the 1990s, the concern over patient safety culminated in a renewed national focus on health care quality. In a groundbreaking 1999 report entitled *To Err Is Human*, the IOM published a set of harrowing statistics:

> At least 44,000 people, and perhaps as many as 98,000 people, die in hospitals each year as a result of medical errors that could have been prevented . . . adverse drug events and improper transfusions, surgical injuries and wrong-site surgery, suicides, restraint-related injuries or death, falls, burns, pressure ulcers, and mistaken patient identities. (IOM, 1999)

The IOM report noted that among the factors contributing to this epidemic were decentralization and fragmentation of our health care delivery system, or what some observers termed a "nonsystem" (IOM, 1999). It further pointed out the unacceptability of harm inflicted by the very system intended to offer healing and comfort (IOM, 1999). In response, President Clinton signed the Healthcare Research and Quality Act of 1999, renaming an existing federal agency the Agency for Healthcare Research and Quality (AHRQ) and authorizing it to promote health care quality improvement through various activities (Healthcare Research and Quality Act, 1999).

In 2001, the IOM released a follow-up report entitled *Crossing the Quality Chasm*, which focused more broadly beyond patient safety and squarely on the alignment of our health care system with patient needs. As alluded to in the introduction, increased life expectancy resulting from earlier public health successes meant that people were living longer and experiencing more chronic conditions. But the IOM found our system incapable of addressing the needs of an aging population with multiple chronic care needs, and instead still "overly devoted to dealing with acute, episodic care needs" (IOM, 2001).

Among other recommendations, the IOM urged "analysis and synthesis of the medical evidence, delineation of specific practice guidelines, identification of best practices in the design of care processes . . . [and] development of measures for assessing quality of care" (IOM, 2001). Essentially, making progress toward a system that maximizes value to the individual patient requires "rigorous, disciplined measurement and improvement of value" (Porter, 2010).

In the next section, we review the types of available quality measures, followed by a discussion of how they are deployed and used to improve quality.

Clinical Quality Measurement in Health Care

Avedis Donabedian, the father of health care quality measurement, set forth three major domains across which a system should measure the quality of care (Donabedian, 1988). These are structure, process, and outcome measures. When measuring structure, we consider the "feature[s] of a health care organization or clinician related to the capacity to provide high quality health care" (Kessell et al., 2015). This includes its human and material resources, such as its size and equipment. This also includes technology, as we measure how well an organization is keeping up with advancements in modern health care delivery, such as the use of electronic medical records (EMRs), e-prescribing capabilities, and other forms of health information technology (HIT). Although structure measurement bears little focus on persons receiving care, it is intended to promote a health care infrastructure that has the tools to deliver optimal care.

In addition to its structure, the process by which an organization or provider delivers care can be measured. The types of measures used are predominantly driven by clinical guidelines. These guidelines draw upon peer-reviewed evidence and represent the consensus as to how a provider should treat a specific patient condition, for example, whether a provider prescribes aspirin at the time of presentation to a patient who has experienced myocardial infarction (heart attack).

Finally, the Donabedian model includes measurement of health care's end result, or the "[h]ealth state of a patient resulting from health care" (AHRQ, 2014b). This might include an intermediate result, such as whether a provider's diabetic patients successfully reduced blood sugar levels or ultimate outcomes, such as mortality. Measures such as these raise the floor for population health outcomes to know how well a provider or health plan performs against it.

Person-Focused Quality Measurement

Some argue that classical quality measurement falls short of measuring what matters most to patients; at worst, it fails to incentivize providers to consider what is best for a particular patient's health or well-being. Donabedian himself said, "Systems awareness and systems design are important for health professionals, but are not enough. They are enabling mechanisms only. It is the ethical dimension of individuals that is essential to a system's success" (Mullan, 2001). The ethical questions surrounding person-focused care are discussed elsewhere in this book; here we focus on policies meant to promote measurement of the patient experience.

In the mid-1990s, the AHRQ developed a different set of quality measures that would add a fourth dimension to quality measurement, the Consumer Assessment of Healthcare Providers and Systems (CAHPS) survey. CAHPS was originally designed to assess "the quality of health plans from their enrollees' perspective" (National Health Policy Forum, 2014). Its results were intended to help consumers evaluate their choice of health plans. Over time, CAHPS measures would broaden to include consumer assessments of the care they received across numerous settings of care. Today, the CAHPS measures the overall patient experience when interacting with our health care systems, as well as the timeliness of care received and how well providers communicate about care. See the examples of several CAHPS measures in Table 7.1.

Patient access to health care is also a domain of measurement. Insurance coverage alone does not guarantee that one will be able to obtain needed care. Access measures are intended to assess whether a health plan or provider's patients receive access to timely and appropriate care. Again reviewing Table 7.1, how do the measures discussed in this section compare with those discussed in the previous section?

Examples of the CAHPS measures and their respective domains are shown in Table 7.1. Although these examples illustrate the different aspects of clinical quality that are typically measured, it is only a small sample of the more than 800 available measures. Data for these measures are collected through various sources, including patient surveys, data from health insurance claims, abstraction of patient charts, and data from electronic health records or patient registries. Accessibility varies across these sources. Claims data is generally considered more accurate, though less useful in monitoring health progress. EMR data is challenging because it is often inconsistent and requires deciphering; however, it has the potential to facilitate better tracking of health progress.

Promoting and Administering Quality Measurement

Effective development and deployment of clinical quality measures relies upon a mix of government agencies, such as AHRQ, and nongovernmental organizations, primarily the National Quality Forum (NQF) and the National Committee for Quality Assurance (NCQA).

AHRQ is housed within the U.S. Department of Health and Human Services. Unlike the Centers for Medicare and Medicaid Services (CMS), AHRQ is not a regulator or payer of health services. Rather, it promulgates quality measures and standards for use across the public and private sectors. Its broad mission is to "produce evidence to make health care safer, higher quality, more accessible, equitable, and affordable, and to work within [HHS] and with other partners to make sure that the evidence is understood and used" (AHRQ, 2014a).

AHRQ conducts extensive provider education campaigns. Beyond mere dissemination of clinical guidelines, these campaigns include promotion of its "SHARE Approach," a five-step process for shared decision making between

TABLE 7.1 – Consider How Each of the Measures and Their Domains Accomplishes or Falls Short of Accomplishing Measurement of How Well Our Health Care Systems Achieve a Person Focus

Clinical Quality Measure Description	Domain	Comment
Adult trauma care: does the trauma system have a protocol directing transport of injured patients aged 18 years and older to specific hospitals?	Structure	Designed to ensure a process is in place so that a person receives timely emergency care.
Planning, organization, and management: percentage of days without the physical presence of an intensivist 24 hr/d.	Structure	Designed to hold facility management accountable for ensuring treatment capacity for the critically ill.
Intensive care unit (ICU) palliative care: presence of room designated for meetings between clinicians and ICU families.	Structure	Designed to ensure the family of a critically ill patient nearing end of life are able to communicate in a dignified environment. Note that this is a structure measure designed to promote person focus.
Weight assessment and counseling for nutrition and physical activity for children/adolescents: percentage of members 3–17 years of age who had an outpatient visit with a PCP or OB/GYN and who had evidence of BMI percentile documentation during the measurement year.	Process	Designed to ensure toddler to adolescent aged health plan beneficiaries receive appropriate weight screening and counseling.
Preventive care and screening: percentage of patients 18 years and older who were screened for tobacco use at least once during the 2-year measurement period *and* who received cessation counseling intervention if identified as a tobacco user.	Process	Designed to ensure adult health plan beneficiaries receive appropriate tobacco use screening and counseling.
Cervical cancer screening: percentage of women 21–64 years of age who were screened for cervical cancer.	Process	Designed to ensure adult females are screened for cervical cancer.
Controlling high blood pressure (BP): percentage of members 18–85 years of age who had a diagnosis of hypertension (HTN) and whose BP was adequately controlled during the measurement year, based on age/condition-specific criteria.	Outcome	Designed to ensure that persons with HTN control their BP.
Acute myocardial infarction (AMI): hospital 30-d, all-cause, risk-standardized mortality rate (RSMR) following AMI hospitalization.	Outcome	Designed to ensure person experiencing a heart attack is treated in a life-saving manner.
Failure to rescue: percentage of patients who died with a complication in the hospital.	Outcome	Designed to quantify hospital failures resulting in death.
Surgical patients' experiences: percentage of surgical patients who reported how well their surgeon communicated with them after surgery.	Patient Experience	Designed to assess patients' satisfaction with their surgeon's communication.
Behavioral health care patients' experiences: percentage of adult patients who reported how often their clinicians communicated well.	Patient Experience	Designed to assess behavioral health patient satisfaction with provider communication.
HIV ambulatory care satisfaction: percentage of HIV-positive women who reported how often their women's health providers knew about the latest medical developments for women with HIV.	Patient Experience	Designed to assess patient satisfaction with provider knowledge. Consider how this differs from a process measure.

BMI, body mass index; PCP, primary care provider.
Source: National Quality Measures Clearinghouse (2016).

providers and patients (AHRQ, 2014c). The SHARE Approach entails "meaningful dialogue about what matters most to the patient" through the following steps (AHRQ, 2014c):

Step 1: Seek your patient's participation.

Step 2: Help your patient explore and compare treatment options.

Step 3: Assess your patient's values and preferences.

Step 4: Reach a decision with your patient.

Step 5: Evaluate your patient's decision.

NQF evaluates and endorses measures, having earned the mantle of "gold standard." Through its consortium of more than 60 public and private entities, known as the Measure Applications Partnership, it advises payers in the government and private sectors on the use of measures in the course of regulating and purchasing health services.

Private, nonprofit accreditors also play an important role in promoting quality care. NCQA is an accrediting organization for many health care entities, including health plans through administration of the Healthcare Effectiveness Data and Information Set (HEDIS), as well as the CAHPS survey. HEDIS is a set of measures, currently 81 in total, that are clarified and revised from year to year as standards of care evolve and new measures are developed and prioritized. The measures vary in their applicability to the commercial, Medicaid, and Medicare markets. Another accreditor, URAC, accredits a wide range of health care entities, including plans, health information websites, and entities organized under distinct payment models, such as ACOs. Other, more niche accrediting entities include organizations such as the Accreditation Association for Ambulatory Health Care (AAAHC), which accredits more than 6,000 such entities.

Industry efforts at self-regulation and accreditation also play an important role in quality measurement. These include The Joint Commission (formerly known as The Joint Commission on the Accreditation of Healthcare Organizations), an accrediting entity for more than 21,000 health care plans, most notably hospitals. Additionally, the Ambulatory Care Quality Alliance (AQA) and Hospital Quality Alliance (HQA) are private sector bodies supported by government that convene stakeholders across providers and payer groups, consumer groups, and government agencies to drive improvement of performance measurement.

Under Title III of the ACA, Congress set forth requirements for a national strategy to improve health care quality. It called upon the secretary of the U.S. Department of Health and Human Services to set national quality priorities and coordinate with states and across federal agencies.

Regulating Quality of Care

The critical reader has likely asked at this stage of reading how a voluntary system of quality measurement, or measurement alone, can improve the quality of care, much less the care experience of a single individual. We endeavor to answer this question throughout the remainder of this chapter by describing payment models that are designed to incentivize high-quality health care. First, though, consider the direct regulation of quality. That is, how our system prohibits the delivery of substandard care.

States are the principal licensers and regulators of the health professions and health facilities. As part of the licensure and regulatory schemes in the states, which vary widely, providers and facilities may be held accountable through inspection and the possibility of discipline where care falls short of professional standards or the conditions of the setting of care pose a risk to patient health. Additionally, as discussed in more detail in Chapter 8, patients have the ability to pursue damages resulting from substandard care, known as malpractice.

Most states also require that health plans are accredited by the organizations discussed earlier, which means they are subject to measurement on a set of predefined quality measures before they can offer insurance products in the state. States do this in two capacities: as direct regulators of plans in the commercial market, and as direct purchasers of Medicaid services provided through managed care plans. As of July 2015, nine states required NCQA accreditation in the commercial market only, six in the Medicaid market only, and 27 in both markets (NCQA, 2016).

Additionally, some states require transparency of quality measurement on a facility, provider, or procedure level. For example, a state might require that facilities publish data on the success of heart surgeries. However, much to the dismay of patient advocates, state transparency laws are generally narrow in scope, if they exist at all, and have done little to facilitate system-wide transparency that would permit a person to meaningfully compare providers.

With 55 million beneficiaries and a total outlay of $630 billion in fiscal year 2015, Medicare accounts for approximately 14% of the federal budget. This makes the program the largest payer in our health care system. Seeking to be a prudent purchaser, Medicare imposes many rules on participating facilities that impact our delivery system more broadly. These are known as conditions of participation (CoPs). For example, in order to participate in Medicare, a hospital's medical staff must be accountable to its board for the quality of care delivered (42 C.F.R. §482.12(a)(5)). Additionally, hospitals must have detailed quality programs in place that identify opportunities, set priorities, and take action to improve quality (42 C.F.R. §482.21).

Are measuring and regulating quality sufficient to guarantee that patients receive the right and best quality care? Or are these mere safeguards that permit unacceptable room for error, patient injury, and dissatisfaction? For the most part, direct regulation, whether state or federal, only sets a floor. It effectively draws a line between acceptable and unacceptable. This, of course, does relatively little to incentivize optimal care. This brings us back to the ultimate incentive—payment—and, more specifically, tying payment to quality.

Paying for Quality Care

In the early 2000s, there was a "common perception that quality of care in the United States remain[ed] unacceptably low despite a decade of benchmarking and public reporting" (Rosenthal, Fernandopulle, Song, & Landon, 2004). Beginning in the 1990s, several public and private experiments were undertaken to shift financial risk to providers for poor-quality care or to reward them for high-quality care through bonus payments.

One of the earliest pay-for-performance models was initiated in 1991 by the Health Care Financing Administration (HCFA, the former name of the agency now known as CMS). Under the Medicare Participating Heart Bypass Center Demonstration project, physicians and hospitals were paid under a bundled arrangement for coronary artery bypass grafts. Although HCFA claimed the arrangement yielded savings, results were mixed for providers and facilities. The model was broadened in the late 1990s to include additional cardiovascular, hip, and knee procedures, but was never made permanent.

In 1998, a group of private sector employers formed the Leapfrog Group to mobilize the collective purchasing power of large employers to reward high-quality care. Its formation, the year before the release of the 1999 IOM report, demonstrated market reinforcement for improved patient safety and quality of care. Other, similar purchasing coalitions were formed. There were concerns in the early 2000s, however, that not enough purchasing power was being brought to bear through these handfuls of small initiatives (Rosenthal et al., 2004). Among them were concerns that provider selection could occur against sicker patients, and that such a system might simply reward already higher performing providers rather than elevate the performance overall (Rosenthal et al., 2004).

It would take several incremental acts of Congress to exercise enough purchasing power to meaningfully transform our health care system. As we review some of these reforms, note that they center predominantly on Medicare payment. This is so because Medicare is the one health insurance program in which the federal government wields the total purchasing power. Contrast this with Medicaid, which is partially federally funded and subject to federal oversight, but predominantly state run. Although regulated to a point at the federal level, government is not the payer in private health insurance markets. But of course, Medicare's sheer size and influence has historically driven the behavior of payers in these other markets, including states, employers, and health insurance plans.

Prior to the ACA, Congress passed two significant Medicare value-based purchasing provisions, each built on top of the FFS model. The Tax Relief and Health Care Act (TRHCA) of 2006 created the Physician Quality Reporting System (PQRS). PQRS operates under the same premise of paying providers on a FFS basis while adding accountability for the quality of care delivered. Under PQRS, providers must report on quality measures, including several measures that emphasize patience experience, or be subject to a future payment reduction. Providers who fail to report, or who report but fail to perform well on these measures, are subject to a 2% payment reduction.

The Health Information Technology for Economic and Clinical Health (HITECH) act, enacted as part of the American Recovery and Reinvestment Act of 2009, was intended to promote the adoption and meaningful use (MU) of HIT. MU incentivizes Medicaid and Medicare providers to demonstrate MU of electronic health records. Providers who refuse to participate are subject to payment penalties. The program has measure providers across three stages. At first, measurement emphasized data capture and sharing, and then advanced clinical processes. It now emphasizes improved clinical outcomes and the delivery of patient education.

Under Title III of the ACA, Congress sought to improve the quality and efficiency of our health care system. These reforms included transforming our health care delivery system by further linking Medicare payment to quality outcomes and encouraging the development of new patient care models. The ACA established within CMS a Center for Medicare and Medicaid Innovation (CMMI; Patient Protection and Affordable Care Act § 3021, 2010). CMMI was given broad authority to test new payment and delivery models. Among the models intended by Congress are those that "transition primary care practices away from fee-for-service based reimbursement and toward comprehensive payment or salary-based payment" (42 U.S.C. § 1315a(b)(2)(B)(ii)).

Additionally, CMMI is required to include in its evaluation of these models the "measurement of patient-level outcomes and patient-centeredness" (42 U.S.C. § 1315a(b)(4)(A)(i)).

The ACA specifically emphasized payment approaches that support the patient-centered medical home (PCMH) concept. The PCMH is more than a payment model. The notion of a "medical home" was first introduced in 1967 by the American Academy of Pediatrics. In 2007, several major provider groups jointly espoused several principles of the PCMH:

- Personal physician
- Physician-directed medical practice
- Whole person orientation
- Coordinated and/or integrated care
- Quality and safety
- Enhanced access to care
- Payment reform

As to the last point, payment reform, many purchasers have instituted payment arrangements that encourage PCMH formation and operation. These include enhanced payments for the PCMH to perform care coordination functions as well as incentives for controlling expenditures for specialty care and hospital services.

Since the ACA's passage, CMS has taken broad and assertive steps toward expanding the use of value-based payment models. In 2015, the secretary of the U.S. Department of Health and Human Services announced that by 2018, 90% of Medicare Part A and B payments will be tied to value or quality. Next, we review several of these models and how they continue to evolve.

The ACO is the most disruptive of these models to traditional FFS. Under the ACO model (Patient Protection and Affordable Care Act § 3022, 2010), Medicare aims to reward FFS providers for their quality and efficiency. That is, providers are paid under the traditional FFS model when they provide services to patients. Additionally, they are incentivized under a range of options involving varied gain and/or loss sharing across. ACOs are measured using 33 quality measures across the four domains discussed earlier. Higher performance results in a reward opportunity in the form of shared savings between Medicare and the ACO. In 2016, there are 405 ACOs providing care to 8.9 million beneficiaries.

The ACO model is evolving to encourage shifting of greater risk to providers, ultimately offering capitation options. CMS introduced the Next Generation ACO model to promote this more aggressive approach.

One of the most direct payment reforms may be the Medicare physician fee schedule value-based modifier (VBM) created by the ACA (Patient Protection and Affordable Care Act § 3007, 2010). Payment to physician practices is automatically adjusted based on a cost-to-quality comparison during a given performance period. Beginning in 2018, it will also apply to eligible nonphysician professionals.

In addition to individual provider-focused payment reform, the ACA established several hospital-focused value-based purchasing reforms. These include the hospital value-based purchasing, hospital-acquired condition reduction, and hospital readmissions reduction programs (Patient Protection and Affordable Care Act §3001, 3008, and 3025, 2010). Under the value-based purchasing program, hospitals will ultimately be subject to a 2% up or down payment adjustment on inpatient services based on patient safety, quality, and satisfaction. Under the hospital-acquired condition reduction program, hospitals ranking in the top 25% of hospital-acquired conditions and infections are subject to a 1% reimbursement penalty. Finally, hospitals with excessive 30-day readmission rates for certain conditions are subject to a reimbursement penalty.

Continuing the Medicare payment evolution, in 2015, Congress passed the Medicare Access and CHIP Reauthorization Act (MACRA). MACRA consolidates the PQRS, MU, and VBM programs. In its place, it creates a new "merit-based incentive payment system" (MIPS). By 2022, Medicare FFS payments will be subject to adjustments ranging from −9% to +27%. These adjustments will be determined based on quality performance using a blend of measurement approaches from the current PQRS, MU, and VBM programs.

MACRA also created a separate payment track called advanced alternative payment models (APMs). Participating providers who meet volume requirements and assume more financial risk will be eligible for 5% bonuses during the years 2019 to 2024. Many models, including ACO, PCMH, and bundled payment approaches, will qualify under APM if they entail sufficient degrees of risk for the provider entities.

In addition to paying individual providers and facilities for value, CMS is bringing its purchasing power to bear under Medicare Parts C and D. Plans under Part C, or Medicare Advantage (MA), are paid on a capitation basis to deliver full Medicare benefits plus supplemental coverage. Under Part D, prescription drug plans (PDPs) charge a set premium for outpatient prescription drug coverage, of which the government pays 75% or more for low-income persons eligible for subsidies. Both MA plans and PDPs are rated based on quality measure performance. Part C measurement focuses across the clinical quality measure domains discussed earlier, whereas Part D measures focus more specifically on patients' adherence to prescribed medication regimens. Plans achieving higher star ratings are eligible for bonus payments up to 5%, whereas plans consistently rated below 3.5 stars may lose their contracts with CMS.

Medicaid Payment Innovation

Medicaid covers 71 million poor and disabled Americans and spent $540 billion on health care services in 2015. Its aggregate market power is second only to Medicare. However, its oversight is shared by CMS and the individual states and territories. CMS sets overarching rules and standards for how states design and run Medicaid, and must approve any deviations by granting waivers. States receive a federal financial contribution ranging from 50% to 80%, or 100% (90% in later years) for the population of adults added under the ACA's Medicaid expansion.

CONCLUSION

The evolution toward payment systems that shift greater financial risk and accountability to providers continues to rapidly take shape. Quality performance measurement that emphasizes patient engagement and provider accountability for patient outcomes helps realize the vision of person-centered care, that is, a system that seeks to understand and fully recognize every patient's individual desires and values.

CASE STUDY

The ACA has encouraged meaningful provider/patient engagement. Today, data about the patient experience is seen as an *influencer of change* that not only improves health but also improves seemingly disparate aspects of health care.

You have been hired to operate a large physician practice located in your state. The practice was awarded a very large funding grant to participate in a primary care initiative funded by the government through the CMS. The program designed by the practice includes innovative ideas to improve the following:

- Access and continuity of care
- Care coordination for chronic conditions
- Prevention
- Risk-stratified care management

The CMS has asked the practice to clarify how patient experience data and patient satisfaction data will be captured throughout the life of the project.

Issues to Consider

1. How will your organization change the way in which it delivers primary care to align with the four items in the case study?

2. What is the difference between patient experience data and patient satisfaction data?

3. How can you measure patient experience data?

4. How can you integrate data gathering about the patient experience into the process of providing care?

REFERENCES

Agency for Healthcare Research and Quality. (2014a). A profile. Retrieved from http://www.ahrq.gov/cpi/about/profile/index.html

Agency for Healthcare Research and Quality. (2014b). Selecting quality measures. Retrieved from www.qualitymeasures.ahrq.gov/tutorial/selecting.aspx

Agency for Healthcare Research and Quality. (2014c). The SHARE approach. Retrieved from http://www.ahrq.gov/professionals/education/curriculum -tools/shareddecisionmaking/index.html

Atlas, R. F. (2015). *HHS declares value-based purchasing goals: Implications for the health care industry* (BNA Medicare Report).

Donabedian, A. (1988). The quality of care: How can it be assessed? *Journal of the American Medical Association, 260*(12), 1743–1748.

42 C.F.R. §482.12(a)(5).

42 C.F.R. §482.21.

42 U.S.C. § 1315a(b)(2)(B)(ii).

42 U.S.C. § 1315a(b)(4)(A)(i).

Healthcare Research and Quality Act of 1999, Public Law 106-129.

Homer, J. B., & Hirsch, G. B. (2006). System dynamics modeling for public health: Background and opportunities. *American Journal of Public Health, 96*(3), 452–458.

Institute of Medicine. (1999). *To err is human: Building a safer health system.* Washington, DC: National Academies Press.

Institute of Medicine. (2001). *Crossing the quality chasm: A new health system for the 21st century.* Washington, DC: National Academies Press.

Kessell, E., Pegany, V., Keolanui, B., Fulton, B. D., Scheffler, R. M., & Shortell, S. M. (2015). Review of Medicare, Medicaid, and commercial quality of care measures: Considerations for assessing accountable care organizations. *Journal of Health Politics, Policy, and Law, 40*(4), 761–796.

Mullan, F. (2001). A founder of quality assessment encounters a troubled system firsthand [Interview]. *Health Affairs, 20,* 1137–1141.

National Committee for Quality Assurance. (2016). Working with states. Retrieved from http://www.ncqa.org/PublicPolicy/WorkingwithStates.aspx

National Health Policy Forum. (2014). Consumer Assessment of Healthcare Providers and Systems (CAHPS) surveys: Assessing patient experience. Retrieved from https://www.nhpf.org/uploads/announcements/Basics_CAHPS_12-18 -14.pdf

National Quality Measures Clearinghouse. (2016). Measure summary. Rockville MD: Agency for Healthcare Research and Quality. Retrieved from https:// www.qualitymeasures.ahrq.gov/content.aspx?id=49248

Patient Protection and Affordable Care Act §§ 3001, 3007, 3008, 3021, 3022, and 3025 (2010).

Porter, M. E. (2010). What is value in health care? *The New England Journal of Medicine, 363,* 2477–2481.

Rajkumar, R., Conway, P. H., & Tavenner, M. (2014). CMS—engaging multiple payers in payment reform. *Journal of the American Medical Association, 311*(19), 1967–1968.

Rosenthal, M. B., Fernandopulle, R., Song, H. R., & Landon, B. (2004). Paying for quality: Providers' incentives for quality improvement. *Health Affairs, 23*(2), 127–141.

Schroeder, S. A. (2011). Personal reflections on the high cost of American medical care: Many causes but few politically sustainable solutions. *Archives of Internal Medicine, 171*(8), 722–727.

CHAPTER  8

LEGAL AND ETHICAL ISSUES IN PERSON-CENTERED CARE

RICHARD H. HUGHES IV

LEARNING OBJECTIVES

- Identify major laws affecting the U.S. health care system.
- Understand areas of law designed to protect patients.
- Explore ways in which health care managers can identify and address potential legal problems in health care.
- Understand how to enhance the person focus of care while adhering to legal requirements.

KEY TERMS

Common law

Duty of care

Emergency Medical Treatment and Labor Act (EMTALA)

Health Insurance Portability and Accountability Act (HIPAA)

Health maintenance organization (HMO)

Informed consent

Malpractice

Patient–provider relationship

Protected health information (PHI)

Regulations

Statutes

Vicarious liability

Although this book emphasizes the clinical aspects of person-focused health care, an understanding of the legal and ethical issues is an important part of the delivery of person-focused care. The reason legal issues are important is that at the heart of person-focused health care is the relationship between the provider and the patient. This relationship is of great concern in the eyes of the law. The role of

117

law is, of course, to protect people and their rights. With respect to providers and patients, this entails defining responsibilities that providers have to patients. Only by defining and effectively enforcing these responsibilities can the law ensure that patients have access to and receive effective, high-quality health services. The same is true for ensuring and upholding a patient's rights to make decisions concerning his or her health or to protect his or her privacy.

After a brief discussion of the types and sources of law affecting the provider–patient relationship, this chapter discusses the formation of a legal relationship between providers and patients and the attendant obligations. That is, when must a provider treat a patient, and what consequences result from failure to provide adequate treatment? We also touch on the obligations of facilities and third parties, such as hospitals and health plans, to the patient. Then, we discuss the necessity of a patient's informed consent in order to be treated. Finally, we discuss the legal privacy and confidentiality protections afforded patients with respect to their medical information.

Many different federal and state laws apply to the health care industry, making it one of the most regulated sectors of our economy. Our legal system consists of statutes—laws enacted by democratically elected legislatures, both in the states and by Congress at the federal level. Many of these laws are administered and enforced by federal and state executive branch agencies. These agencies create, or promulgate, detailed rules and regulations, or issue guidance to the public and regulated entities to implement and clarify statutes. Among the agencies with jurisdiction over health care issues are the U.S. Department of Health and Human Services (HHS), Centers for Medicare and Medicaid Services (CMS), and state health agencies. Laws and the manner in which they are enforced vary significantly between the states, adding an additional layer of complexity. Finally, our courts have the important task of interpreting our laws to ensure they are consistent with our constitution, state of federal statutes and regulations, and the body of law created by the courts themselves, in an English tradition known as common law.

Most of the legal concepts discussed in this chapter are derived from common law, or decisions by courts. Many of these concepts or rules have evolved over time to accommodate social change, legal precedent, and advancements in how our society views the patient–provider relationship. Like the practice of medicine itself, the law that governs it has grown and continues to be more complex and nuanced. Although we could not possibly capture every nuance or legal rule in this chapter, we present some of the most important legal concepts for providers and managers of health services in this chapter:

- Patient–provider relationship
- Medical standard of care for medical malpractice
- Liability of third-party entities
- Hospital responsibility to emergency patients under the Emergency Medical Treatment and Labor Act (EMTALA)
- Informed consent
- Patient privacy and confidentiality under HIPAA

This chapter is intended to equip a health care manager to spot these issues as they potentially arise and think critically. It is important to note that laws often vary across jurisdictions and the guidance of skilled counsel is always advisable.

- Common law—judicial decisions, by state or federal courts, which create legal precedents or binding rules
- Statute—legislatively created laws, whether at the state or federal level
- Regulations—rules created by government agencies to clarify or implement statutes, which have the same effect as law

THE PATIENT–PROVIDER RELATIONSHIP

The relationship between the patient and the provider is fundamentally important because it creates legal accountability of the provider to the patient. Therefore, the first question is usually whether a legal relationship exists between a particular patient and a provider. It might seem reasonable to assume that when a patient seeks care from a provider, the provider is obligated to treat the patient. However, this is not ordinarily the case. Perhaps surprising to you, as a general matter, no one has the duty to help an injured person in need. The same is generally true for physicians. As discussed later in the chapter, although a facility or provider has to treat patients in emergency situations, both patients and providers must ordinarily enter their relationship willingly.

We must first consider then how a relationship between the patient and the provider is created. Ordinarily, a court might look for a contract to see what the parties agreed to. But providers do not often enter into a written contract with their patients. Hence, the law recognizes that when a patient seeks care and a provider agrees to treat the patient, or simply initiates treatment, an implied contract is formed (*Childs v. Weis*, 1969). This is usually memorialized by the medical record created for the treatment and by the subsequent act of billing for services rendered.

Additionally, when a provider enters into an agreement with a third-party payer, he or she ordinarily is obligated to treat the patients covered by a health plan. Providers or facilities contracting with the federal Medicare and Medicaid programs are also obligated to accept patients covered by those programs. When an on-call physician agrees to abide by a hospital's medical staff bylaws, which may, and often do, require the physician to treat patients in an emergency, this too creates a legal relationship between the provider and the patients of the facility. This is important because it helps to define the provider's obligation to the third party and all patients to which the third party is responsible for covering or treating.

Once a patient–provider relationship is established, the provider has a duty to provide treatment until it is no longer necessary. The patient may terminate the relationship at any time. If the provider wishes to terminate the relationship, however, the patient must be given sufficient notice to secure continuing care (a substitute provider). Failure to provide sufficient notice constitutes abandonment of a patient (*Ricks v. Budge*, 1937).

MEDICAL STANDARD OF CARE AND MALPRACTICE

Once a relationship is established between the patient and the provider, it is incumbent on the provider to render care of a certain standard. This is what is known as a duty of care. Laypersons going about their ordinary lives owe a duty of care to everyone around them. We are all held to a reasonable person standard. For example, a reasonable person would not walk down the street wielding a shovel horizontally, because this is likely to cause injury to others. A person disregarding this risk and acting unreasonably violates his or her duty of care. Professionals, such as health care providers, are held to a higher standard of care than the ordinary person. Failure to act in accordance with this standard of care is a breach of the provider's duty to his or her patient. This violation of the provider's duty is known as "malpractice." For example, if a provider diagnoses a patient with a medical condition and then fails to treat the patient appropriately, that is according to the standard of care for that condition, that provider has committed malpractice.

> *Medical malpractice is a legal fault by a physician or surgeon. It arises from the failure of a physician to provide the quality of care required by law. When a physician undertakes to treat a patient, he takes on an obligation enforceable at law to use minimally sound medical judgment and render minimally competent care in the course of services he provides.* (Hall v. Hilbun, 1985)

By what method do we determine whether a physician has met his or her standard of care? In the early 20th century, a physician's standard of care was determined according to what was known as the "locality rule." This meant that the physician's standard of care was "that of the local community where the physician practiced" (Starr, 1982, p. 111).

A malpractice plaintiff was therefore required to prove how another local physician would have acted and show that the defendant physician's conduct departed from the expected conduct. This was problematic for plaintiffs alleging malpractice, because it was difficult to find a local physician willing to testify against another physician in the community, a necessary step to establishing the standard of care at a trial. Illustrating the adaptability of common law and the concurrent evolution of both law and medicine, over time, courts came to recognize the locality rule's collective detrimental impact on our health care system:

> *Rather than encouraging medical practitioners to elevate the quality of care and treatment of patients to that existing in other communities, the [locality rule] may serve to foster substandard care, by testing the conduct of medical professionals by the conduct of other medical professionals in the same community.* (Morrison v. MacNamara, 1979)

Judicial approaches to defining a standard of care have evolved in response to this problem. Some courts adopt a "same or similar community" standard, which permits comparison with what a physician would do in the same or a similar locality (*Morrison v. MacNamara*, 1979).

This assists in overcoming the local physician testimony conundrum, because it enables the plaintiff to look outside of the immediate community to prove the standard of care. Others apply a national standard of care, which significantly eases the burden on plaintiffs to prove how a physician should have acted. For example, when a physician or practitioner is certified through a national board, courts must necessarily apply a national standard of care. In these cases, courts look to the national standard established by the board that certified the provider.

Thus, the national standard of care approach amplifies the importance of health care providers staying abreast of advances within a particular category or specialty area of care.

Therefore, standard of care in modern health care is heavily impacted by best practices supported by scientific consensus. Therefore, providers are typically guided by adherence to clinical practice guidelines. Contrast this with the quality measures discussed in the chapter on quality and payment. Does failure to perform well on a particular quality measure constitute malpractice? Not necessarily. For instance, failing to adequately control a patient's blood pressure (BP) could be the result of many factors, including contributory patient behavior. On the other hand, discharging a patient too early or infecting a patient by mistake increases the risk of malpractice. Failure to treat represents an even greater risk. Hence, there is no bright line and courts have recognized that while patient injury due to physician failure may create liability, "[a] competent physician is not liable per se for a mere error of judgment, mistaken diagnosis or the occurrence of an undesirable result" (*Hall v. Hilbun*, 1985).

Consider then that a provider's legal duty perhaps stops short of providing optimal, person-focused care. In that same way, the legal duty does not make the provider the "insurer of the right result."

LIABILITY OF THIRD PARTIES TO THE PATIENT–PROVIDER RELATIONSHIP

Facilities or other health care entities (e.g., hospitals, health plans) can also be held liable for undesirable health outcomes or patient injury resulting from malpractice on the part of individual providers. For instance, when a practice group or hospital employs a physician, the employing entity might be held vicariously liable for the acts of the physician.

Generally, the entity must have the power to hire and fire the physician or set working conditions; for example, a hospital binds the physician to its bylaws and practice guidelines. However, even in the absence of an employment relationship or a facility's control over a provider, a plaintiff might also hold these entities liable under the doctrine of apparent agency. That is, if there is a sufficient impression for a reasonable patient to conclude that the physician was acting under a hospital's control, courts have ruled that the hospital might also be liable for the physician's malpractice (*Jackson v. Power*, 1987).

Like individual physicians, facilities or health care entities are also subject to malpractice risk. Like providers, hospitals and other facilities owe a duty to their patients. Under a theory of corporate liability, these entities are responsible for supervising, credentialing, and monitoring their employees. Failure to do so, or to do so adequately, may constitute negligence on the part of the facility (*Darling v. Charleston Hospital*, 1965; *Thompson v. Nason Hospital*, 1991). An entity's risk increases when a patient can demonstrate that it interfered, through policy or practices, with medical judgment. For example, when a hospital policy forces discharge when the discharge would be premature, the hospital can be found negligent (*Muse v. Charter Hospital of Winston-Salem, Inc.*, 1995). In more egregious cases, such as one deeply unfortunate case in which a hospital's nurses allowed a man to bleed to death, a hospital may be held liable under a theory of gross negligence (*New Biloxi Hospital, Inc. v. Frazier*, 1962).

In addition to health care delivery entities, third-party payers may also be held liable in certain circumstances. For example, a patient may seek care through a health maintenance organization (HMO) and the HMO holds itself out to a patient as a reliable source of health care. By design, the HMO model constrains a patient's choice of providers, and malpractice on the part of a provider in this context may give rise to liability on the part of the HMO, known as ostensible liability (*Petrovich v. Share Health Plan*, 1999).

Similarly, health insurance plans that offer networks of contracted providers owe a duty to patients. For example, a health plan that negligently credentials its network providers or fails to offer an adequate network may risk liability for injuries to patients under the doctrine of corporate negligence. Likewise, utilization management practices that can be construed to interfere with patient care create risks on the part of plans. In sum, third-party payer liability for malpractice turns largely on how tightly integrated the payer arrangement is, payer involvement or interference in medical decision making, or the degree to which a payer makes and fulfills assurances to an insured individual with regard to health services access.

HOSPITAL RESPONSIBILITY TO EMERGENCY PATIENTS

As discussed earlier, providers are generally not obliged to render services to patients in the absence of an established relationship between them. It might seem reasonable to assume that when a patient seeks care from a provider, the provider is obligated to treat the patient. However, this is not always the case. In general, citizens have no duty to help an injured person in need. The same can be true for physicians. Some states, however, have enacted "good Samaritan laws," which do create a legal duty to render assistance, or, in a physician's case, medical treatment.

However, emergency services are a significant departure from this principle. Hospitals with an emergency department (ED) have an affirmative duty, a legal obligation to treat patients regardless of their insurance, or ability to pay. In some jurisdictions, courts have imposed this duty under common law (*Wilmington General Hospital v. Manlove*, 1961). However, the lack of uniformity across states proved itself to be a problem. As a result, after tragic refusals to treat emergency patients and an epidemic known as "patient dumping," Congress enacted the EMTALA in 1986 (42 U.S.C. §§ 1395cc, 1395dd).

Legal analyses under EMTALA are legally complex and require an understanding of many carefully defined legal terms. Familiarity with these terms and their practical application is important to all providers and managers involved in the work of a hospital ED (see Table 8.1). Under EMTALA, Medicare-participating hospitals must screen and treat patients presenting to the hospital ED. This must occur without regard to the patient's ability to pay. Moreover, registration and other routine matters must not interfere with screening and treating the patient.

After appropriate screening, if a patient is determined to have an emergency condition, the hospital is obligated under EMTALA to render necessary treatment to stabilize the patient's condition. However, whether the duty to continue rendering treatment continues past stabilization is the subject of great legal dispute.

TABLE 8.1 – Key EMTALA Statute Definitions

The term *emergency medical condition* means a medical condition manifesting itself by acute symptoms of sufficient severity (including severe pain) such that the absence of immediate medical attention could reasonably be expected to result in—

(i) placing the health of the individual (or, with respect to a pregnant woman, the health of the woman or her unborn child) in serious jeopardy,
(ii) serious impairment to bodily functions, or
(iii) serious dysfunction of any bodily organ or part, or
(iv) with respect to a pregnant woman who is having contractions—
    (a) that there is inadequate time to effect a safe transfer to another hospital before delivery, or
    (b) that transfer may pose a threat to the health or safety of the woman or the unborn child.

The term *to stabilize* means, with respect to an emergency medical condition described [above], to provide such medical treatment of the condition as may be necessary to assure, within reasonable medical probability, that no material deterioration of the condition is likely to result from or occur during the transfer of the individual from a facility, or, with respect to an emergency medical condition described [above, where involving pregnancy], to deliver (including the placenta).

The term *stabilized* means, with respect to an emergency medical condition described [above], that no material deterioration of the condition is likely, within reasonable medical probability, to result from or occur during the transfer of the individual from a facility, or, with respect to an emergency medical condition described [above, where involving pregnancy], that the woman has delivered (including the placenta).

The term *transfer* means the movement (including the discharge) of an individual outside a hospital's facilities at the direction of any person employed by (or affiliated or associated, directly or indirectly, with) the hospital, but does not include such a movement of an individual who (A) has been declared dead, or (B) leaves the facility without the permission of any such person.

Source: Emergency Medical Treatment and Labor Act (EMTALA), codified at 42 U.S.C. § 1395dd.

CMS has consistently interpreted the EMTALA duty to cease upon a patient's admission for inpatient care (42 C.F.R. 489.24). In fact, CMS takes the position that once admitted, patient protections are limited to Medicare Conditions of Participation (CoPs), state laws, and professional considerations (see CMS, 2003). Despite CMS's position, federal courts are split as to whether the EMTALA duty continues beyond inpatient admission. The Fourth and Ninth Circuit Courts of Appeals agree with CMS (see *Bryan v. Rectors and Visitors of the University of Virginia*, 1996; *Bryant v. Adventist Health System/West*, 2002); the United States Courts of Appeals are intermediate courts, hearing appeals from the federal district courts. Courts of Appeal decisions are reviewable by the Supreme Court of the United States.

The Sixth Circuit Court of Appeals, however, came to the opposite conclusion, finding that inpatient services are a part of stabilization as protected under EMTALA (*Moses v. Providence Hospital and Medical Centers, Inc.*, 2009; cert. denied). In that rather extreme case, a psychiatric inpatient who was admitted and discharged after visiting the hospital's ED later killed his wife.

EMTALA also requires hospitals to maintain a list of on-call physicians and establish on-call procedures to ensure physicians come to the hospital within a timely manner to screen a patient or render stabilizing emergency care. Hospitals must have backup procedures in place in the event a physician or particular specialist is unavailable. EMTALA also imposes specific reporting, signage, and recordkeeping requirements to ensure that emergency patients understand their rights and that hospitals can be reviewed for their compliance with EMTALA.

THE DOCTRINE OF INFORMED CONSENT

A fundamental and jealously guarded right in American society is that to be in control of one's own person, "free from all restraint or interference of others unless by clear and unquestionable authority of law" (*Union Pacific Railway Co. v. Botsford*, 1891).

In other words, one has a right to be "let alone," to self-determine his or her actions. This right forms the basis of the common law doctrine of informed consent. Although the provider obligations to patients are of great importance, the doctrine of informed consent attracts greater relational consideration by the courts (Hall, 2015, pp. 233, 241). This is so because of the presumably superior medical knowledge and the reliance thereupon by the medically needy patient. Under the doctrine of informed consent, a person must consent to medical care before it is rendered. In fact, "[a] physician who treats a patient without consent commits a battery, even though the procedure is harmless or beneficial" (*Leach v. Shapiro*, 1984, citing *Lacey v. Laird*, 1956).

Consider the scenario wherein a patient undergoes surgery for the removal of his or her left kidney. He or she completes a series of preoperation forms, including a statement specifically consenting to the removal of the left kidney. What if the provider removes the right kidney by mistake? This constitutes malpractice because the provider was negligent in his or her failure to locate and remove the correct kidney. However, when the provider intentionally removes the wrong kidney, contrary to the patient's consent, what is the result? Traditionally, courts held this unauthorized "touching" to constitute the intentional tort of battery, as well as malpractice. But as with any area of law, there are important exceptions to these rules.

Under certain circumstances in which consent cannot be obtained, it may be implied. First, when a patient consents to a particular treatment and a provider determines additional procedures are necessary to perform the treatment, consent may be implied. Borrowing from the aforementioned example, if a provider needed to operate on a nearby organ to remove the left kidney, he or she may infer consent absent some material reason that would cause the patient to withhold consent. Second, under emergency circumstances when the patient's life is in danger and the provider can presume the patient would consent, the provider may infer the patient's consent.

In order to effectively obtain an informed consent, the provider must give the patient all relevant information to make an informed decision. This includes an explanation of the patient's condition and the nature of the treatment that is proposed. Additionally, the provider must give the patient the necessary information to weigh the benefits that can reasonably be expected from treatment alongside its material risks. When the provider fails to disclose risks that later materialize in an injury and the patient would have declined the treatment had he or she been informed, this constitutes lack of informed consent (*Nickell v. Gonzalez*, 1985).

Analyzing what information should have been given and what the patient should expect to receive is not necessarily a straightforward task. Historically, courts would ask what a reasonable physician would have disclosed under the circumstances. However, the modern judicial trend is toward asking what a reasonable patient would want to know. Some jurisdictions disregard the element of reasonableness and simply inquire as to what the patient in an instant case would want to know. One important exception to the doctrine of informed consent is the physician's privilege to withhold information for therapeutic reasons (*Canterbury v. Spence*, 1972). This privilege recognizes that "patients occasionally become so ill or emotionally distraught on disclosure as to foreclose a rational decision, or complicate or hinder the treatment, or perhaps even pose psychological damage to the patient" (*Canterbury v. Spence*, 1972). Accordingly, the therapeutic exception privilege is narrowly restricted to these instances, and is not appropriately exercised by the provider simply to overcome the patient's anticipated refusal of treatment.

A patient may generally confirm informed consent orally or in writing, although state statutes often require the completion of written consent forms. Hospital accreditors, state licensing agencies, and CMS impose additional requirements and guidelines for obtaining and documenting a written consent. HIV testing and abortion services commonly require special consent under state law. Obtaining a written consent is particularly advisable in high-risk treatment situations.

For minor children, parental consent is ordinarily required prior to treatment. However, there are exceptions in emergencies, when a child has been emancipated, or under specific state common laws or statutory exceptions. For example, some courts recognize a "mature minor" doctrine, whereas others permit minors to consent to an abortion without parental consent (see *Younts v. St. Francis Hospital & School of Nursing*, 1970; see also *Planned Parenthood of Central Mo. v. Danforth*, 1976).

Ultimately, the constitutionally protected interest of parents to make decisions in the best interest of their children may clash with the medical needs of the child. Enforcing medical judgment over parental wishes may invite legal dispute. Courts have rejected parental objections of a religious nature, and state neglect laws go so far as to criminalize some refusals (*Commonwealth of Pennsylvania v. Nixon*, 2000).

Despite historic uncertainty surrounding the rights of incompetent patients to make medical decisions, these individuals now have an established right to informed consent. However, when incompetency extends to incapacity, consent should be obtained from an appropriate third party. In the absence of a legal guardian or state statute specifying to the contrary, this may be the patient's next of kin. When the treatment of an incompetent patient is of a life-saving nature, states typically require one of three standards to be used to determine how a decision must be made. Under a subjective standard, a court would look to a patient's wishes, ordinarily indicated by an advance directive. Under a substituted-judgment standard, a proxy may substitute judgment based on a belief as to what the patient would want. Finally, when there is no way to ascertain a patient's wishes, the patient's best interest standard may be applied.

A particularly challenging scenario involves the patient who is unable to consent to care and her family wishes to make end-of-life decisions. The Supreme Court of the United States has held the right to refuse treatment is a protected liberty interest under the Fourteenth Amendment of the Constitution (*Cruzan v. Director, Missouri Department of Health*, 1990).

However, a state regulation that is rationally related to a legitimate state interest may override the right to refuse. The Supreme Court has recognized four such interests: (a) protection of third parties; (b) prevention of suicide; (c) preservation of medical ethics; and (d) preservation of human life (*Cruzan v. Director, Missouri Department of Health*, 1990).

In *Cruzan v. Director, Missouri Department of Health*, a family wished to remove a feeding tube from their comatose daughter. The state imposed, and the Court upheld, a requirement of proof that the patient would have refused the treatment. Suffice it to say, end-of-life decision making and life-sustaining treatment decisions will often present legal hurdles when informed consent is not readily ascertained. Without an advanced directive or living will, this is typically difficult to prove, emphasizing the importance of careful advanced planning for patients and their guardians. Providers too can play a significant role by counseling patients and their guardians as appropriate to their needs.

PATIENT PRIVACY AND CONFIDENTIALITY

Like informed consent, privacy is also a jealously guarded patient right. Privacy protection occurs under legislatively created law at the state and federal level and under common law. Traditional state medical licensure schemes are designed so that professional misconduct, including improper release of patient information, is punishable by license revocation or suspension, or by fine, though such schemes have been criticized for lack of meaningful enforcement. Additionally, patients litigate and courts remedy breaches of privacy in a manner similar to malpractice. A patient's so-called right of action, or right to sue for a breach of privacy, may arise out of the common law. For example, defamation, invasion of privacy, and breach of confidentiality are actions that have enabled patients to recover for improper release of their medical records. Although most of these are recognized common law, some states have created such rights of action by statute.

Though state privacy protections vary significantly, to successfully defend against a breach of privacy claim generally requires a provider to show that the release of patient information was done with patient consent. Therefore, consent remains just as important to the handling of patient information as it does to actual patient treatment. The legal practitioner would likely urge providers to obtain broad patient consent for the release of patient information for purposes beyond treatment to ensure that the providers are protected. For example, consent might include any range of provider business purposes for which disclosure might be necessary.

A unique challenge arises when a patient's medical history is the subject of litigation. Judicial disclosure generally requires full disclosure of all relevant information in the course of litigation, including patient medical information. However, states have created many exceptions or privileges from litigation-related disclosure in the interest of protecting the patient–provider relationship. Such protection ensures that patients and providers have open honest conversations to ensure health care meets the needs of the patients. For example, a patient who feared the repercussion of having his or her sexual history publicized could not very well receive timely and accurate testing and treatment for sexually transmitted diseases. Additionally, protecting patient privacy ideally fosters medical ethics. Although privacy protection may exist through state law privileges in state court cases, federal courts do not recognize such privileges between patients and providers. However, the Supreme Court has recognized a narrow privilege between patients and psychotherapists (*Jaffee v. Redmond*, 1996). Importantly though, federal regulations do provide confidentiality protection for patients who undergo alcohol and substance abuse treatment covered by federally funded programs (42 C.F.R. Part 2, Confidentiality of Alcohol and Drug Abuse Patient Records).

One significant departure from the principles of safeguarding patient information is that of the duty to warn. As discussed earlier, providers have a duty to their patients to provide care of a certain standard. Moreover, providers have a duty of confidentiality to their patients. However, our society recognizes an important exception in the interest of public safety. That is, when a provider adjudges a patient to pose a direct threat to a third party, that provider has a duty to warn the third party and must take steps to do so (*Tarasoff v. Regents of the University of California*, 1976). When a psychiatrist failed to warn an identifiable woman whom the psychiatrist knew the patient intended to kill, the psychiatrist violated the duty to warn (*Tarasoff v. Regents of the University of California*, 1976).

Although health professionals remain obligated under state professional licensing schemes to protect the confidentiality of patient information, and risk litigation for failure to do so, variation in standards ultimately led to federal action. In 1996, Congress enacted the Health Insurance Portability and Accountability Act (HIPAA), setting forth privacy rules and patient rights related to health information (HIPAA). According to HHS, "[a] major goal of the [HIPAA] Privacy Rule is to assure that individuals' health information is properly protected while allowing the flow of health information needed to provide and promote high quality healthcare and to protect the public's health and wellbeing."

If anything, HIPAA is designed to permeate a health care organization with a culture of privacy protection. Among its requirements for covered individuals and entities are the designation of a privacy officer and the organizational privacy training. More specific requirements relate to protected health information (PHI). Without patient consent, PHI cannot be released for purposes other than for treatment, payment, or operations. Table 8.2 outlines the elements of an HIPAA authorization form, as required by HHS regulation. Absent patient consent, full disclosure of PHI may be made for treatment purposes, such as internal disclosure or to another provider involved in the patient's care. For payment or operation purposes, only minimum necessary information may be disclosed without patient consent. The minimum necessary standard applies even between providers or staff within an institution. Therefore, limiting information sharing in institutional settings and training staff accordingly is crucial.

TABLE 8.2 – Required Elements of an HIPAA Authorization Form

Required Elements:

- Description of the information to be used or disclosed that identifies the information in a specific and meaningful fashion.
- Name or other specific identification of the person(s), or class of persons, authorized to make the requested use or disclosure.
- Name or other specific identification of the person(s), or class of persons, to whom the covered entity may make the requested use or disclosure.
- Description of each purpose of the requested use or disclosure.
- An expiration date or an expiration event that relates to the individual or the purpose of the use or disclosure.
- Signature of the individual and date. If the authorization is signed by a personal representative of the individual, a description of such representative's authority to act for the individual must also be provided.

Required Statements:

- The individual's right to revoke the authorization in writing.
- For provider-covered entities, the provider's inability to condition treatment (except in research-related treatment) on the obtainment of a release.
- The potential for information disclosed pursuant to the authorization to be subject to re-disclosure by the recipient and thus longer protected.

HIPAA, Health Insurance Portability and Accountability Act.
Source: 45 C.F.R. 164.508 - Uses and disclosures for which an authorization is required.

HIPAA also affords patients specific rights, including the ability to restrict how their information will be used and to inspect and copy their information. Patients also have a right to request and receive an accounting of how their information has been disclosed, except for treatment, payment, or operation purposes. Additionally, covered entities must provide patients with a notice upon the initial visit of their privacy practices, as well as any subsequent changes to said practices. Unlike the PHI authorization, providers need only provide a written copy and make a good-faith effort to obtain a written acknowledgment of the notice of privacy practices.

Because health care payment and delivery necessarily involve the transmittal of information to other entities, HIPAA goes further. These other entities, called business associates, must enter into written contracts with covered entities, binding them to handle PHI in a similar manner as covered entities.

Failure to comply with HIPAA carries substantial penalties. The HHS Office of Civil Rights (OCR) enforces the act through both civil and criminal actions and compliance oversight. Unintentional violations of the act carry a $100 per occurrence penalty, up to $25,000 per year for violations of the same type. When an entity discovers and corrects an unintentional failure to comply within 30 days, no penalties will be assessed. In addition to such penalties, OCR actively monitors and audits covered entities and business associates for noncompliance.

CONCLUSION

Health law is a vast and complex web of interrelated statutes, regulations, and binding case law at multiple levels of government. Here, we have focused thematically on those areas of greatest significance to the provider–patient relationship itself. Delivering health care in a manner that is both person focused and legally appropriate requires conscientiousness on the part of the provider. A keen awareness of where one risks failure to meet his or her duty to a patient and seeks the advice of skilled counsel is always advisable.

CASE STUDY

In 1986, Congress enacted the Emergency Medical Treatment & Labor Act (EMTALA) to ensure public access to emergency services regardless of their ability to pay. Section 1867 of the Social Security Act imposes specific obligations on Medicare-participating hospitals that offer emergency services to provide a medical screening examination (MSE) when a request is made for examination or treatment for an emergency medical condition (EMC), including active labor, regardless of an individual's ability to pay. Hospitals are then required to provide stabilizing treatment for patients with EMCs. If a hospital is unable to stabilize a patient within its capability, or if the patient requests, an appropriate transfer should be implemented. (CMS, n.d.)

EMTALA has several provisions that are applicable to situations where persons present themselves to an emergency department. One fundamental question pertaining to EMTALA is "did an appropriate screening take place when the patient was examined in the emergency department?" Special provisions exist for pregnant women in active labor.

(continued)

CASE STUDY (*continued*)

In a case titled *Nolen v. Boca Raton Community Hospital, Inc.* (2004), a woman presented herself to the emergency department pregnant with triplets. She was having symptoms that looked like the onset of labor. Her physician instructed her to go to the emergency department at the hospital. Nolen was experiencing cramping and discharge. The physician in the emergency department examined her and concluded that she was not in labor and sent her home. The next day Nolen was examined by her doctor and found to be in preterm labor. She was sent to the hospital. Her first baby was stillborn and the other two babies failed to survive.

Issues to Consider

1. What are the facts of the case?
2. What did the judge decide?
3. Which provisions of EMTALA applied to the facts of this case?
4. Change up the facts of the Nolen case to reflect procedures and processes where person-focused care is very pronounced. How does that change the legal result?

REFERENCES

Bryan v. Rectors and Visitors of the University of Virginia, 95 F.3d 349 (4th Cir. 1996).

Bryant v. Adventist Health System/West, 289 F.3d 1162 (9th Cir. 2002).

Canterbury v. Spence, 464 F.2d 772, 789 (D.C. Cir. 1972).

Centers for Medicare and Medicaid Services. (n.d.). Emergency Medical Treatment & Labor Act (EMTALA). Retrieved from http://www.cms.gov/Regula tions-and-Guidance/Legislation/EMTALA

Centers for Medicare and Medicaid Services. 2003 Final Rule, 68 Fed. Reg. 53245 (September 9, 2003).

Childs v. Weis, 440 S.W.2d 104 (T.X. Ct. Cv. App. 1969).

Commonwealth of Pennsylvania v. Nixon, 761 A.2d 1151 (Pa. 2000).

Cruzan v. Director, Missouri Department of Health, 497 U.S. 261 (1990).

Darling v. Charleston Hospital, 211 N.E.2d 253 (Ill. 1965).

Emergency Medical Treatment and Labor Act (EMTALA), 42 U.S.C. § 1395dd.

45 C.F.R. 164.508.

42 C.F.R. 489.24.

42 C.F.R. Part 2, Confidentiality of Alcohol and Drug Abuse Patient Records.

42 U.S.C. §§ 1395cc, 1395dd.

Hall, M. A. (2015). Toward relationship-centered health law. *Wake Forest Law Review, 50*(2), 233–250.

Hall v. Hilbun, 466 So.2d 856, 866 (Miss. 1985).

Health Insurance Portability and Accountability Act (HIPAA) of 1996, Public Law 104-191.

Jackson v. Power, 743 P.2d 1376 (Alaska 1987).

Jaffee v. Redmond, 518 U.S. 1 (1996).

Lacey v. Laird, 166 Ohio St. 12 (Ohio 1956).

Leach v. Shapiro, 13 Ohio App. 3d 393 (Ohio Ct. App. 1984).

Morrison v. MacNamara, 407 A.2d 555 (D.C. Ct. App. 1979).

Moses v. Providence Hospital and Medical Centers, Inc., 561 F.3d 573 (6th Cir. 2009).

Muse v. Charter Hospital of Winston-Salem, Inc., 452 S.E.2d 589 (N.C. Ct. App. 1995).

New Biloxi Hospital, Inc. v. Frazier, 146 So.2d 882 (Miss. 1962).

Nickell v. Gonzalez, 17 Ohio St.3d 136, 139 (Ohio 1985).

Nolen v. Boca Raton Community Hospital, Inc., 373 F.3d 1151 (2004).

Petrovich v. Share Health Plan, 719 N.E.2d 756 (Ill. 1999).

Planned Parenthood of Central Mo. v. Danforth, 428 U.S. 52 (1976).

Ricks v. Budge, 64 P.2d 208, 211–212 (Utah 1937).

Starr, P. (1982). *The social transformation of American medicine.* New York, NY: Basic Books.

Tarasoff v. Regents of the University of California, 17 Cal. 3d 425, 131 Cal. Rptr. 14, 551 P2d 334 (1976).

Thompson v. Nason Hospital, 591 A.2d 703 (Pa. 1991).

Union Pacific Railway Co. v. Botsford, 141 U.S. 250 (1891).

Wilmington General Hospital v. Manlove, 54 Del. 15, 174 A 2d 135 (1961).

Younts v. St. Francis Hospital & School of Nursing, 469 P.2d 330 (Kan. 1970).

CHAPTER 9

REGULATORY COMPLIANCE AND POLICY

CHARLES R. WHIPPLE AND DENISE G. OSBORN-HARRISON

LEARNING OBJECTIVES

- Gain exposure to health care corporate compliance and select laws.
- Consider how regulatory compliance in a health care environment impacts the entire enterprise and can be leveraged to support person-focused care.
- Connect quality measures used by Centers for Medicare and Medicaid Services (CMS) to person-focused care and select regulations.
- Begin to understand the plethora of laws that pertain to health care and consider how to create a culture that enforces those laws while supporting person-focused care.

KEY TERMS

American College of Healthcare Executives (ACHE)

Anti-Kickback Statute

Enforcing agency

Health Insurance Portability and Accountability Act (HIPAA)

Informed consent

Legal regulations

Occupational Safety and Health Administration (OSHA)

Stark Law

Health care is the most highly regulated industry in the United States. A range of regulatory bodies across all levels of government, including federal, state, and local, conduct industry oversight. Since the passage of the Affordable Care Act (ACA), providers are experiencing increasing pressure to report and prove compliance with the law, and penalties are being assessed with increasing rigor by the government. The federal government reported that in fiscal year 2014 it collected

$2.3 billion in health care false claims judgments and settlements involving federal health care (Medicare, Medicaid, and TriCare), bringing the 5-year total to $14.5 billion in false claims recoveries.

The American College of Healthcare Executives (ACHE) surveyed hospital chief executive officers (CEOs) across multiple providers nationwide. Those CEOs unequivocally characterized government audits and other regulatory reviews as a number one priority. These audits are ongoing, require a huge investment of resources, and could result in impactful consequences, such as monetary penalties, criminal convictions, or both. Health care providers are routinely surveyed by agencies that focus on patient care, such as the CMS, The Joint Commission (TJC), state-specific boards of registration in medicine, and state departments of public health. Those same providers are also bound by regulations promulgated by agencies that are not per se chartered with improving patient care, such as the Occupational Safety and Health Administration (OSHA), which regulates employee safety, and local boards of public health, which address food service functions. All regulatory bodies, however, have the power to impose monetary penalties, corrective action plans, and other consequences upon a health care organization found to be noncompliant with the law. In health care, an entire industry has developed dedicated to assisting health care institutions to interpret laws and implement systems that ensure compliance.

Laws have evolved over time in response to unfortunate circumstances arising out of unethical practices, medical malpractice, fraud, and other harmful activities. It can be easily argued that every law associated with health care directly or indirectly affects the well-being of the patient. For this reason, a person-focused health care organization works to devise approaches to health care corporate compliance that reflect a genuine desire to go beyond patient-centered care into the realm of enhancing the patient experience where the well-being of the patient drives the design and implementation of every system and process within the enterprise.

PRIMARY OPERATIONAL AREAS COVERED

Depending on the size of a health care organization, the domain in which regulatory compliance is enforced lies with a corporate compliance officer or division of compliance. This domain is responsible for managing adherence to regulations set forth by governmental agencies, certifying organizations, and other entities with jurisdiction over regulatory compliance. Other domains within a health care organization tasked with ensuring regulatory compliance may also include the risk manager, patient safety officer, quality assurance officer, legal department, a peer review committee, and the board of directors. All of these domains work with a wide spectrum of operational systems within the provider organization, thereby affecting how managers manage people and processes across the enterprise. In a person-focused environment, leadership will actively socialize a corporate culture that strives to continually enhance every patient's experience. To that end, managers must be asked to connect how the *reason* for a regulation leads to enhancing the well-being of the patient.

One can argue that it is relatively easy to map the underlying objective of any regulation back to the patient's well-being. Four examples of important laws and how they protect the well-being of the patient are described in Table 9.1.

TABLE 9.1 – Types of Laws That Protect the Patient's Well-Being	
Regulation and Enforcing Agency	**How Patient's Well-Being Is Served**
Regulations enforced by CMS, state, and local authorities focused on the patient's physical safety require health care organizations to construct and maintain rooms that adhere to strict codes and standards.	Safe clean patient rooms and hospital areas reduce the risk of infection. Specialty behavioral areas are required to have "breakaway" pipes and safety glass to prevent compromised patients from hurting themselves.
To meet the objective of delivering high-quality health care, organizations must legally verify physician and other clinical staff qualifications both before and during employment.	Qualified medical practitioners assist patients. Preemployment screenings seek to ensure a competent workforce.
Information management must be done in compliance with complex HIPAA laws to protect individual identifiable health information.	Policies and procedures limit access to a patient's health information to only staff who "need to know" to assist the patient with care or insurance paperwork.
Billing for services provided must comply with rigorous coding laws to avoid inaccuracies that could place unnecessary burdens on patients.	Rules help ensure that the proper bills are generated and submitted for only the care that is provided.

CMS, Centers for Medicare and Medicaid Services; HIPAA, Health Insurance Portability and Accountability Act.

Domains that span across operational units within a health care organization must work in concert to ensure regulatory compliance. What then can health care managers working within those domains do to ensure regulatory compliance while improving the *patient's personal experience* and clinical quality of care?

HOW DOMAIN CONTRIBUTES TO LARGER SYSTEM-WIDE "INSTITUTIONALIZATION" OF CARE

Characteristics of a health care organization such as size, location, and culture often drive the nature of its internal policies, as well as their overall approach to achieving compliance with applicable regulations. The best policies and procedures adopted by a health care organization do not function independently of other domains within the organization. Rather, they constitute systems that are literally woven into several aspects of the organization's operations, touching multiple subprocesses and promoting behaviors that put the patient first. Such subprocesses promote the notion that regulatory compliance need not be seen as burdensome. Rather, understanding, promoting, and complying with those processes that support rules specifically designed to protect the patient should always feel right and be rewarded.

Due to the nature and complexities of regulatory compliance, it is easy to compartmentalize the activities associated with it, effectively separating it from the day-to-day operations. A person-focused organization will not fall to this approach; rather, it will work to demystify the process by integrating compliance efforts holistically across the enterprise. Operationalizing compliance laws with the well-being of the patient at the center of the cause requires a focused corporate culture.

In a healthy, nonpunitive culture of transparency, information is highly valued and feedback of any kind is viewed as "a gift." Some organizations have successfully created a culture of learning and sharing all types of information whereas others are still on the road to achieving the same. Nevertheless, even under the best circumstances culture change is difficult and requires strong, steady focused leadership. Change is best achieved from the top down, preferably by using techniques from organizational development research, which provides proven methods used to change perceptions and help people embrace change.

A high-performing health care organization, for example, builds a culture around its mission, vision, and values. It empowers its associates, encourages them to meet patient and customer needs, measures their performance, and rewards them for improvement.

Why would a health care organization need to address culture change to devise a holistic approach to regulatory compliance? There are many conceivable answers to this question. Each domain within an organization is chartered with keeping the organization compliant and therefore safe. The information being gathered and studied is often delicate in nature and could expose the organization to future liability. Confidentiality often plays a role in the processes as do laws pertaining to legal discovery of evidence. For example, risk managers address potential medical errors on the front lines assessing potential liability for the organization and clinicians involved. They must follow strict procedures both internal and external to the organization. Compliance officers are often the first to discover a deficiency or violation that could force the provider to voluntarily disclose a regulatory violation to the government or another entity providing oversight. So, how can these individual domains modify their processes, connect with other domains appropriately, protect the organization, and enhance the patient experience? What would that look like?

On a practical level, it surely makes sense for the internal domains within an organization tasked with enforcing regulatory compliance to embrace processes that simultaneously protect both the patient and the organization. In essence, processes are designed to align the patient's well-being with the well-being of the entire organization. It would not, however, be enough to simply design a process that appears to achieve those two objectives. The impact of those processes must be measured and studied. What becomes paramount is how the patient *personally experiences* the processes or the by-product of the processes during his or her time of medical treatment.

Making the connection between how a certain domain of management is related to the personal experience of care is a precursor to designing processes that address regulatory compliance *and* enhance the patient experience. Moreover, the processes created by managers must fully enable their staff to connect with patients in a meaningful way so that the patient experiences a positive difference.

HOW DOMAIN OF MANAGEMENT IS RELATED TO THE PERSONAL EXPERIENCE OF CARE

A significant set of federal regulations pertaining directly to patient care exist and are enforced by the federal government. One example is the conditions of participation (CoPs) for the CMS. This body of regulatory requirements has been established to protect the public interest and provide guidelines for how patients receive medical care. These rules set standards for types of medical services to which providers must be in compliance. Once a provider is deemed to be in compliance, he or she is certified to the CoPs and able to participate with and receive payment from Medicare and Medicaid.

The CMS is the largest payer of health care claims and holds providers accountable to standards promulgated by the federal government. Providers work very hard to establish robust policies and procedures to maintain their certification status for the CoP. As a result, during the journey of a patient through a patient care setting, the patient will encounter a process or policy that supports the CoP. Although the intent of these policies and procedures is to ensure safe patient care, it is possible that complying with them can be so time-consuming and complex that staff may put less time into patient care. The sheer volume of regulatory standards that need to be met by health care providers forces managers to commit a substantial amount of time teaching and monitoring their staff on how to collect and analyze relevant data. When staff are focused primarily on completing a lengthy "checklist" of activities to ensure compliance with internal processes, the connection between the staff and the patient can be lost, leaving the patient feeling like a number rather than a person. To avoid this phenomenon, managers within every domain should have a clearly defined role within an efficient process that includes overt behaviors that map back to enhancing the patient experience.

The case study in this chapter touches upon a TJC enforced rule (NPSG 01.01.01 [TJC, 2016]) that requires at least two patient identifiers when providing care, treatment, and services. Activities associated with this rule happen on an ongoing, daily basis and can therefore easily become rote. Managers need to train their staff how to use language effectively. There should be some sense of standardization across the organization in terms of both how and what staff communicates to patients. At the same time, staff should be trained to pay close attention to the patient's words and behaviors to ascertain how the patient is processing the information. The key to improving a patient's personal experience is picking up on cues that bring insight into what the patient is thinking and feeling—during a moment in time. Gaining insight into a patient's individuality is then followed by words and conduct that make the patient feel respected or heard. Asking questions and listening intently to the answers will usually provide a positive experience for both parties involved.

PRIMARY TASKS THAT MUST BE PERFORMED WITHIN DOMAINS OF MANAGEMENT

In order for an organization to be compliant with applicable regulations, it must understand which regulations apply to the health care institution and the requirements of each regulation. There are regulations that apply to the institution as a whole, whereas other specific rules and regulations apply only to individual departments.

For regulatory requirement issues that pertain to the organization as a whole, most organizations have established specific departments that oversee and coordinate compliance. The most common of these departments are a quality improvement department and a corporate compliance department. In many organizations, these two departments divide the responsibility for the applicable regulations into clinical and nonclinical subject matter. The quality improvement department oversees compliance with clinical regulations, whereas the corporate compliance department handles nonclinical areas, such as billing and coding compliance, health information release, and physician–hospital relationship laws, such as Stark Law or Anti-Kickback Statute. The clinical and nonclinical lanes of activities appear to run in parallel with very little overlap. A person-centered health care organization, however, should think about converging the two lanes into one when appropriate. The result could be processes that address both clinical and nonclinical compliance issues in a way that enhances quality of care and patient safety. This approach would bring together multidisciplinary teams of staff that could collectively author innovative approaches to enhancing the patient experience.

Every domain must plan, do, and act relative to the regulatory mandates that are within its realm of responsibility. The process in which most domains within organizations engage in to find the best way(s) to monitor compliance is relatively standard in nature. These planning activities provide a foundation for their day-to-day operations and could provide a venue for robust collaboration with other domains. Rather than having domains plan in silos, they should join forces with other domains to discover innovative ways to ensure compliance with a focus on bettering the patient experience.

ORGANIZATION OF KEY TASKS TO ACHIEVE THAT DOMAIN'S GOALS

Each department within an institution must know the regulations that apply to its area and establish a process to comply with those regulations. In doing so, an organization that is committed to optimizing the patient experience should routinely consider socializing concrete suggestions. The steps to set up this process include:

1. **Identify applicable regulations/rules:** To complete this first step in meeting regulatory compliance, a manager should look to the agencies that address their department's scope. As an example, a clinical laboratory would review the CMS Clinical Laboratory Improvement Amendments (CLIA), state laboratory licensing boards, as well as the Centers for Disease Control and Prevention (CDC). A tremendous resource for managers can be the professional society dedicated to their area of expertise. The professional societies often have summaries or checklists of regulations that must be adhered to. *Consideration:* One might include information from national associations and government-funded nonprofits that represent the public. What information do they offer from the patient perspective that can be leveraged?

2. **Review workflow to assess compliance with rules:** The second step in meeting regulatory compliance is to review the operations of the manager's department to assess compliance with the regulations. This process can take on several different forms ranging from direct observation of workflow to a review of a selection of charts (medical records) to determine if the necessary information or clinical protocol has been followed. *Consideration:* Managers may have their own audit tool or may work with the quality improvement or compliance department to assist with the assessment of current practice.

3. **Redesign workflow and data collection to comply with rules:** It is likely that the initial assessment of the department's workflow will yield areas where improvement or changes are needed in order to achieve regulatory compliance. The completion of this step is critical as the

identification of an issue and failure to correct it is not viewed favorably by investigators from agencies. *Consideration:* This process provides a myriad of opportunities to incorporate steps that foster an ongoing dialogue with the patient population.

4. **Audit process to ensure compliance with policies established:** Once necessary changes in departmental policies and workflow and training of staff in these changes have been done, it is necessary to establish a periodic review process to ensure continued regulatory compliance. A manager should work with his or her organization's quality improvement or compliance department to conduct audits of the department to assess if the department is continuing to follow the policies and procedures put in place. The schedule of these reviews or audit will vary depending on the size of a department and the potential risk associated with noncompliance. A practical consideration would be to have departmental reviews/audits vary across shifts/days/nights/weekends. This is because many health care departments operate on nights and weekends. *Consideration:* If an audit is conducted during regular business hours, such as Monday through Friday—how can a manager be certain that patients are getting the same level or quality of care at night or on the weekend? Audits should be constructed to make sure that off-shifts are reviewed.

5. **Set up monitoring process for rules changes:** The laws and regulations that cover health care are not static. It is necessary for managers or for their organization to have a process to keep up to date with changes in the laws and regulations. Many of the regulations that organizations need to maintain compliance with are issued through the administration law process of the federal or state government. This process requires that the notice of the proposed rule changes must be published for public review and comment before they can be implemented. This process allows for organizations to have time to review and prepare for changes if they are adopted and put into effect.

   An organization's compliance department can assist with helping managers keep up to date on regulatory changes that may impact an operational area. In addition, professional societies and provider groups such as state hospital associations are excellent resources to monitor to keep abreast of changes to regulations. If there is a change to a rule or regulation that a department must comply with, the manager would repeat steps 1 through 4. *Consideration:* How do changes impact the patient? Are these rules available to patients in an easy-to-understand format?

THE INTERCONNECTIONS BETWEEN THAT DOMAIN'S TASKS AND THE CENTRAL TASKS OF OTHER DOMAINS

The domain of regulatory compliance does not stand on its own within an organization. It is connected to and part of every area of an organization. Regulatory compliance is not the sole responsibility of an entity's compliance department. Compliance is everyone's responsibility—each manager, each employee. Everyone in an organization needs to be part of a culture that believes in doing the right thing or takes steps necessary to correct what is wrong. Many organizations formalize this concept that "compliance is everyone's job" by instituting codes of conduct or standards of behavior that all employees agree to uphold as a condition of their employment. It is these types of requirements that work in conjunction with an organization's compliance program. If it is part of an employee's job to report an event or try to correct an issue—the compliance program provides the method for him or her to do so. Whether that process is an anonymous reporting line or online reporting form, the compliance department provides the structure and a process for staff and managers to do the right thing.

STRENGTHS AND LIMITATIONS OF KEY INFORMATION TYPICALLY USED TO MEASURE DOMAIN PERFORMANCE

Measuring performance in the regulatory compliance domain can be challenging in certain instances; however, the data can clearly speak for itself in most instances and is collected on an ongoing basis pursuant to law. There are a number of methods that a manager and organization can use to measure their effectiveness in achieving regulatory compliance.

First, in the area of clinical quality, CMS and other third-party payers publish data on compliance with quality measures. This data is robust and permits organizations to benchmark themselves against both state and national averages on a consistent set of patient safety goals and other measures. The data is reliable and readily accessible to the public.

Second, surveying by monitoring/certifying entities could lead to ongoing violations that have gone undiscovered. Sometimes, these audits can be infrequent, which is why internal auditing is important to support continuous process improvement. There are several reputable entities that offer consulting services to assist health care organizations with conducting internal audits.

Third, assuming the health care organization embraces a culture of transparency, employees can voluntarily report violations. If the environment in a health care organization invites punishment on those who point out regulatory violations, this mechanism becomes thwarted. Punitive culture in health care does exist due to fear and unjust leadership practices. Transforming a punitive culture can be done and there are plenty of best practices being shared among providers in this regard.

Fourth, most health care organizations are mandated to report certain events such as unexpected clinical outcomes to TJC, or an unauthorized release of patient information in violation of the HIPAA law must be sent to the Office of Civil Rights (OCR) and/or a local state authority.

CONCLUSION

Why is this culture important? Every health care provider enters into agreements with payers to provide services to patients in return for compensation. These agreements outline the rules about how a provider is expected to carry out delivery of the services delineated in the agreement. If providers do not meet the requirements in their payer contracts—whether from the federal government or a private health insurance company—the provider may have to return the monies earned from the payer or face fines and penalties. In extreme circumstances, providers can be excluded from the payer's network, preventing the provider from caring for certain patients.

If each member of an organization believes that compliance is part of his or her job, then an organization can more easily integrate compliance into care delivery. Embracing regulatory compliance and the primary impetus behind the rules and policies—ensuring safe quality patient care—will help staff members understand the need to "do things the right way" and be able to convey this message to patients.

If regulatory compliance is viewed as a "have to" item, then the performance of the necessary steps to be compliant may become seen as arbitrary boxes to be checked off as complete and are not viewed as being necessary to protect patients. If this is the attitude of viewing regulatory compliance as a burden embraced by an organization, then it will be very difficult to explain why compliance is necessary to a patient as part of person-centered care delivery.

CASE STUDY

An elderly patient is on an inpatient stay with the need for an unexpected surgical procedure. The physician wants to have a discussion with the patient to explain why the procedure is needed. The physician wants to share data pertaining to the diagnosis, purpose of the proposed treatment/procedure, possible risks and benefits of the proposed treatment/procedure, possible alternatives to the proposed treatment/procedure, and the possible risks of not receiving the treatment/procedure. The unit nurse manager and the surgeon are working together to deliver this information to the patient who is not following the conversation well. The patient's family is present; however, they are indecisive about the procedure. The surgeon just wants to push forward and begin the procedure so she tells the nurse manager to obtain the signature of the patient and bypass the family.

Issues to Consider

1. What should the unit nurse manager do in this instance?

2. What sort of techniques can the nurse manager utilize to effectively communicate with the patient?

3. Who can assist the nurse manager to navigate through this situation effectively?

4. Can the nurse manager proceed without family involvement?

LEGAL RESOURCES

To find state case law and state codes, see www.findlaw.com/casecode/state.html

To find state and federal law cases, see www.findlaw.com/casecode/courts/fed.html

To find provisions in the U.S. code, see uscode.house.gov

To find the Code of Federal Regulations, see www.ecfr.gov/cgi-bin/ECFR?
page=browse

To find law review articles, see stu.findlaw.com/journals/law-review.html

To align with best practices and ensure the accuracy of any law, check for revi-
sions.

To find information on the Health Care Compliance Association, see www
.hcca-info.org

REFERENCES

Anti-Kickback Statute, 42 U.S.C. §1320a-7b(b).

Centers for Medicare and Medicaid Services, 42 C.F.R. 482.

Centers for Medicare and Medicaid Services Clinical Laboratory Improvement
Amendments, 42 C.F.R. 482.

Stark Law, 42 U.S.C. § 1395nn.

The Joint Commission. (2016). Standards FAQ details. Retrieved from https://
www.jointcommission.org/standards_information/jcfaqdetails.aspx?Standa
rdsFaqId=1178&ProgramId=46

CHAPTER 10

HEALTH CARE MANAGERS LEADING THE WAY TO HIGHER ADOPTION RATES OF INFORMATICS DESIGNED TO ENHANCE THE PATIENT EXPERIENCE ACROSS THE CONTINUUM OF CARE

KATHLEEN MARTINEZ

LEARNING OBJECTIVES

- Understand the role of informatics within accountable care organizations.
- Identify how informatics supports chronic disease management and why that is important.
- Learn about how certain federal agencies support activities supporting informatics.
- Identify ways in which health care managers can implement informatics initiatives.

KEY TERMS

Accountable care organizations (ACOs)

Evidence-based practice (EBP)

Health care informatics

Patient advisory councils

Patient portals and personal health records

Telehealth and telemedicine

As defined by the U.S. National Library of Medicine, health informatics is the interdisciplinary study of the design, development, adoption, and application of information technology (IT)–based innovations in health care services delivery, management, and planning. Informatics plays a huge role in providing quality, safe, patient-centered care mostly because it assists in acquiring the necessary information for clinicians and patients to make informed choices (Bates & Bitton, 2010). Informatics can equip providers and consumers to acquire, store, analyze, use, and leverage information that leads to better health outcomes. Some examples of informatics include electronic health records (EHRs), web portals, personal health records, telehealth, and telemedicine. These tools facilitate physician–patient communication to take place and are tools that are known to drive patient satisfaction. The patient experience can be significantly enhanced and optimized through the use of these informatics tools when the data is collected, tracked, and *acted upon*.

Adoption of certain informatics by health care organizations has been somewhat problematic due to high cost, policy barriers, and lack of interoperability across other platforms. Regardless, most health care organizations are cognizant of the promise of informatics and continue to pursue implementation of technology that directly supports patient-centered care. Health care managers are keenly aware of their responsibility to comply with laws and regulations; and supporting such technology is part of adhering to the quality of care provisions in the Affordable Care Act (ACA). Using informatics to capture important medical data also supports new delivery of care models described in the ACA, such as accountable care organizations (ACOs).

What is an ACO? A good place to learn more is www.cms.gov/Medicare/Medicare-Fee-for-Service-Payment/ACO/index.html?redirect=/ACO

What does the ACA say about ACOs? Find summaries of the provisions within the ACA, including those pertaining to ACOs, at www.whitehouse.gov/healthreform

---

In the ACO setting, data is studied very carefully to ensure that patient care is properly integrated to support a model of care that supports accountability. Informatics like a patient portal or telemedicine foster proper integration of key data points that support ongoing patient–clinician communication (Snyder et al., 2011). In that setting, informatics can provide patients with a feeling of being in control of monitoring their own health care. Patients will feel like they are partnering with their clinicians and that they have a shared strategy that will lead to the best health outcome possible. Such feelings experienced by patients are crucial to an optimal patient experience.

This chapter explores some of the challenges associated with adoption and proper usage of EHR, patient portals, and telemedicine, and how the health care manager can exhibit patient-centered leadership by leveraging these tools to create a better patient experience.

ELECTRONIC HEALTH RECORDS

The U.S. Government has sent a message to the health care industry about the importance of adopting EHRs. The Health Information Technology for Economic and Clinical Health (HITECH) Act of 2009 was put in place to encourage and support health care providers to increase utilization of the EHR.

Are you up to date on the most recent federal government funding activities pertaining to EHR? You can find out here: www.cms.gov/Regulations-and-Guidance/Legislation/EHRIncentivePrograms/index.html?redirect=/ehrincentiveprograms

Under HITECH, the U.S. Government allocated approximately $20 billion to develop health information infrastructures and for the acquisition, implementation, and adoption of health information technology (HIT; Kaplan & Harris-Salamone, 2009).

An important part of the government's message to industry is that the government will only fund efforts that advance EHRs in a meaningful way. To be meaningful, organizations must generate data proving that their EHR system made a significant impact on patient safety, minimized health discrepancies, improved communication, and decreased costs. Criteria defining meaningful use (MU) of EHR was based on goals from a variety of government agencies, affecting mostly populations of people who suffer from one or more chronic diseases.

How do EHRs assist with battling incidents of chronic diseases? The Agency for Healthcare Research and Quality (AHRQ) recommends using HIT for chronic disease management. Learn more at www.healthit.ahrq.gov/ahrq-funded-projects/emerging-lessons/health-it-improved-chronic-disease-management

Chronic disease management met through EHR implementation remains a thread throughout every government-supported EHR initiative. These programs collect data for health conditions, such as heart disease, stroke, cancer, diabetes, obesity, and arthritis (National Center for Chronic Disease Prevention and Health Promotion, 2016).

The damage that chronic disease is doing to our national health care budget and the people of the United States is a tragedy. Chronic diseases are responsible for 86% of our health care budget nationally (Gerteis et al., 2014; National Center for Chronic Disease Prevention and Health Promotion, 2016).

How many deaths in the United States each year are due to chronic disease? What percentage of our nation's health care costs are due to these diseases? Data are available from the CDC at www.cdc.gov/chronicdisease

People are dying prematurely due to preventable chronic diseases because they lack knowledge or access to evidence-based interventions. These statistics provide a platform to advocate for swift adoption of informatics tools, such as EHR.

From the beginning, the goal was for all EHRs to have the ability to share information and "talk" to other software products, including other EHR systems. As of early 2016, unfortunately, this has not been the case. There are many products on the market today that are not able to "talk" to other EHR systems. Some health care systems have highly customized EHRs, making it difficult to achieve interoperability between EHR and other important data collection mechanisms.

This type of customization can make it difficult to share data captured within the EHR, making it hard to establish benchmarks across similar settings or identify best practices. By renaming fields, or alternating the original product, it interferes with the ability to categorize findings and interventions, thus making it more difficult to collect the "big data" necessary to identify key components of care. Fortunately, new products are emerging that allow for health information exchange (HIE) and the interfacing of key information reflecting multiple encounters with the patient. Next generation EHR will need to include sophisticated interoperability design to allow full integration of the patient medical record.

> What are some of the more recent challenges facing implementation of EHRs according to the federal government? Read more here: www.cms.gov/regula tions-and-guidance/legislation/ehrincentiveprograms/downloads/faqs_oct _2012.pdf

In 2015, there was a tremendous shift in the health care landscape when the U.S. Department of Defense (DoD) and Veterans Administration (VA) decided to move away from their customized, homemade EHR and contract with an existing EHR commercial vendor (Healthcare IT News, 2015). The decision was made to ensure that the DoD EHR would be interoperable with systems in the private sector, ensuring that the 60% to 70% of care that occurs outside the DoD is communicated with government agencies. This type of care coordination is imperative to ensure smooth transitions of care from levels of care and between care providers. How much was the U.S. government willing to invest in integrative care delivery? The answer is approximately $4.33 billion (Kern, 2015). When the project is completed in 2022, it will coordinate care for 9.5 million military personnel across 1,000 Military Health System sites, including 55 hospitals, 350 clinics, ships, submarines, and other locations in the military theater of operations.

However, despite their promise, EHRs have not enjoyed rapid adoption in all settings. As of early 2016, only about 40% of U.S. hospitals have a comprehensive EHR system (Charles, Gabriel, & Searcy, 2015). This is partially because EHRs are seen as cumbersome or difficult to use. Medical staff working in acute care settings suggested that duplicative documentation was at times common, and that a significant amount of their work day was spent documenting data to implement EHR (Lavin, Harper, & Barr, 2015). Nurses spend about 75% of their day in nursing care and 35% of that time is spent on documentation activities (Hendrich, 2008). Over a period of 2 years, from 2010 to 2012, staff reported a decrease in overall satisfaction with the EHR and 34% of users were "very dissatisfied" with the ability of the EHR to decrease their workload. Approximately 32% of users were unable to return to preimplementation workloads. Less than half of the users were satisfied with the ease of use. Almost 40% of clinicians would not recommend their EHR to a colleague (American College of Physicians, 2013).

A 2013 time and motion study reviewed the documentation practices of physicians in an acute care setting. It found that the documentation practices were highly fragmented related to disruptions and interruptions (Lavin et al., 2015). Interruptions include phone calls, patient requests, and requests from other care providers. Even more frustrating is the fact that current EHRs often require transitioning between different modalities. These disruptions create the perfect storm where errors and omissions can occur.

The leader manager is in an ideal position to evaluate the care delivery setting and identify risky documentation behaviors as well as best practice opportunities. Health care leader managers must petition for a seat at the table with IT and clinical application specialists (CASs) so they can share their valuable observations and insights. Too often, managers abdicate their right to influence informatics because they do not understand the significance of their contributions. No one has a better understanding of the overall flow of the department and the impact on the patient experience than the manager. The manager is close enough to the point of care delivery to hear the frustrations and suggestions of the care providers. The leader manager can advocate for newer technologies that support synthesis rather than demanding complete composition of a note. Synthesis entails highlighting and capturing single words or phrases, then constructing new notes descriptive of the patient's current status. This decreases redundancy and ensures that the note is patient centered and relevant (Lavin et al., 2015).

The ever-increasing abundance of data requires that health care providers synthesize and make decisions using large amounts of complex information. Unfortunately, data quickly degrades; for example, critically ill patients have many clinical parameters that are being monitored frequently. Decisions need to be based on trends in the data and current information, which is essential to making informed decisions. Tremendous amounts of information are constantly being generated, such as monitored clinical parameters, diagnostic tests, and multidisciplinary assessments. When this large amount of information is combined with the numerous individuals—clinical and nonclinical—who come in contact with a patient during a treatment episode and data transmission, not all members of the health care team may be aware of all the information pertinent to each patient.

A steady but slow increase of interest has evolved over recent years; however, attitudes must change if we are to adequately address the poor health of Americans coupled with a broken health care industry. The overarching goal is to improve the health and health care of all people on a population level.

> What is population health, and how do we measure health outcomes? According to the CDC, outcomes can be measured; see data on this page: www.cdc .gov/nccdphp/dph

In order to meet that goal, we must actively gather and analyze medical data, learn from the information, and leverage it throughout the entire continuum of care in a way that enhances the patient experience. This is a challenging environment for managers. How do you engage and empower staff when a significant amount of their day is spent wrestling with an unwieldy companion? Health care managers are uniquely positioned to lead the way.

EHR TRACKING DATA THROUGH THE CONTINUUM OF CARE

EHR is an important clinical tool that is particularly helpful for tracking data associated with complex health conditions, such as cancer. The EHR tool can be used to assist with treatment, such as chemotherapy, where multiple handoffs may be involved throughout different phases of the treatment protocol (Friesen, White, &

Byers, 2008). Accurate patient records are necessary to ensure that safe, high-quality care is delivered across all delivery systems. A study of the records in one EHR system found that 84% of progress notes contained at least one documentation error, with an average of 7.8 documentation errors per patient (Bowman, 2013).

The use of "cut and paste" instead of EHR has led to faulty decision making and serious patient safety situations (Bowman, 2013). Leaders must educate their staff regarding safe documentation practices and the dangers of seemingly safe practices, such as "copy forward." They must also be willing to audit documentation, observe workflows, recognize pain points for staff and clinicians, and work with software developers and vendors to correct the root problems, rather than allow their staff to put themselves and their patients in risky situations. We know that patients who have access to key information and test results in their records are more engaged in their care (Schnipper et al., 2012). There is an increasing move to ensure all patient health information is transparent and available to patients and families. Nothing will erode the trust of our patient partners faster than the presence of erroneous information in patient records. Health care managers acting as transformational leaders impresses upon staff the importance of accuracy in all recordkeeping as it is instrumental in maintaining the sacred trust of our patients and families.

PATIENT PORTALS AND PERSONAL HEALTH RECORDS

A patient portal allows patients, families, and caregivers to access specific information from the EHR in a timely and convenient fashion. A patient portal allows patients to request appointments, ask their care providers specific information, request records, and enter information. Some portals offer a simple platform that simply reports test results, whereas others may respond to patient inquiries by providing hyperlinks that offer additional information. By reviewing patterns of use, we can improve and enhance current products so that they are more useful and appealing to patients (Jones, Weiner, Shah, & Stewart, 2015). A key barrier to use is that patients often have to sign up for the service in-person, during an in-person health encounter. Enrollment rates tend to be very low at this point of care, which has a direct impact on use between visits and limits the ability of the patient to interact with his or her health care provider. Based on requirements set out by the Centers for Medicare and Medicaid Services (CMS), providers can earn MU stage 2 federal incentives if they demonstrate that 5% of patients are using secure portals to view, download, and transmit their health information.

STAGE OF MEANINGFUL USE CRITERIA BY FIRST-YEAR HHS/CMS

- How can a provider participate in HER incentive programs? See www.cms.gov/Regulations-and-Guidance/Legislation/EHRIncentivePrograms/index.html?redirect=/ehrincentiveprograms
- The CMS blog on MU lives here: blog.cms.gov/2016/01/19/ehr-incentive-programs-where-we-go-next

CMS lowered the objective from 10% to 5% when it published its MU stage 2 final rule. Less than 720 hospitals of the 5,686 hospitals in the United States have met MU stage 2 requirements so far (CMS, 2014). Health care managers can lead the way in advocating for the necessity of patient portals and personal health records among staff and patients.

A health care manager can carefully evaluate the process and workflows of staff to identify barriers for enrollment. Taking the time to educate and inform staff about the importance of a patient portal and the potential impact on patient health and satisfaction can be critical. Helping them realize the importance of certain tasks over others will allow them to prioritize actions that have the biggest impact on patient care. Organizations that have successfully operationalized patient portals, including secure messaging and online appointment requests, are able to utilize less hours to accomplish the same volume of work (Goldzweig et al., 2013).

Using e-mail, texts, and secure messaging decreases time spent playing phone tag and unsuccessful attempts to connect with patients.

Current research has demonstrated that patients' interest and ability to use patient portals is strongly influenced by personal factors, such as age, ethnicity, education level, health literacy, health status, and role as a caregiver. Ultimately, adoption by patients and endorsement by providers will come when existing patient portal features align with patients' and providers' information needs and functionality (Irizarry, DeVito Dabbs, & Curran, 2015).

On the other hand, current research demonstrates the difficulty in aligning information management tools, such as the patient portal, with current provider workflow and care delivery priorities. A greater understanding of the essential adjustments in provider workflow, including potential changes in the roles and responsibilities of the care team overall, is necessary in order to translate findings into practice. Few studies have focused on exploring how patient portal use should unfold within the context of the patient–provider interaction, or how it might impact the overall organization and workflow of the health care team including potential liability concerns, reimbursement, and relationships with patients (Irizarry et al., 2015). Again, the health care manager sits at the intersection of provider workflow and patient experience. They are in a unique position to evaluate how patient information is integrated into care visits. Research is needed to design, implement, and evaluate new workflows that integrate patient-generated information into the care process. Health care managers can partner with researchers, recognizing that direct care areas provide ideal settings for patient-centered and patient-engaged research.

TELEHEALTH AND TELEMEDICINE

Telehealth and telemedicine are seen by some as somewhat of a "hot commodity" because they allow clinicians to interact with patients from an alternative setting. These tools are often used to facilitate triage situations. Many scheduled visits to a health care facility are a single focus of short duration, for example, a blood pressure (BP) check or weight check for a patient with congestive heart failure. Now, technology-enabled equipment allows the care provider to capture and interpret a BP reading or daily weight and incorporate it into the patient's record. A more thorough assessment allows the health care provider to create or edit the plan of care to accurately address current trends. If the patient's condition is stable, there is no reason to interrupt his or her schedule with a visit to the provider. This also frees up valuable time in the schedule for same day and urgent appointments.

Patient satisfaction is high when care can be delivered in the home rather than across town, or across the state.

Telemedicine is especially valuable in rural settings, or areas that are underserved by certain specialties. With telemedicine, a patient can be seen in his or her local office or clinic and technology-enabled communication devices allow the local provider to consult with a specialist in a distant location. This can be used for follow-up appointments, when the initial care was delivered at a distant medical center and the patient has returned home. This eliminates the cost and inconvenience of traveling to another city and permits high-quality care to be delivered in the patient's preferred location, thus improving the patient experience (Herendeen & Deshpande, 2014).

Apps and wearables are the new frontier in health care informatics. In 2015, the National Academies of Sciences, Engineering, and Medicine hosted a 1-day workshop with key leaders to explore health literate practices in HIT, including consumer-facing technology, that is, apps and wearables. Currently, there are over 40,000 health care-related apps (Alper, 2015). Many are static, providing information only, which is no different than a handout or brochure. However, new apps are emerging that integrate patient data with the app and transmit it to that patient's EHR. One large EHR vendor has an app that communicates with the patient's digital scale and a wireless BP cuff to record readings and transmit the information to the patient's iPhone app and then to the EHR. The appropriate member of the health care team is notified that there is a new entry in the patient record for review. For patients who manage chronic diseases, this decreases the number of required health care visits since the information is gathered while they are at home. Fewer visits equate to less interruptions in the family schedule, lower absenteeism from school or work, and a decreased burden on caregivers. The care coordinator can contact the patient by phone to discuss results and alter the plan of care if necessary (Health Data Management, 2014). This is a great example of enhancing the patient experience by delivering care in the setting that the patient prefers—home.

A potential drawback with using new apps and wearables is the time required to inform and educate patients on their use. There is significant variability in patients' health literacy and comfort level with health technology. Again, this is an area where health care managers have the opportunity to introduce innovative models of care to provide new services. Ochsner Health System, based in New Orleans, created an "O Bar" modeled after the Apple Genius Bar (HIT Consultant, 2014). It is staffed by trained members of the health care team and stocked with iPads. The iPads have hand-picked apps that can help patients achieve their health and fitness goals. It is a pressure-free setting where patients can try out the apps with support and direction from knowledgeable staff members. Once they are comfortable using the technology, they can download the app to their own device and turn on the HealthKit integration to submit data to their EHR. In a clinical setting, health care managers can manage staffing and budget restraints by identifying appropriately trained personnel to evaluate patient knowledge and comfort with technology. Using teams to deliver care allows all members to operate at the top of their scope. Among the most important roles of the health care manager are career development and coaching. Many organizations offer career development through mentoring, on-site classes, and tuition reimbursement. Informatics is an opportunity for staff who are not interested in traditional patient care roles, such as nursing or medicine, to have a meaningful role in the patient's journey. Creating opportunities for staff in nonlicensed roles to interact with patients in a meaningful way may increase employee satisfaction and engagement.

HEALTH CARE MANAGERS LEADING CHANGE

It is imperative that managers function as leaders in the health care organization. Clinicians have a place at the table when electronic systems are created, tested, and implemented. A well-designed EHR should support staff and clinicians by streamlining processes and workflows, standardize documentation, assist with clinical decision making at the point of care, and make data entry and retrieval easier and more accurate. These elements are promised by all EHR vendors, yet the reality is that it takes a lot of work and effort to transform an out-of-the-box system to a thoughtfully customized product that can meet the specific demands of each unit in a health care system. A wise leader will ensure that key staff are invited to the table to participate in implementation and usability testing. Even after implementation, there are ongoing adjustments and refinements to improve functionality and align with workflows. Staff must be encouraged to voice their opinions and concerns and have the opportunity to engage in work to find solutions that can work across all care delivery areas.

Too often, managers feel compelled to force staff to accept and adapt to systems and processes that do not meet the needs of the organization, staff, or patients. It takes a lot of courage to field honest concerns and empower staff to impact their work environment in a positive way. But that is what makes a great manager.

A leader within the health care environment understands the needs of his or her specific patient population, and will be the champion for the most appropriate technology to meet patient needs. Leaders also have the opportunity to ensure that staff have adequate training and experience to optimize technology through continuing education offerings, conference attendance, and webinars. Staff and clinicians who are engaged in lifelong learning have greater satisfaction and contribute to improved patient outcomes.

The reality is that we live in a world of limited resources and competing priorities. Every day the health care manager is asked to juggle pressing needs with financial accountability. A thoughtful assessment of patient, provider, and staff needs will help identify true priorities among the cacophony of competing agendas. Creating alliances with key partners and stakeholders will help ensure success in achieving identified goals.

Little can be accomplished in today's health care setting without IT personnel, performance improvement specialists, and project managers. Information gleaned from the EHR must be transformed into data and displayed on dashboards. Patient satisfaction data is collected, analyzed, interpreted, and distributed by department or area. Productivity, utilization, error rates, and quality data can all be quantified, measured, and compared. No matter how sophisticated the operating system in an area, there is information that can be gleaned and used to improve patient satisfaction and safety or improve processes.

Health care is moving so quickly that there often is not information in the published literature to support new practices. In these situations, using internal data creates the evidence needed to support evolving technology. In the following example, one organization carefully collected the information needed to support and fund a program to address an unmet need in their community.

VIGNETTE: CHILDREN'S HOSPITAL COLORADO

Leadership Decision Making That Has a Positive Impact on the Personal Experience of Care

Written by: Lindsey Shaw, MS, RN, CPNP | Clinical Practice Specialist | Network of Care Children's Hospital Colorado

Also represented: Amy J. Lewis, MS, RN, CPEN | Director, Patient Care Services | Network of Care, Sondra Valdez, MSN, RN, CPEN Manager South Campus Network of Care

One in five children are affected by mental health issues, including everything from attention deficit hyperactivity disorder (ADHD) to severe depression. Although the rates of these issues have continued to increase over the past few decades, the numbers of resources available to families to help their children continue to evaporate. In many communities, crisis providers such as the local emergency department are considered the primary behavioral health provider for these children (Masi & Cooper, 2006). Oftentimes, the lack of psychiatric specialists in these settings results in potentially unnecessary admissions or costly and potentially traumatic ambulance transfers. Numerous studies have indicated that barriers such as lack of access, maldistributed specialists, costs, and risks associated with travel can be addressed through telemedicine.

In 2015, Children's Hospital Colorado deployed telemedicine capacity to its Network of Care (NOC) satellite emergency department (ED) and urgent locations with the purpose of providing telepsychiatry consults from its main campus location. Experience from the prior year informed us that if one of these patients presented in a NOC acute care setting, he or she had a 93% chance of being transferred by ambulance to Children's Hospital's main campus emergency department. This, even though the likelihood of them being discharged upon arrival and triage was 50%. Data from 2013 indicated that behavioral health emergencies constituted an average of 4.9% of all ED visits, more than twice the national average. NOC aims of introducing telemedicine are as follows:

- Evaluate differences in quality of care (transfer versus discharge disposition from NOC location, patient satisfaction with telemedicine services, and provider satisfaction with telemedicine services) among children who received psychiatric consult in the NOC locations.

- Evaluate the difference between admission and transfer rates among children who received telemedicine psychiatric consults.

- Compare the economic efficiency of care provided to children receiving telemedicine consultations using economic evaluations, including cost effectiveness analysis.

The NOC South Campus was the first location to go live for utilizing telemedicine for patients presenting for a behavioral health chief complaint. NOC's primary data included 108 patients between January 2015 and August 2015. When a patient was triaged as being at risk using our Rapid Psych Assessment

(continued)

VIGNETTE: CHILDREN'S HOSPITAL COLORADO (*continued*)

in the electronic medical record, and once the patient was medically cleared, we called our emergency psychiatric attending that was located at our main psych ED. This process required that this patient would be prioritized to the psychiatric attending, due to the limited amount of resources at our NOC locations. Once the psychiatric attending was available, an e-mail was sent to the primary nurse of the patient at the South Campus, and the video software (HIPAA-compliant and encrypted) was utilized to connect the attending to our patient. This assessment usually took no more than 1 hour to complete, and included an interview of the patient, and possibly family members (if present). Figures 10.1 and 10.2 summarize data obtained in 2015.

The data in Table 10.1 includes all 228 patients seen throughout our NOC locations that utilized telemedicine for a behavioral complaint.

We also conducted a survey to determine the patient/family satisfaction of the process. The survey consisted of 10 questions, and was weighted as a total

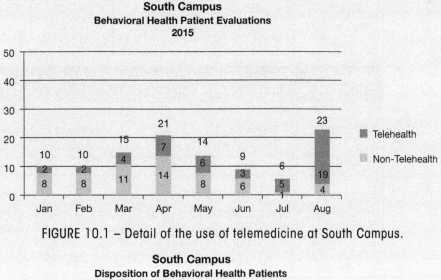

FIGURE 10.1 – Detail of the use of telemedicine at South Campus.

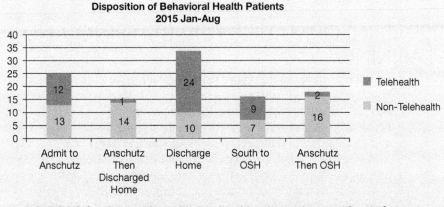

FIGURE 10.2 – Disposition of behavioral health patients at South Campus.
OSH, occupational safety and health.

(*continued*)

VIGNETTE: CHILDREN'S HOSPITAL COLORADO (*continued*)

score. As is evidenced in Table 10.2, 97% of the patients completing the survey had a positive experience with telemedicine being used in their care.

TABLE 10.1 – Demographics of Pediatric Psychiatric Patients Who Either Received Telemedicine Consultations in the Emergency Department or Were Transferred by Ambulance

	Overall	Telemedicine	Transfer	*p*-value
	n =	*n* =	*n* =	
Age in years, *M* (SD)	228	158	70	.42
Gender, *n* (%)				
Male	98 (42.7)	76 (48.1)	22 (31)	.015
Female	131 (57.2)	82 (51.9)	49 (69)	
Race, *n* (%)				
Caucasian	181 (79.7)	128 (81.5	53 (75.7)	.61
Non-Caucasian	34 (15.1)	21 (13.3)	13 (18.5)	
Unknown	12 (5.29)	8 (5.1)	4 (%)	

TABLE 10.2 – Overall Patient Satisfaction With the Use of Telemedicine for Psychiatric Consultation

Total Score	Frequency	%	Cumulative Frequency	Cumulative %
0–9	0	0	0	0
10–18	0	0	0	0
19–27	3	2.97	3	2.97
28–36	36	35.6	39	39
37–45	62	61.4	101	100

USING INFORMATICS FOR STAFFING AND PLANNING

Less is known about the ability to leverage informatics in staffing decisions. In most health care settings, salaries are by far the greatest expense. Predicting, planning, and ensuring adequate staffing for safe patient care is a primary responsibility of health care managers in all settings. Safe staffing levels increase staff satisfaction, and staff satisfaction impacts patient satisfaction (Rathert & May, 2007).

As we have stated, strong patient satisfaction promotes customer loyalty, which in turn encourages consistency of care, decreases duplicative services, and controls costs. Managers often oversee complex care delivery settings where physicians, nurses, various health care specialists, clinic staff, and business operations staff interact. Many patient care services are delivered in academic settings where time for teaching, professional growth, and research must be considered. This impacts the amount of time available for direct patient care.

A wise manager will investigate all possible data sources to build an informed staffing model. This may include pulling patient diagnosis data, trending seasonal variation in patient visits over the years, and anticipating the impact of new services and patient demands. It also involves communicating with staff to keep abreast of anticipated schedule changes and adjustments to determine anticipated time off. A staffing tool or dashboard will allow the manager to predict patient utilization patterns and plan accordingly.

EVIDENCE-BASED PRACTICE AND QUALITY IMPROVEMENT

Value-based purchasing (VBP) is part of the CMS's long-standing effort to link Medicare's payment system to a value-based system to improve health care quality. It is based on improved patient care outcomes and decreased safety events. In the initial Institute of Medicine (IOM)'s report *To Err Is Human*, we learned that a staggering number of patients were harmed within the very institutions and settings where they went to receive care and seek healing (Institute of Medicine, 2000). The IOM executive statement recommended that "the external environment should create a set of incentives that will clearly signal the need for change and serve as a spur for actions by health care delivery settings, including academic health centers" (IOM Committee on the Roles of Academic Health Centers in the 21st Century, 2004). This is the contextual basis of VBP.

To financially incentivize health care providers to deliver the safest, most expedient, patient-centered care, evidence-based practice (EBP) is the cornerstone of achieving this mission.

> *EBP is the integration of clinical expertise, patient values, and the best research evidence into the decision making process for patient care. Clinical expertise refers to the clinician's cumulated experience, education and clinical skills. The patient brings to the encounter his or her own personal preferences and unique concerns, expectations, and values. The best research evidence is usually found in clinically relevant research that has been conducted using sound methodology.* (Sackett, 2002)

EBP allows clinicians and managers to identify and replicate best practices leading to optimal patient outcomes. Quality improvement is the application of systematic and continuous actions to improve the processes of health care delivery to improve patient outcomes. The IOM defines quality in health care as a direct correlation between the level of improved health services and the desired health outcomes of individuals and populations. Quality improvement often uses rapid cycle strategies such as plan, do, study, act (PDSA) to implement and evaluate process changes and their impact on patient outcomes. PDSA cycles are data rich. Collecting and synthesizing this data is an important step and informs the health care manager of potential risks and opportunities for improvement within the care delivery system.

Organizations often use dashboards to collect and report quality improvement across the system. These dashboards are frequently displayed in patient care areas to inform and engage patients in the quality work of the health care organization. The patient experience is enhanced when patients are invited to speak up related to safety concerns and provide insights from their perspectives. Often, the patient is the only member involved in care experience that sees the entire continuum of care. The tragedy is that we so rarely engage them as equal members of the health care team. Transparency, in the form of shared metrics, opens the door for honest conversation and appreciative inquiry. This involves asking questions because we are interested in the answer, not just to complete a checklist.

The most revolutionary aspect of EBP is that patient preference is just as important as the other two measures: current research and provider experience and expertise. This is a significant paradigm shift in care delivery. For too many years, physicians and other care deliverers have been authoritative and prescriptive, always telling the patient what must be done, rather than explaining options and working as a team to create and implement care plans. The health care manager has the opportunity to serve as a patient advocate, ensuring that the patient experience is central in all discussions of care delivery.

SERVICES ADMINISTRATION: PATIENT ADVISORY COUNCILS LEVERAGING DATA THROUGH THE CONTINUUM OF CARE

Utilizing patient advisory councils or family advisory councils to help identify "pain points" or areas of frustration will help the leader manager to prioritize tasks and projects. Often, it is hard to see what is not working when you are within a broken system. But, it is easy for those on the outside to immediately spot areas of dysfunction. Patient advisory councils have the direct experience of illness and of navigating the health care system. Health care professionals often approach health care delivery from their own perspective, not the patients' or families'. Patients' feedback and suggestions are often insightful, straightforward, and easy to implement. Council responsibilities may include input into or involvement in:

- Program development, implementation, and evaluation
- Planning for major renovation or the design of a new building or services
- Staff selection and training
- Participation in staff orientation and in-service training programs
- Development and review of patient education materials
- Design of new materials or tools that support the doctor–patient relationship (Gerteis, 2014)

A "Getting Started" kit is available from the patient advisory councils at c.ymcdn .com/sites/www.theberylinstitute.org/resource/resmgr/webinar_pdf/pfac_tool kit_shared_version.pdf

Soliciting feedback from patients, and then acting on their feedback to improve the patient experience, are empowering. It builds relationships and heightens customer loyalty. This is reflected in increased patient satisfaction scores, and also staff satisfaction scores. Satisfied staff are often highly engaged staff. Highly engaged staff are the people who move your organization forward and make it a better place to work. Higher staff satisfaction scores are also associated with better patient outcomes and increased patient safety (Rathert & May, 2007). A key characteristic of an effective leader is that he or she listens to and values the feedback of all team members. A leader who collaborates with staff to set department priorities is more likely to navigate the waters of competing priorities successfully.

ENSURING A POSITIVE PATIENT EXPERIENCE FOR ALL PEOPLE IN THE PATIENT ROLE

The central truth of patient-centered care is that the patient is an equal partner in all health care decisions. It is important to note the recent shift away from terms such as *patient centered* to a more neutral *person centered*. *Patient* infers that a person is in a position of receiving care from another. Yet, as we move toward a platform of population health, health promotion, and disease prevention, the term *patient* may be too limiting. Are you a patient if you are engaging in health-promoting activities? The goal of high-quality health care is to empower the person to own his or her own behaviors, decisions, and outcomes. Informatics allows us to share information and decision making with patients, enabling them to ask questions and evaluate treatment options.

This hierarchy is important to remember: data, information, knowledge, and wisdom. In many areas of health care, we are still in the data phase. We have statistics, but have not organized it into meaningful components. In its raw stage, it does not inform our decision making or impact our choices. A wise leader will always look beyond the data and try to determine what it means. Much of the key information pulled from HIT is raw data. We look at indicators in isolation and so are not empowered to act upon them. Reports indicate that a clinic has a low number of on-time starts for appointments, but there is no understanding as to why that is or how to improve it. Patient satisfaction may dip in a certain month, but we do not know why. Data can be pulled from discrete fields, but discrete fields do not include narratives or subjective information. So although we have our dashboards, they are often only the first step.

CONCLUSION

The leader manager must look beyond numbers to understand driving forces and barriers to improvement. This is where strong communication skills and leadership abilities come in. It is important to take the time to observe your staff, ask them questions, identify obstacles, and ensure they have the tools and resources necessary to be successful. Focus on an area where you have some understanding of the structure, process, and outcomes and engage your staff to commit to improvements in that area. Celebrate small victories and acknowledge all efforts toward improvement. Reward sincerity and earnest effort. Honor the sacred trust of your patients through acts of kindness and compassion in every setting. Remember that you make the greatest impact on staff satisfaction and intent to stay with the organization. Be great.

CASE STUDY

"Re-Mission" is a video game for kids and young adults with cancer to help them take on the "fight of their lives" (Miller, 2013). The game gives patients a sense of power and control while encouraging treatment adherence. It uses "super powers," such as chemotherapy, antibiotics along with the body's own healing powers, and natural defenses to combat cancer within the human body. The game won a Parent's Choice Gold Award and a Common Sense Media Award. The game was created in collaboration with medical professionals, game developers, and young cancer patients. A nurse manager at Hospital Y wants to purchase and implement the gaming system for the pediatric cancer patients. The upper management does not support the idea, stating that it may be offensive to some parents of children suffering from cancers that are incurable. A survey was taken by the nurse manager of parents asking for their thoughts on the idea of using "Re-Mission." The nurse manager received a reprimand from human resources.

You are the nurse manager who received the reprimand from human resources. The chief medical officer (CMO) met with you and the human resources manager to explain why you were reprimanded. The crux of the problem was that you did not present data and/or best practices regarding how such a program should be implemented that demonstrates a sensitivity to the parents' psychological plight. The CMO is going to reconsider your idea to use the video game after you present some supplemental data and go through proper channels. She wants you to advise her on how to set up a patient family advisory committee to focus solely on this project.

Issues to Consider

1. Why was the risk manager reprimanded?
2. How will setting up an advisory committee help to address this issue?
3. Should the risk manager decline to continue to work on the project?
4. What best practices can be gleaned from other children's hospitals, such as St. Jude Hospital, relative to creating an effective strategy to engage an advisory committee?

REFERENCES

Alper, J. (Ed.). (2015). *Health literacy and consumer-facing technology: Workshop summary*. Washington, DC: National Academies Press.

American College of Physicians. (2013). Survey of clinicians: User satisfaction with electronic health records has decreased since 2010. Retrieved from https://www.acponline.org/newsroom/ehrs_survey.htm

Bates, D. W., & Bitton, A. (2010). The future of health information technology in the patient-centered medical home. *Health Affairs, 29*(4), 614–621. http://dx.doi.org/10.1377/hlthaff.2010.0007

Bowman, S. (2013). Impact of electronic health record systems on information integrity: Quality and safety implications. *Perspectives in Health Information Management, 10*(Fall), 1c.

Centers for Medicare and Medicaid Services. (2014). Meaningful use stage 2 overview tipsheet. Retrieved from https://www.cms.gov/regulations-and -guidance/legislation/ehrincentiveprograms/downloads/stage2overview_tip sheet.pdf

Charles, D., Gabriel, M., & Searcy, T. (2015, April). Adoption of electronic health record systems among U.S. non-federal acute care hospitals: 2008–2014 (ONC Data Brief, no. 23). Washington, DC: Office of the National Coordinator for Health Information Technology.

Friesen, M. A., White, S. V., & Byers, J. F. (2008). Handoffs: Implications for nurses. In R. G. Hughes (Ed.), *Patient safety and quality: An evidence-based handbook for nurses* (Chapter 34). Rockville, MD: Agency for Healthcare Research and Quality.

Gerteis, J., Izrael, D., Deitz, D., LeRoy, L., Ricciardi, R., Miller, T., & Basu, J. (2014). *Multiple chronic conditions chartbook.* Rockville, MD: Agency for Healthcare Research and Quality.

Goldzweig, C. L., Orshansky, G., Paige, N. M., Towfigh, A. A., Haggstrom, D. A., Miake-Lye, I., . . . Shekelle, P. G. (2013). Electronic patient portals: evidence on health outcomes, satisfaction, efficiency, and attitudes: a systematic review. *Annals of internal medicine, 159*(10), 677–687.

Healthcare IT News. (2015, August 5). Cerner rides high with DoD deal. Retrieved from http://www.healthcareitnews.com/news/cerner-rides-high-dod-deal

Health Data Management. (2014). Epic ties MyChart App to Apple HealthKit. Retrieved from http://www.healthdatamanagement.com/news/Epic-Ties-My Chart-App-to-Apple-HealthKit-48845-1.html

Hendrich, A., Chow, M., Skierczynski, B. A., & Lu, Z. (2008). A 36-hospital time and motion study: How do medical-surgical nurses spend their time? *The Permanente Journal, 12*(3), 25–34.

Herendeen, N., & Deshpande, P. (2014). Telemedicine and the patient-centered medical home. *Pediatric Annals, 43*(2), e28–e32. http://dx.doi.org/10.3928/0090 4481-20140127-07

HIT Consultant. (2014). Ochsner health's epic EHR integrates with Apple Health-Kit. Retrieved from http://hitconsultant.net/2014/10/06/ochsner-healths-epic -ehr-integrates-with-apple-healthkit

Institute of Medicine. (2000). *To err is human: Building a safer health system.* Washington, DC: National Academies Press.

Institute of Medicine Committee on the Roles of Academic Health Centers in the 21st Century. (2004). Executive summary. In L. T. Kohn (Ed.), *Academic health centers: Leading change in the 21st century.* Washington, DC: National Academies Press. Retrieved from http://www.ncbi.nlm.nih.gov/books/NBK221671

Irizarry, T., DeVito Dabbs, A., & Curran, C. R. (2015). Patient portals and patient engagement: A state of the science review. *Journal of Medical Internet Research, 17*(6), e148.

Jones, J. B., Weiner, J. P., Shah, N. R., & Stewart, W. F. (2015). The wired patient: Patterns of electronic patient portal use among patients with cardiac disease or diabetes. *Journal of Medical Internet Research, 17*(2), e42. http://dx.doi.org/10.2196/jmir.3157

Kaplan, B., & Harris-Salamone, K. D. (2009). Health IT success and failure: Recommendations from literature and an AMIA workshop. *Journal of the American Medical Informatics Association, 16*(3), 291–299.

Kern, C. (2015, August 12). Cerner, Leidos, Accenture win $4.33 billion DoD EHR contract. *Health IT Outcomes.* Retrieved from http://www.healthitoutcomes.com/doc/cerner-leidos-accenture-win-billion-dod-ehr-contract-0001

Lavin, M. A., Harper, E., & Barr, N. (2015). Health information technology, patient safety, and professional nursing care documentation in acute care settings. *Online Journal of Issues in Nursing, 20*(2), 6.

Masi, R., & Cooper, J. (2006). *Children's mental health: Facts for policymakers.* New York, NY: National Center for Children in Poverty, Columbia University Mailman School of Public Health.

Miller, T. (2013, May 6). Can video games fight cancer? Re-Mission 2 aims to give young patients a fun way to battle their serious diseases. *New York Daily News.*

National Center for Chronic Disease Prevention and Health Promotion. (2016). Chronic diseases: The leading causes of death and disability in the United States. Retrieved from http://www.cdc.gov/chronicdisease/overview

Rathert, C., & May, D. R. (2007). Health care work environments, employee satisfaction, and patient safety: Care provider perspectives. *Health Care Management Review, 32*(1), 2–11.

Sackett, D. (2002). *Evidence-based medicine: How to practise and teach EBM* (2nd ed.). London, UK: Churchill Livingstone.

Schnipper, J. L., Gandhi, T. K., Wald, J. S., Grant, R. W., Poon, E. G., Volk, L. A., . . . Middleton, B. (2012). Effects of an online personal health record on medication accuracy and safety: A cluster-randomized trial. *Journal of the American Medical Informatics Association, 19*(5), 728–734.

Snyder, C. F., Wu, A. W., Miller, R. S., Jensen, R. E., Bantug, E. T., & Wolff, A. C. (2011). The role of informatics in promoting patient-centered care. *Cancer Journal, 17*(4), 211–218. http://dx.doi.org/10.1097/PPO.0b013e318225ff89

ADDITIONAL RESOURCES

Conway, J., Johnson, B., Levitan, S., Schlucter, J., Ford, D., Sodomka, P., & Simmons, L. (2006). Partnering with patients and families to design a patient- and family-centered health care system: A roadmap for the future: A work in progress. Retrieved from http://www.ipfcc.org/pdf/Roadmap.pdf

Sackett, D., Rosenberg, W., Gray, J. M., Haynes, R. B., & Richardson, W. B. (1996). Evidence based medicine: What it is and what it isn't. *British Medical Journal, 312*(7023), 71–72. http://dx.doi.org/10.1136/bmj.312.7023.71

CHAPTER 11

CRITICAL FACETS OF A PERSON-FOCUSED SUPPLY CHAIN MANAGEMENT HOSPITAL SYSTEM: INCLUDING LESSONS LEARNED FROM THE UNIVERSITY OF MICHIGAN HEALTH SYSTEM, ANN ARBOR, MICHIGAN

ROLANDO R. CROOCKS AND KORI JONES

LEARNING OBJECTIVES

- Understand the scope of operation for supply chain management.
- Understand how supply chain management typically contributes to the larger, system-wide "institutionalization" of care.
- Provide examples of how supply chain management is related to the personal experience of care.

KEY TERMS

Affordable Care Act (ACA)

Environmentally preferred purchasing (EPP)

Group purchasing organizations (GPOs)

Laundry management

Patient-centric supply chain

Personal experience of care

Procurement management

Supply chain management

Every area of business provides opportunities for person-centered managerial decision making. Managing supply chains often requires approaches that emphasize the bottom line. That is, the patient's needs, desires, or opinions will often remain a nonissue. However, every aspect of operations can embrace protocols that enhance person-focused care. The University of Michigan has an extremely large laundry management department that has successfully met patient needs and desires while maintaining the bottom line. Its approach to supply chain management relative to laundry is highlighted in this chapter.

WHAT ARE THE PRIMARY OPERATIONAL AREAS COVERED BY SUPPLY CHAIN MANAGEMENT?

Supplies are the second largest cost after labor in the health care industry (Butvilofsky, 2014). The supply chain typically accounts for up to 40% of a hospital's budget (Lee, 2012).

The passage of the Affordable Care Act (ACA) has brought about many changes that impact the way in which hospitals do business. These changes support health care reform and the IHI Triple Aim, which calls for improvements in care, health, and cost within health care (Institute for Healthcare Improvement, 2016). Supply chain management is viewed by health care executives as an important mechanism to achieve those changes.

The well-known publication titled *Crossing the Quality Chasm: A New Health System for the 21st Century* by the Institute of Medicine (IOM) lists areas for improvement for the entire health care industry: providing care that is safe, timely, effective, efficient, equitable, and patient focused (IOM, 2001). Supply chain management can address those areas for improvement on a large scale in a way that benefits the patient experience.

Supply chain management encompasses many different areas within a hospital. Processing of purchase orders, requisitions, invoices, and other administrative paperwork are classic examples. Inventory management, recall management, leveraging group purchasing organizations (GPOs), and building business relationships with suppliers are important aspects of the supply chain. Ideally, these processes are centralized to optimize data collection and a global view of expenditures. When a hospital commits to an enterprise-wide culture that puts the patient experience first, supply chain management takes a different form.

The University of Michigan Health System (UMHS) through its Patient and Family Centered Care (PFCC) program has successfully supported supply chain management activities that are making a difference. The UMHS is the largest hospital in Michigan and a premier academic medical center made up of hospitals, health centers, clinics, family group practices, a medical school, a nursing school, and one of the largest biomedical communities (UMHS, 2016a).

Like other similarly situated provider systems, UMHS grapples with the day-to-day operations touching supply chain management and works hard to keep costs under control. Unique to UMHS is a top-down culture that embraces a structured program for patient- and family-centered health care. This program strives to achieve the ideal patient care experience by embracing the four PFCC principles at the point of care: respect and dignity, information sharing, participation, and collaboration (Patient and Family Centered Care, 2016). Inputs are derived from volunteer patient and family advisors who are placed in a variety of venues, including on-site patient/family advisory councils and hospital committees, E-Advisors, community boards, peer mentoring, PFCC theater activities, speaking bureaus, and task forces (Patient and Family Centered Care, 2016). Online surveys and structured, collaborative conversations with UMHS patients and family advisors serve to provide real-time data regarding services that directly affect the patient experience, such as facility design, room design, laundry services (including clothes, blankets, and linens), and other services offered by UMHS. This data is used to influence redesign processes and modify the patient's environment to improve his or her experience. Outcomes are captured and studied to ensure change is moving in the right direction.

This chapter highlights lessons learned, approaches to leadership, employee management, and successful outcomes from the UMHS health system's division of laundry management. This division is made up of 84 employees, spans across a 44,000 sq. ft warehouse, and is tasked with cleaning over thousands of pieces of clothing and linens per day. The number of employees necessary to run this operation and the monetary expenditures are significant due to the size of the health system. At the core of all processes adopted within this division and the leadership style exhibited by management is respect for the patient experience. The case study in this chapter is based on activities that currently take place within the UMHS division of laundry management.

HOW DOES SUPPLY CHAIN MANAGEMENT TYPICALLY CONTRIBUTE TO THE LARGER, SYSTEM-WIDE "INSTITUTIONALIZATION" OF CARE?

All facets of hospital operations, including supply change management, have had to make significant changes to support health care reform. The role of the supply chain and its impact to the patient experience is not lost on health care executives and managers. Most executives understand the importance of creating a patient-centric approach to every aspect of the supply chain. However, making the switch from operational techniques based purely on improving the bottom line to a patient-focused model is not easy.

Managers across the hospital enterprise use tools to track costs and waste associated with product purchases. Trends in labor costs are studied. Ways to achieve savings and increase value for the dollar are constantly being explored. Simplification of processes is ongoing.

Hospitals committed to putting the patient experience first for every line of business, including the supply chain, will at times make decisions that may not always be 100% cost-effective. This is because the patient experience becomes the driver that will influence the decision-making process for every aspect of the supply chain. It is important to note that achieving a balance between quality and cost is the goal. The goal is not to completely ignore the importance of cutting costs.

Health care executives have shared how noticeable outcomes from linking supply chain to the patient experience have improved quality and consistency of products/services and improved relations with clinical staff (Patient and Family Centered Care, 2016). For the fifth consecutive year, the University of Michigan Hospitals and Health Centers has been given the Greenhealth's Environmental Leadership Circle Award. This award is a most prestigious honor from a national membership organization of health care facilities committed to environmentally responsible operations (UMHS, 2016b).

Among several other activities that led to the Greenhealth Award is the way in which UMHS enters into environmentally preferred purchasing (EPP), which incorporates environmental sustainability practices into the supply chain processes (University of Michigan Health System, 2016b). The award is evidence of UMHS's commitment to reengineering the supply chain to reflect practices that are good for people. The act of purchasing products/services whose environmental impacts have been considered and found to be less damaging to the environment and human health can be the key to saving money and reducing waste while meeting the needs of patients (Practice GreenHealth, 2016). Another impressive showing by UMHS that demonstrates commitment to the patient experience lies within its PFCC program.

The PFCC program has provided critical data to the division of laundry services that have led to positive change. A success story worth noting evolved from information shared by the PFCC program that focused on patient dignity issues relative to hospital gowns. Data was gathered and a prototype was developed and piloted. This led to the idea of providing pajama bottoms made with linen designed to reduce the likelihood of pressure ulcers. These new pieces of clothing that could potentially combat a serious and common medical condition are currently being assessed.

HOW IS SUPPLY CHAIN MANAGEMENT RELATED TO THE PERSONAL EXPERIENCE OF CARE?

Supply chain processes that enhance the patient experience work to impact effective care delivery in the proper environment. They also avoid waste and lower administrative costs. The person-focused supply chain has the potential to overtly affect the patient continuum of care.

Processes supporting a supply chain that is influenced by the patient experience may exhibit the following practices:

- Join supply chain systems with technology to achieve specific objectives around quality, safety, and cost
- Create systems designed to positively impact how supplies are selected, moved, and delivered to the patient care setting
- Design systems that reflect data inputs derived directly from patients and their families
- Work to provide clinicians and patients with everything that is needed in a timely fashion and support safe quality clinical care
- Routinely conduct a value analysis including outcome measures and a process improvement methodology to show how the patient experience is enhanced
- Create employee incentive programs to support patient-focused approaches to supply chain management

These practices must all take under consideration the insight, preferences, wisdom, desires, suggestions, observations, and needs of the patient. Hence, direct contact with patients and/or data collection reflecting patient preferences is critical. But how do we capture and act upon patient preferences? Basically, direct patient contact matters to get real-time data that can be acted upon.

Equipping patients to directly influence the supply chain comes in different forms. The electronic health record is a tool that can be of assistance. Some would argue that patients will only be incentivized to influence the process if it is going to save them money. This attitude is more akin to the traditional way of managing the supply chain where cost savings are the main focus. Sometimes, a value stream identified from important data will not result in a cost savings per se. The choice to redesign or implement a new process that does not save money or clearly cost more money can be difficult to achieve.

The following section uses information gleaned from the UMHS using the division of laundry services as the referred to domain.

WHAT ARE THE PRIMARY TASKS THAT MUST BE PERFORMED WITHIN THE DOMAIN OF MANAGEMENT?

The laundry supply chain must ensure that the entire UMHS has a reliable supply of linens 24 hours/7 days. This division is chartered with supporting the tri-part institutional mission that emphasizes education, research, and clinical care. The division is responsible for linen specification, inventory procurement, inventory management, and processing, finishing, and transporting clean linen to all user areas in a reliable manner. Every step requires constant vigilance to cost. Laundry is not a revenue-generating cost center, yet must remain competitive with the local suppliers while providing outstanding service. Management must keep things moving, monitor quality, and ensure the timely delivery of laundry to over 300 distinct locations in the health care system.

HOW SHOULD THE ORGANIZATION OF KEY TASKS TO ACHIEVE THAT DOMAIN'S GOALS BE APPROACHED?

The laundry supply chain division at UMHS is a diverse environment when it comes to employees. The work is a repetitive process that poses certain challenges. A traditional hierarchical approach to management does not work very well in an environment where promotion is not likely and teamwork is necessary to get the job done. Leadership actively exhibits the need for respect of self and others. The importance of what they do is highlighted through large pictures throughout the facility displaying images of patients wearing their gowns and linens and holding a sign with a thank you message for laundry staff. Much of the laundry staff work off-site and never see the fruit of their labor in use. Linen is an essential part of a patient's care; these pictures were designed to bring the patient to the staff in a display of gratitude. These pictures were a result of a joint initiative with the PFCC program, patient and family advisors, and laundry services leadership. Language used by leadership is devised to keep morale high.

Staff accountability is part of the culture within the division of laundry. Inspections of finished goods are frequent. Good quality work is reinforced and poor quality is seen as an opportunity for training. Management must stay abreast of changes in the industry to help the operations reduce cost through efficiencies while providing value to the patients.

WHAT ARE THE INTERCONNECTIONS BETWEEN THAT DOMAIN'S TASKS AND THE CENTRAL TASKS OF OTHER DOMAINS?

Deliveries are prioritized by units based on information gleaned from hospital staff. Early delivery takes place to operating rooms, emergency, and labor/delivery units. Rehabilitation and/or early morning scheduled procedures have special needs that are addressed. Understanding the type of products needed by units within the hospital system is critical and changes with time. Constant dialogue is necessary to stay abreast of expectations expressed by physicians, nurses, volunteers, patients, families, and other sources.

WHAT ARE THE STRENGTHS AND LIMITATIONS OF KEY INFORMATION TYPICALLY USED TO MEASURE DOMAIN PERFORMANCE?

At the UMHS, the laundry division is fortunate to receive ongoing feedback, allowing for continuous process improvement. The existence of the PFCC program is a huge advantage as it actively partners with the division and reports our activities and successes to leadership. Daily huddles with staff are effective. Policies on how staff should interact with patients and clinical staff count.

CONCLUSION

A holistic approach to supply chain management that always puts the patient experience first is an evolution. Phases in support of culture change may be in order and should include determining readiness, raising awareness, educating staff and families, holding staff accountable, and measuring success. Basically, over time, "doing the right thing" by treating patients as individuals becomes the right way to do business and achieve clinical outcomes. The patient and family voice becomes an integral part of all core functions: education, research, governance, policies, quality, safety, patient–clinician interactions, and the like. Senior leadership set expectations and determine measurable ways to hold staff accountable. They also allocate funding and put "barrier busters" into place. Staff that comply and succeed are rewarded.

Lessons learned from the UMHS's PFCC program that provides data provided by patients to all operational units, including those that manage the supply chain, include:

- Understand top-down commitment is necessary
- Teach people how to be open
- Create policies for the majority
- Provide tools to staff to manage expectations
- Use your language wisely—nuances are impactful
- Realize moments of truth jobs are frequently entry-level positions

- Understand human resources needs to be part of the process
- Educate staff on how to support family involvement

Suggestions on how to stay connected with stakeholders to keep your efforts alive include the use of social media to recruit advisors and solicit feedback; create a website, portal, and/or mobile app; advertise events through webinars; build peer relationships through video clips; and provide private feedback.

CASE STUDY

You work for the corporate office that manages a chain of long-term care facilities that are located across the entire nation. Most of the facilities are in rural areas. A significant number of family members of patients have reported to the corporate office that the facilities seem to lack enough supplies. For example, the towels and sheets are not replaced daily, meals are staggered due to a lack of utensils, there is a shortage of gowns in certain sizes, there are an insufficient number of medical devices such as mobile oxygen tanks, and the like. The corporation and all of its facilities are accredited by The Joint Commission (TJC). Several of the nursing homes have been cited by TJC pertaining to the lack of supplies.

Some preliminary research was done showing that the corporation is paying top dollar for all supplies across the board. The corporation does not use a GPO, but is now interested in doing so because it wants to buy more supplies in bulk at a lower cost. Executive management asked you to research and inform them on how a GPO works.

Issue to Consider

1. How do GPOs achieve cost savings without compromising quality when it comes to purchasing supplies, including medical devices that will support a more patient-centered environment?

2. Can you propose ideas for training and implementation of a corporate-wide program that places the patient experience as the highest priority?

3. How can the corporation achieve top-down commitment to change culture to support a person-focused framework?

4. Does TJC include data focused on the patient experience in its accreditation process?

5. What is a high-reliability organization in health care and how can it use data reflecting person-focused care?

REFERENCES

Butvilofsky, R. (2014). Efficient supply chain management presents a range of benefits for healthcare institutions. Retrieved from http://www.beckershospitalreview .com/hospital-management-administration/efficient-supply-chain-management -presents-a-range-of-benefits-for-healthcare-institutions.html

Institute for Healthcare Improvement. (2016). IHI Triple Aim initiative. Retrieved from http://www.ihi.org/engage/initiatives/tripleaim/pages/default.aspx

Institute of Medicine. (2001). *Crossing the quality chasm: A new health system for the 21st century.* Washington, DC: National Academies Press.

Lee, J. (2012). Purchasing practices at hospitals and health systems continue to evolve, with the supply chain continuing to be a target for large non-labor cost savings. Retrieved from http://www.modernhealthcare.com/article/20120818/MAGAZINE/308189932

Patient and Family Centered Care. (2016). Nothing about me, without me. Retrieved from http://www.uofmhealth.org/patient-visitor-guide/patient-and-family-centered-care-pfcc

Practice GreenHealth. (2016). Environmentally preferable purchasing. Retrieved from https://practicegreenhealth.org/topics/epp

University of Michigan Health System. (2016a). About the system. Retrieved from http://www.uofmhealth.org/about

University of Michigan Health System. (2016b). U-M Hospitals and Health Centers receives top environmental award. Retrieved from http://www.uofmhealth.org/news/awards%20practice%20greenhealth

CHAPTER  12

PREVENTING MEDICAL ERRORS: USING THE SEVEN PILLARS APPROACH TO ADVANCE AUTHENTIC PATIENT-CENTERED CARE AND IMPROVE THE SAFETY OF CARE

MARTIN J. HATLIE, ROBERT MALIZZO, AND BARBARA MALIZZO

LEARNING OBJECTIVES

- Understand the statistics showing injuries and deaths due to medical errors.
- Describe best practices reflected in the Seven Pillars approach.
- Recommend process improvement changes based on the review of a case study.
- Devise a managerial approach to implementing a disclosure program.

KEY TERMS

Disclosure of medical errors program

Quality improvement processes

Seven Pillars approach

Medicine is not a perfect science. There is risk associated with almost every medical procedure that can lead to patient harm or, in certain instances, death. Patients provide consent for such risk prior to a medical procedure because the risk cannot be totally alleviated. Preventable medical errors are different from forseeable risk, because preventable errors were unanticipated and could have been avoided.

Thousands of people die or are injured every day in hospitals due to medical errors. The IOM's report *To Err Is Human: Building a Safer Health System* (IOM, 1999) estimated that as many as 98,000 deaths in the United States result each year from medical mistakes. A 2016 study by Johns Hopkins University researchers found that death caused by medical error is grossly underreported; they estimated the number to be 2.5 times higher than IOM estimates, making medical error the third highest cause of death in the United States (Makary & Daniel, 2016). On any given day, more than 1,000 preventable deaths and 10,000 preventable serious complications occur in U.S. hospitals. More than 90% of these deaths are a result of failed systems or procedures. Typically a protocol was worked around, test results were not routed effectively, or medications interacted unexpectedly, leading to a series of events that cause harm. This type of error is called a systems failure; it usually involves multiple contributing causes and is much more complex than straightforward physician negligence.

Guided by engineering principles, systems failures are analyzed to identify contributory factors that led to the patient harm and holes in risk management defenses that allowed it to occur. Once those causes and gaps in defenses are identified, processes can be improved so that future patients are reliably protected.

ROOT CAUSE ANALYSIS

The Joint Commission (TJC) has published a template to assist nurses in conducting valid root cause analysis for medical errors. It can be found at www .jointcommission.org/framework_for_conducting_a_root_cause_analysis _and_action_plan

---

Identification of root causes requires a robust exchange of information from multiple stakeholders, including risk managers, attorneys, patient safety officers, physicians, nurses, staff, the patient, and family members. This exchange depends on a culture trusted to be just. Stakeholders must trust that one contributing factor—often a human mistake—will not be cited as the main or only cause. If not, people will not openly and honestly communicate their thoughts and ideas and thereby undermine the integrity of the process.

See The Joint Commission on High Reliability Healthcare Organizations at www.jointcommission.org/assets/1/6/chassin_and_loeb_0913_final.pdf

---

Unfortunately, it is difficult and sometimes impossible for health care personnel to thoroughly analyze the root causes of a medical error because the threat of being sued thwarts transparent communication. The culture within the legal system is to sequester information until it is formally requested via a subpoena or other legal mechanism. Legal culture shapes health care culture. Thus, medical personnel are often discouraged from openly communicating facts and circumstances that contributed to a medical error, precluding the system of stakeholders from discovering the root causes of the event. Hence, without a thorough understanding of why the event occurred, clinicians are unable to avoid the same mistake from happening again.

National experts dedicated to decreasing medical errors have identified the need for greater transparency about the problem of medical errors nationwide. Those same experts have testified before the U.S. Congress, emphasizing the necessity for clinician–patient engagement to decrease the number of medical errors and advance a culture of trust, as well as the need for hospitals to embrace "high-reliability organization" concepts and strategies committed to a culture of safety that continuously learns from error. Such organizations are committed to modeling through leadership and supporting a "just culture" where persons are held accountable for intentional or reckless acts, but never blamed for good faith mistakes even when they contribute to patient harm. Reducing the rate of preventable injuries and deaths in a hospital setting can be done; however, it requires a well-defined systematic approach. The University of Illinois Hospital & Health Sciences System (UI Health) has created and implemented an approach called the Seven Pillars.

THE SEVEN PILLARS APPROACH

Report the event
Communicate with the patient and/or family
Care for the Caregiver
Investigate the event
Compensate the family
Educate the staff
Improve the process

UI Health applied for a demonstration project grant in 2010 from the Agency for Healthcare Research and Quality (AHRQ), whose mission is to improve the quality, safety, efficiency, and effectiveness of health care. UI Health received $3 million to prove that the Seven Pillars could be replicated in varied settings, including nonacademic institutions such as community hospitals with nonemployee physicians. Initially proposed for 3 years, the grant was extended to 4 years and ended in mid-2014.

Implementation of the Seven Pillars includes a bundle of core protocols. Errors must be reported immediately. Communication with the patient and/or family members starts promptly after the event is reported, and hospital staff are supported as they engage in these emotionally difficult conversations. An investigation quickly ensues that includes a root cause analysis type process that seeks to identify all contributing factors. When the investigation determines that a medical error occurred and caused harm, this is openly and honestly communicated to the patient and discussion is started about an appropriate remedy (e.g., compensation to the patient and his or her family as well as meaningful responses or actions that may be nonmonetary). An explanation of how the hospital will actively improve its protocols and train its staff to avoid the same mistake in the future is offered to the patient and his or her family. Clinical staff receive education focused on improving process and safety measures, and there is "care for the caregiver" emotional support and peer counseling offered to those staff involved in the harm event. Both errors and the positive impact due to the system changes are measured.

The Seven Pillars program has yielded good data to date. The data derived from these efforts includes best practices to be used by other providers who desire to implement a disclosure of medical errors program. The Seven Pillars approach drives home the importance of top-down support as described in high-reliability organization models. All of these protocols must be endorsed and visibly supported by the hospital's executive leadership, including legal counsel, as part of the organizational just culture. Health care leaders looking to adopt the Seven Pillars approach within their organization must be ready and committed, which is to say they must have leadership buy-in and support.

The Seven Pillars program is an innovation different from other disclosure or conflict resolution programs, because of the emphasis it places on an early offer of a remedy that usually includes monetary compensation. In doing so, it stands in stark contrast to the traditional "deny and defend" risk management approach, which impedes organizational learning from error. The Seven Pillars also has the potential to help physicians and other providers sustainably maintain patient and community trust by earning a reputation for "doing the right thing" when error occurs. By quickly offering fair compensation or other meaningful responses when a breach of the standard of care is determined to have occurred, legal claims are often avoided. Research strongly supports the fact that most lawsuits are filed because patients and family members believe physicians, nurses, or hospital leaders have kept information from them. Under the Seven Pillars program, early investigation and communication allow patients and families to get better and more accurate explanations—within days or week, rather than the years it takes a liability claim to be fully developed. For those cases requiring resolution, families are willing to accept reasonable compensation up front rather than waiting 5 years or longer after a lawsuit is filed to receive any award.

So how does the Seven Pillars approach impact the patient experience? The intent and design of the Seven Pillar approach naturally optimizes person-centered care. Proper execution of the approach aims to make the patient experience, including the experience of the family, the best that it can be under sorrowful circumstances. The typical alternative to the Seven Pillars program is either a system that fosters an incomplete disclosure of the medical error or a system that does not provide fair and early remedies. Both are suboptimal from the patient's perspective.

Discussion of the components of the Seven Pillars approach and the story of two hospitals that committed to implementation of the approach are discussed in this chapter. Case studies in this chapter coupled with questions to be answered provide ideas for practical application of the approach that can be emulated in any provider setting.

RESOURCES TO EXPLAIN KEY POINTS ABOUT THE IMPACT OF MEDICAL ERRORS

What is the issue? Preventable medical errors injure and kill thousands of people in U.S. hospitals on a daily basis. Hospitals need a system whereby errors are fully disclosed in a timely fashion, an apology is communicated, and changes are made to avoid a repeat of the same error in the future. Listen to true stories of people who died or been injured due to medical errors:

- Ted Talk on medical errors, Carol Gunn: www.youtube.com/watch?v=Lu-HcylvuU8

(continued)

> **RESOURCES TO EXPLAIN KEY POINTS ABOUT THE**
> **IMPACT OF MEDICAL ERRORS** (*continued*)
>
> - Transparency, compassion, and truth in medical errors: www
>   .youtube.com/watch?v=qmaY9DEzBzI
>
> - Medical errors and the Quaid twins: www.youtube.com/
>   watch?v=XEbf9bliOus
>
> Who are the main stakeholders? Patients, families, hospitals, physicians,
> nurses, hospital staff, providers, government, liability insurers, and attorneys.
>
> What can be done to address the issue? The current tort system jeopardizes
> patient safety, offers an intimidating liability environment, and often has no
> assurance of legal protection for hospitals and/or physicians in the event of
> disclosure. For these reasons, some providers shy away from disclosing. To
> reduce rates of preventable injuries and promote open communication, medical
> errors must be disclosed in a timely and appropriate fashion. A well-constructed
> program committed to open and honest communication is necessary to pro-
> vide a foundation for this process. The Seven Pillars demonstration project
> funded by AHRQ and piloted at the UI Health provides best practices.
>
> - The Seven Pillars: Summary of the comprehensive approach:
>   www.youtube.com/playlist?list=PLEBDdt7RnWsPoW2rBiOm2EAp
>   MtpIQM9F_
>
> - The Seven Pillars: Leadership, structure, and courage: www.you
>   tube.com/playlist?list=PLEBDdt7RnWsPoW2rBiOm2EApMtpIQM9F_
>
> - The Seven Pillars: Culture transformation: www.youtube.com/playli
>   st?list=PLEBDdt7RnWsPoW2rBiOm2EApMtpIQM9F_
>
> The AHRQ defines full disclosure of a medical error (www.psnet.ahrq.gov/
> primers/primer/2) as disclosure of all harmful errors, an explanation as to why
> the error occurred, how the error's effects will be minimized, and steps the
> physician (and organization) will take to prevent recurrences.
>
> The University of Michigan model—which includes full disclosure of adverse
> events, appropriate investigations, implementation of systems to avoid recur-
> rences, and rapid apology and financial compensation when care is deemed
> unreasonable—has resulted in fewer malpractice lawsuits and lower litigation
> costs since implementation. Both providers and practitioners have concerns
> regarding openness and transparency in health care delivery. A shift is needed
> from placing blame on health care organizations to developing systems for
> improving quality of our patient safety practices. The overarching goals are to
> (a) reduce rates of preventable patient injuries; (2) promote open communica-
> tion between providers and patients; (c) ensure patient's access to fair com-
> pensation for legitimate medical injuries; and (d) reduce liability insurance
> premiums for health care providers.

WHAT IS THE SEVEN PILLARS APPROACH?

The Seven Pillars approach offers a proven protocol to be followed in the event of
a medical error. Every component must be followed and performed in order. A
brief description of that process is set forth next followed by a case study, *Michelle's*

Story, about a woman who died of a preventable error and how UI Health used the Seven Pillars approach to reach resolution with the family and support physicians and nurses involved.

Pillar 1: Report the Event

The first pillar involves ensuring that events were reported. Events are reported online, through a 24/7 telephone hotline, and/or in person to the patient safety and risk management department.

Anyone can report an event to one of three risk managers; these individuals are assigned to specific units and clinical services, which helps them form relationships with the staff in each unit. Failure to report an event to patient safety and risk management, which results in a lawsuit, is taken very seriously.

Pillar 2: Communicate With the Patient and/or Family

Providing known information coupled with emotional support to patients and families is critical. An adage among the patient safety team at UI Health is that every hour that goes by after patient harm occurs, during which we are not effectively communicating, equates to another harm. Timothy McDonald, the thought leader whose team developed the Seven Pillars at UI Health, learned from patient advocates that "it's not about saying you're sorry, because that alone does not work." The teams at UI Health preserve the integrity of an apology. They apologize when—and only when—a harm event is caused by error, and then they acknowledge the mistake.

After talking to patient advocates, UI Health created a critical part of the program—a team of people known as the Patient Communication Consult Service—that reaches out to the patient, the family, and the care delivery team to help facilitate effective communication. The team supports clinicians involved to provide honest and ongoing communication in very rapid time. Supporting the patients and family members is akin to providing cardiopulmonary resuscitation (CPR)—it does not do any good if you start CPR an hour after the person needs it—you need to do it immediately.

UI Health has learned from other patients and family members the importance of staying in contact with families, because their feelings will change over time and their perception, questions, or concerns about the event may change over time, as well.

Pillar 3: Care for the Caregiver

In the aftermath of a harm event, many physicians and nurses feel isolated and fearful that their actions will be judged and misunderstood. They feel better when they can talk with someone who knows what they are going through. Recognizing the need for an immediate response for the caregiver, UI Health created a team to quickly contact the caregivers involved in a patient harm event and provide ongoing support. Their model is peer based: Doctors support doctors, nurses support nurses, and so on. The care for the caregiver program now has deep resonance in the organization.

For example, when a harm event occurs, the patient safety officer sets into motion the following events for clinicians involved:

- They identify the people involved.
- They inform persons involved of the availability of peer support, while providing informational pamphlets.
- They notify the Peer Support Program which pairs the persons involved in the event with a peer who has volunteered for this work and been assessed to be skilled in offering it. Oftentimes, staff feel strongly about becoming a peer supporter due to their own personal experience with medical errors.

Learn more about the Peer Support Program at the UI Health at www.youtube .com/watch?v=O0xh9cojKpQ

The peer clinician may send an e-mail or text introduction before initiating the first call or visit. Staff know that someone will call them; it is not a surprise. If a clinician is really distressed, this may impact his or her duties, as well as the clinician's personal health and well-being, so follow-up may include referral to the employee assistance program.

Pillar 4: Investigate the Event

When an event is reported, the office of patient safety goes into action immediately. Evidence is preserved. A timeline for the event that happened is created by talking to all individuals associated with the event. The patient safety officer meets with each person privately to allow the individual to describe the sequence of events from his or her perspective. In an expedited time frame, the team meets with the patient if possible or family members to bring them into the timeline and to hear their take on the event. Then all of the interviews and medical record reviews are compiled into a case summary of events. At this point, the risk management and clinical review team seeks a consensus on the events that transpired, as well as makes sense of the timeline. When the facts are as clear as can be determined, the team presents the case to the medical review board, which is charged with reviewing the event, performing a root cause analysis, endorsing suggested improvements, and offering recommendations.

Pillar 5: Compensate the Family

The team at UI Health has received permission from the board of trustees and the legal department to offer patients and families an appropriate remedy. Remedies could range from parking and childcare to waiving professional and hospital fees, for both past services rendered and for future care. Nonmonetary remedies, if important to the family, also are considered. In resolution discussions, patients and families are represented by their own counsel even when no claim has yet been filed.

WHAT ARE THE DUTIES OF A RISK MANAGER?

See the description published by the American Society for Healthcare Risk Management, available at www.ashrm.org/about/HRM_overview.dhtml

Pillar 6: Educate the Staff

In addition to one of the largest medical schools in the country, the UI Health has multiple other programs that train nurses and other health science students, along with hundreds of resident physicians. UI Health also offers a certificate and a master's program in patient safety leadership through its medical school for people from multiple disciplines who are interested in obtaining an advanced degree in patient safety.

Pillar 7: Improve the Process

UI Health engages in ongoing scrutiny of its many, complex hospital processes. Learning is continuous and focused on ensuring patient safety. Providers interested in gleaning learnings from the UI Health experience should contact the office of patient safety.

THE SEVEN PILLARS APPROACH AS IMPLEMENTED BY UI HEALTH: MICHELLE'S STORY

UI Health has applied the Seven Pillars approach to real-life situations of system failure that harm patients. *Michelle's Story* is a true story drawn from events that took place 2 years after UI Health implemented the Seven Pillars. Interviews of Michelle's parents and caregivers involved in her case can be viewed online by accessing the web addresses listed in the next section. It has also been reported in a 2011 *Chicago Tribune* news story that was syndicated nationwide. Michelle's parents speak frequently in public forums about UI Health's actions after their daughter was injured and died. Additional facts regarding Michelle's story are set forth next.

Background

A 39-year-old named Michelle Malizzo Ballog entered the hospital, accompanied by her parents, to undergo what should have been a short medical procedure. During a similar procedure some weeks before, Michelle woke up.

In preparation for the second procedure, she expressed concern about waking up again. She was assured that she would be given appropriate sedation.

The day of the second surgery, after a long wait, the medical team prepared her for what was estimated to be a 20-minute surgery. At that time, Michelle was told that the anesthesiologist was delayed. If she wanted an anesthesiologist, she would have to wait another 2 or 3 hours. She agreed to undergo surgery without an anesthesiologist.

Learn More About Michelle's Story

Family of woman who died after a medical error joins hospital's safety panel, *Chicago Tribune*, October 11, 2011 (articles.chicagotribune.com/2011-10-07/ health/ct-met-medical-errors-20111007_1_medical-errors-safety-panel-patient -advocates)

(continued)

> ### Learn More About Michelle's Story (*continued*)
>
> Michelle Malizzo Ballog Story: Overview: www.youtube.com/playlist?list=
> PLEBDdt7RnWsPoW2rBiOm2EApMtplQM9F_
>
> Michelle Malizzo Ballog Story: Engaging the Malizzo family to improve
> care: www.youtube.com/playlist?list=PLEBDdt7RnWsPoW2rBiOm2EAp
> MtplQM9F_
>
> Michelle Malizzo Ballog Story: Caring for the caregiver: www.youtube.com/
> playlist?list=PLEBDdt7RnWsPoW2rBiOm2EApMtplQM9F_
>
> Michelle Malizzo Ballog Story: Organ donation: www.youtube.com/playlist
> ?list=PLEBDdt7RnWsPoW2rBiOm2EApMtplQM9F_

Michelle's parents, Bob and Barb Malizzo, had been waiting for about an hour when they began to wonder why the doctor had not finished the surgery. The last time Michelle had a similar procedure it only took 30 minutes.

Shortly thereafter, the Malizzos were brought to their daughter and found her on life support. They still believed that their daughter would be fine and would leave the hospital soon thereafter. A hospital physician brought the Malizzos to a private room. He told them that he thought some mistakes had been made during the procedure. He explained that he did not yet have all the facts and that he would contact them within a couple of days.

Nurses and doctors who had been with Michelle when the incident occurred were interviewed immediately. The operating room where her surgery took place was secured to keep it from being cleaned, and to keep material in waste receptacles from being discarded.

Within a couple of days, Michelle's husband and her parents were told what had happened to their daughter. It was explained that the hospital staff had committed numerous errors and Michelle was in the intensive care unit (ICU) because of those mistakes. Michelle's parents explained that they expected the hospital to make excuses for what happened to their daughter. They were upset and angry but, as they explained, that was tempered because the truth was volunteered, they did not have to search for it, and their questions were answered. The Malizzos felt that knowing the truth helped with their healing process.

Michelle was an organ donor. In the conversations between the provider and the family prior to the withdrawal of life support, this was discussed. With the help of Timothy McDonald, MD, JD, UI Health's chief patient safety officer at the time of Michelle's tragic event and the driver of the Seven Pillars process, a dear friend of Mr. Malizzo, who was at the end of his dialysis with his body rejecting the procedure, became the self-directed recipient of Michelle's kidney.

The Malizzos wanted reassurance that the hospital would make changes to its protocols to avoid the same mistakes from reoccurring. Approximately 1 year after their daughter's death, the Malizzos were asked by a hospital representative to join the medical review board, an entity that reviews incidents stemming from medical errors that have occurred at UI Health, as part of the root cause analysis and continuous improvement processes. Appointment of patients or their family members to the medical review board was unprecedented.

In interviews, Mrs. Malizzo shared that her "anger was taking much of her energy." She knew that "Michelle wouldn't want that to be the case." By serving on the medical review board, Mrs. Malizzo believed that she was doing something that might help other families "so that they would never have to go through what she and her husband went through" regarding the death of their daughter.

"All hospitals should have patient advocates, because the medical community sometimes is too close," Mr. Malizzo has stated. "We bring a layman's perspective. We're not vindictive people; we are there to help, but you have to be willing to accept our help and some hospitals don't want to be transparent."

Dr. McDonald describes the role the Malizzos played as the "conscience of the community." Their opinions were valued; their participation on the medical review board and in educational activities across the university's many health professional training programs was inspiring and motivating.

The Malizzos have traveled to several hospitals and insurance companies nationwide to speak to the value of the Seven Pillars program, in addition to speaking at large national conferences convened by the Centers for Medicare and Medicaid Services (CMS), National Quality Forum (NQF), and others.

During one of those visits, a doctor shared her story of shame when a patient was harmed and she could not face the family. Mrs. Malizzo countered with her sympathetic understanding that "Caregivers grieve and need help, too."

Michelle's Legacy

On Thanksgiving Day, November 24, 2011, the *Chicago Tribune* published an editorial commenting on the legacy of Michelle Ballog (articles.chicagotribune .com/2011-11-24/opinion/ct-edit-families-20111124_1_declan-sullivan-michelle -malizzo-ballog-bob-malizzo). It read in part

> *This is a day for giving thanks. It is also a day when, as families gather, the pain of losing a loved one can be most acute. We thought it was a good day to reflect on the grace of [a family that has] suffered sudden losses, and from those losses ha[s] accomplished great things. Michelle Ballog . . . will be honored, not just by . . . families and friends, but by all those . . . hospital patients who will survive surgery because of enhanced safety procedures. Those are wonderful legacies.*

Change Impact

Several changes were made in the first hour after the event. From that time forward, all similar procedures would only be done with an anesthesiologist present. Working together with the Malizzo family, hospital leaders analyzed the contributing factors that led to Michelle's death, and practice standards were changed to improve capnography monitoring of patients like Michelle undergoing "routine" procedures. The hospital contacted the American Society of Anesthesiologists, and its policy was modified to ensure that all patients receiving sedative medications would have a device that monitors their breathing throughout the procedure.

One of the most remarkable changes made in Michelle Ballog's memory was establishing a new protocol for managing when conditions are perceived to be unsafe. The hospital acknowledged that it needed to teach nurses how to speak up when they are uncomfortable with something, such as administering additional medicine.

Dr. McDonald has shared this protocol in interviews. The protocol is to say, "Stop. Michelle told me to tell you to stop." According to McDonald, "Everyone within the organization knows what it means if a nurse holds up their hand and says that."

CASE STUDY: MICHELLE'S STORY

Watch the videos for *Michelle's Story* and read the written rendition provided earlier. Use information within this chapter, the videos, and the written case study to consider the two questions. Your answers may include information gleaned from this chapter coupled with your own questions or concerns. Your ideas may include questions characterized as "food for thought" that remain unanswered within the content of your response. Your ideas posed within your answers, however, may not solely be comprised of "food for thought" questions.

Issues to Consider

1. Give one example of how this case study illustrates how managerial decision making (how the Seven Pillars approach was implemented) positively impacted the disclosure of the medical error and offer of compensation to the patient's family. How did those decisions positively affect the personal experience of patient care? What other managerial options were available that would have enhanced the positive impact?

2. Give one example of how this case study illustrates managerial decisions (how the Seven Pillars approach was implemented) that negatively impacted the disclosure of the medical error and offer of compensation to the patient's family. How did those decisions negatively affect the personal experience of patient care? What other managerial options were available that would have mitigated the negative impact?

MacNEAL HOSPITAL IMPLEMENTS THE SEVEN PILLARS PROGRAM: LEONARD'S STORY

At MacNeal Hospital in Berwyn, Illinois, a western suburb of Chicago, chief medical officer Chuck Bareis, MD, had been tracking the Seven Pillars model implemented across town at UI Health for some time. MacNeal Hospital is a 427-bed community hospital with a medical staff consisting of employed, private practice, and contracted physicians, who are responsible for their own malpractice insurance. Dr. Bareis had an interest in disclosure of medical error in a way that could sustain relationships in the community that MacNeal Hospital serves.

Bareis felt that MacNeal Hospital leadership was ready for change because no one feels good when something bad happens and they are not able to talk about it. MacNeal Hospital's governing board and attorney were supportive of the effort. The chairman of the board, an attorney, cited her first impressions of the Seven Pillars program as a very good way to interact with patients and families early on and pursue resolutions that would impact the hospital positively. With strong support from the hospital board and physicians, the MacNeal Hospital team joined the AHRQ-supported Seven Pillars demonstration project.

Leonard's story, another true story of hospital response after a serious patient safety event, happened very shortly after MacNeal Hospital implemented the Seven Pillars program.

Background

Colorful balloons floated above Leonard's head as the staff in the transitional care unit at MacNeal Hospital fussed over one of their favorite patients celebrating his 86th birthday. Ready to be discharged in a couple of days, Leonard had spent 4 weeks in rehabilitation recovering from open-heart surgery.

"We all thought the world of him," says one of his nurses interviewed after his death. "He was such a nice person with a dynamite smile."

It was Christmas Eve, and a couple of days away from discharge, as Leonard got out of bed without waiting for assistance to arrive from the nurses' station. As he made his way to the bathroom, he stumbled and fell, hitting his head on the floor. The Seven Pillars rapid response was implemented and the risk management office was immediately alerted. The investigation started and care for the caregiver began.

Emergency surgery was needed to relieve the pressure caused by bleeds on Leonard's brain as a result of the fall. Leonard refused treatment, electing to die rather than undergo further medical procedures. Despite efforts to change his mind, Leonard was adamant about not wanting surgery.

A few hours later he passed away. The staff who had seen him through 4 weeks of rehabilitation were devastated.

Leonard's Legacy

Leonard's Story: www.youtube.com/playlist?list=PLEBDdt7RnWsPoW2rBiOm2EApMtplQM9F_

Leonard's closest relative, an older brother, met with the risk manager, Carol Hafeman. "It was quite sad," she recounts. "The staff was devastated. I was devastated." Leonard's brother "shared with us stories about him and his brother, who both served in World War II. Leonard had never married and he had no children, and his brother was concerned about a proper funeral."

Stepping away from the meeting, Hafeman consulted the hospital chief executive officer (CEO), who was made aware of this concern. The CEO immediately approved the release of $5,000 to assist the family in planning the proper funeral that they wanted to give Leonard.

Further discussion with Leonard's family, using the Seven Pillar process, resulted in a settlement reached by the parties 1 week after Leonard's death.

Change Impact

In the investigation portion of Seven Pillars, MacNeal discovered that the team members on duty at the time of Leonard's fall were at another end of the unit helping a patient in need. As a result of the learning from this incident, policies for staffing nurses at MacNeal have changed. There is always someone within earshot to hear an alarm and visually see what is happening in the rooms.

The Care for the Caregiver program was an important part of events following Leonard's death. A MacNeal nurse shared about a medical error involving harm to a baby she was involved in, prior to MacNeal Hospital adopting the Seven Pillars approach. A root cause analysis revealed that a baby was given a double dose of medicine inadvertently because the weight was in kilos, not pounds.

The nurse explained how difficult it was mainly because she had "no one to talk to about the incident." That same nurse has become an advocate for and has benefitted from the Seven Pillars program and the Care for the Caregiver aspect of the program at MacNeal Hospital.

Interviews with MacNeal Hospital personnel highlight some of the lessons learned from applying the Seven Pillars program:

1. **Manage an event right away:** As soon as a code event is identified, a number of people will likely be notified immediately. If an unexpected outcome occurs, a chain of command is followed. Depending on the event, this could include managers; operators; the 24/7 administrator; a senior lead, such as the chief nursing officer; physicians; the medical team; the chief medical officer and those in risk management.

2. **Communicate with the family within 30 minutes:** No longer is MacNeal Hospital reluctant to talk with the family; rather, it immediately embraces the transparency of speaking to the family about the event. A specific person is designated to speak with the family, which is, oftentimes, the director of patient safety and risk management who talks to the family about the ongoing investigation. If an interpreter is needed, a few are on staff; special "blue telephones" allow immediate access to an interpreter.

3. **Start taking care of caregivers:** Seven Pillars is one of the first programs to address the needs of the caregiver, sometimes referred to as the second victim of an event. The team that assists is comprised of clinicians including medical students and residents.

   Oftentimes after a medical error occurs, there is no institutional support for physicians or frontline staff, making it extraordinarily difficult for the caregivers involved. The Care for the Caregiver program from UI Health coupled with the Care for the Caregiver course at the Institute of Healthcare Improvement (IHI) was the model for the MacNeal Hospital program.

4. **Investigate the event:** Immediately after an error has occurred, the area and/or the equipment is sequestered. For example, a pump may be taken off line. The team gathers in the room and explores all aspects of the event, as well as interviews all participants as the timeline is created.

5. **Provide a commitment to offer compensation to the family:** The hospital's attorney, working with liability insurers, decides on the settlement offer.

6. **Educate the staff about the event:** Every code event includes an education segment for the staff. After a code event and a thorough investigation, there are always lessons to be learned. Managers are given the educational tools to provide feedback to their staff; and

findings are also shared at the daily morning huddle with hospital leadership. Training is continually done with staff at all levels of the organization regarding the importance of reporting.

7. **Measure and improve:** In an effort to prevent future events, the investigation under the Seven Pillars is more aggressive and timely.

CASE STUDY: LEONARD'S STORY

Watch the videos for *Leonard's Story* and read the written rendition provided earlier. Use information within this chapter, the videos, and the written case study to consider the two questions. Your answers may include information gleaned from this chapter coupled with your own original ideas. Your ideas may include questions characterized as "food for thought" that remain unanswered within the content of your response. Your ideas posed within your answers, however, may not solely be comprised of "food for thought" questions.

Issues to Consider

1. Give one example of how this case study illustrates how managerial decision making (how the Seven Pillars approach was implemented) positively impacted the disclosure of the medical error and offer of compensation to the patient's family. How did those decisions positively affect the personal experience of patient care? What other managerial options were available that would have enhanced the positive impact?

2. Give one example of how this case study illustrates managerial decisions (how the Seven Pillars approach was implemented) that negatively impacted the disclosure of the medical error and offer of compensation to the patient's family. How did those decisions negatively affect the personal experience of patient care? What other managerial options were available that would have mitigated the negative impact?

CONCLUSION

An important aspect of efforts demonstrated by UI Health and MacNeal Hospital is that they both had the undeniable support of hospital executive leadership from the board of directors downward. How can this type of support be secured? Based on lessons learned in the Seven Pillars demonstration project and other AHRQ-funded programs, a new toolkit has been developed that includes tools to use to assess readiness to adopt a Seven Pillars type program and procedures for doing a gap analysis between existing protocols and those that will support this kind of program. Entitled Communication and Optimal Resolution (CANDOR), the toolkit published in May 2016 is available at: www.ahrq.gov/professionals/quality-patient-safety/patient-safety-resources/resources/candor/introduction.html.

UI Health has reported significant savings in legal fees realized by negotiating compensation up front for patients who have been injured by medical errors. They also have experienced a decrease in their annual medical liability premiums.

REFERENCES

Institute of Medicine. (1999). *To err is human: Building a safer health system.* Washington, DC: National Academies Press.

Makary, M. A., & Daniel, M. (2016). Medical error—the third leading cause of death in the US. *British Medical Journal, 353,* i2139.

SECTION III

PATIENT (PERSON) MANAGEMENT

CHAPTER 13

WHY PERSON- AND FAMILY-CENTERED CARE?

JOANNE DISCH

Crossing the Quality Chasm, a publication by the Institute of Medicine (IOM, 2001), emphasized the importance of treating the patient as a real partner. Patient-centered care is seen by the IOM as an important foundational precept for safe, effective, and equitable health care.

Providing care that is respectful of and responsive to individual patient preferences, needs, and values and ensuring that patient values guide all clinical decisions. (IOM, 2001, p. 40)

With the implementation of health care reform both prior to the Affordable Care Act (ACA) and afterward, how health care is delivered has changed. The ways health care is provided to the consumer have become much broader with an emphasis on prevention of disease rather than simple medical treatment after it has occurred. Prevention requires ongoing and sustained patient engagement. Providers need to "engage the person to treat the patient" (Schenck & Churchill, 2012, p. 138).

This chapter touches upon the following:

• Why *person-* and family-centered care?

• Dimensions of person- and family-centered care

• System-level changes

• Leadership commitment

WHY *PERSON-* AND FAMILY-CENTERED CARE?

In 2001, the IOM offered a definition of patient-centered care: "Providing care that is respectful of and responsive to individual patient preferences, needs, and values and ensuring that patient values guide all clinical decisions."

Although many caregivers responded by saying, "This is what we've always done," a subsequent report by the IOM 10 years later (*The Future of Nursing: Leading Change, Advancing Health*) disagreed.

While affirming the need for patient-centered care to improve quality, access, and value, they observed that "practice still is usually organized around what is most convenient for the provider, the payer, or the health care organization and not the patient" (IOM, 2011, p. 51). Many would agree.

Achieving patient-centered care is important and challenging. Yet it has become increasingly clear that this concept is actually inadequate to describe what is needed in health care today. Barnsteiner, Disch, and Walton (2014) advocate for *person- and family-centered care.* In their text of that same name, along with multiple authors from nursing, medicine, law, ethics, business, and literature, they offer several reasons why we must move beyond focusing on the patient, to not only the patient and family, but also the *person* and family, as they define it.

These reasons include:

• Many individuals engaging in a care relationship are not patients in hospitals but are receiving care in ambulatory facilities, clinics, community centers, and their own homes. Children often receive health care in the school setting. Homeless individuals may receive some of their care on the street. Some individuals are residents in long-term care facilities rather than patients receiving care for a particular condition. Does the term *patient* adequately capture the full range of experiences here?

• Many individuals have a chronic illness that they live with on a daily basis. Are these people all "patients" or, rather, individuals who have a chronic condition requiring care?

- Some of us, myself included, had an experience with a serious illness, such as cancer, many years ago. I certainly do not consider myself a cancer patient when I go for follow-up.

- Even if someone is a patient in a hospital, Schenck and Churchill would say that we should "engage the person to treat the patient" (2012, p. 138).

- Koloroutis and Trout (2014) would go further and say there is universal appeal for all of us to the concept: *See me as a person.*

And finally, the term *patient* can perpetuate a hierarchical imbalance between caregiver and care receiver, which can compromise health care outcomes. A growing body of evidence shows that improved care outcomes occur when a partnership exists whereby the care provider brings professional knowledge and expertise, and the individual and family bring expert knowledge of the individual's background, preferences, experiences, and values. Examples of these outcomes reflect that individuals who are more involved in their care are better able to manage complex chronic conditions, seek appropriate assistance, point out incorrect information in the chart or plan of care, experience reduced lengths of stay, and avoid unnecessary readmissions and emergency department (ED) visits. Furthermore, they experience increased satisfaction with the care episodes (Agency for Healthcare Research and Quality [AHRQ], 2012; Aronson, Yau, Helfaer, & Morrison, 2009; Charmel & Frampton, 2008; Charmel, Stone, & Otero, 2013; Jarousse, 2011).

To be clear, there are still patients in hospitals receiving care, and they would obviously be called patients. However, the concept and principles of person- and family-centered care would still apply, that is, "Recognize the patient or designee as the source of control and full partner in providing compassionate and coordinated care based on respect for the patient's preferences, values and needs" (Cronenwett et al., 2007, p. 123). This emphasizes the need to fully engage the patient's family when the patient is unable to express his/her own preferences; to keep the patient and family fully informed and engaged in the decision making; to respect their input and wishes; and to encourage their participation and presence, now allowed to be round-the-clock if desired by the patient or designee (Centers for Medicare and Medicaid Services [CMS], 2010).

DIMENSIONS OF PERSON- AND FAMILY-CENTERED CARE

The Quality and Safety Education for Nurses (QSEN) initiative defines person- and family-centered care as "recognize the patient or designee as the source of control and full partner in providing compassionate and coordinated care based on respect for patient's preferences, values and needs" (Cronenwett et al., 2007, p. 123).

Dimensions of person- and family-centered care include:

1. Respect for patients' values, preferences, and expressed needs
2. Coordination and integration of care
3. Physical comfort, including freedom from pain

Patients should direct their own care, and clinicians and staff should honor what the patient wants (Berwick, 2009). A growing body of evidence demonstrates that patients who are more involved in their care are better able to:

- Manage complex chronic conditions
- Seek appropriate assistance
- Have reduced lengths of stay
- Avoid readmissions
- Experience patient satisfaction
- Achieve employee engagement (Jarousse, 2011)

SYSTEM-LEVEL CHANGES

Achieving system-level changes that enhance person- and family-centered care should be viewed as a journey. Once achieved, to sustain the changes there must be core components in place that support the system. Clinicians, patients, and families must view themselves as change agents. These stakeholders work together as partners within a collaborative process across the enterprise to improve safety, quality, and the patient experience. This approach to health care is respectful and ethical. Families become active participants and are better prepared to care for their family members. These factors lead to positive financial outcomes for the health care organization (Charmel & Frampton, 2008).

Hospitals that provide person- and family-centered care have demonstrated numerous financial benefits, such as increases in patient satisfaction, staff retention, and market share. Staff recruitment was improved and operating costs were reduced along with an improvement of the liability claims experience. Patients' lengths of stay were decreased as were readmissions, and the number of medication errors was reduced (Charmel & Frampton, 2008).

LEADERSHIP COMMITMENT

Health care leaders are being called to implement and support cultures within their organizations that are safe, effective, and of the highest quality. In doing so, they are being asked to place patients and families actively within the decision-making process. Several key national organizations are mandating that we move in the direction of person- and family-centered care:

- The IOM (2014)
- The Joint Commission (TJC, 2009)
- The National Patient Safety Foundation (NPSF, 2015)
- The AHRQ (2012)

To meet the challenge, providers need:

- Visible commitment from senior leadership
- An infrastructure that supports patient engagement
- A shared vision between clinicians and patients
- Multidisciplinary teams

- Empowered local leaders
- A plan of action
- Adequate resources

The clinician or health care executive must no longer be seen as the person with all of the answers. The role of the leader today is to create systems, processes, and structures for providing care that is respectful of and responsive to individual patient preferences, needs, and values and ensuring that patient values guide all clinical decisions (Disch, 2014, p. 415). This requires leaders to listen to and learn from the experiences of individual patients and their families.

PRACTICAL STEPS FOR HEALTH CARE MANAGERS

Person- and family-centered care is based on the premise that the basic relationship among individuals, their families, and the caregivers has to change in two fundamental ways: (a) from caregivers caring for individuals toward partnering with them; and (b) from caregivers having all of the expertise toward caregivers having the expertise in the disease or treatment and the person and his family being the experts in the life experiences of the individual. This requires significant change in how care is planned, organized, and delivered and how outcomes are evaluated. Health care managers play a key role in modeling the appropriate values and in creating systems that support the staff in executing a person- and family-centered approach to care.

Assess the Individual's Ability and Motivation to Participate in His or Her Care

Individuals present themselves with varying degrees of knowledge, competency, motivation, and skill in engaging in their care. Caregivers need to determine the individual's understanding of the condition and the plan of care, what the anticipated benefits and possible outcomes are, and actions that they can take to improve their health. The Patient Activation Measure (PAM) by Judith Hibbard and colleagues (2005) provides a simple framework to use in this strategy.

Solicit the Opinions of the Patient and Family in All Discussions About Care and Progress

The preferences and perspectives of the patient and family member should be routinely sought in discussions about the plan of care, desired outcomes, progress within treatments, and possible alternative options and choices. This can occur in rounds, handoffs at the end of a shift, care conferences, consultations, and discharge planning. These opportunities should be explicitly built into the day's schedule and not allowed to happen by chance or caregiver preference.

Tailor Educational Materials and Communication Strategies to Fit the Level of Health Care Literacy of the Patient and Family

Individuals approach health care with diverse value systems, beliefs, cultural norms, languages, and personal characteristics. This requires that education and communication must be individualized to both understand and meet the learning needs of the individual patient and family. One size does not fit all, and for individuals to actively participate in their care, information must be presented in ways that are meaningful to them. Preprinted materials can help but must be augmented by communication to ensure that the information has been accurately understood.

CONCLUSION

In conclusion, we are moving from a system where the caregivers were the experts and anyone receiving care was considered a patient to one based on the concept of partnership. For a variety of reasons, health care is much more complex today—and active engagement by caregivers, individuals, and their families, working together, offers the best—some would say only—opportunity to improve health care outcomes.

CASE STUDY

A 50-year-old man is hospitalized on the surgical floor after having a nephrectomy (surgical removal of a kidney), with the incision on his right side. As a result of the surgery, the most comfortable position for him is on his left side with his back to the door. During his hospital stay, he hears the door open and close but is unable to see individuals who come in unless they come around the foot of his bed and speak to him directly. During his 2-day stay, numerous people come into his room and speak to him facing his back. One nurse actually comes around the bed and looks at him as she speaks to him. He tells the nurse that while it probably seems like a small thing, it means a lot to have someone come around the bed and actually look at him while he or she is speaking.

Issues to Consider

1. How could the nurses have identified this preference on the patient's part?

2. How could they communicate across the shifts that this approach worked better for him?

3. What questions could nursing staff ask to personalize a surgical patient's care?

4. What actions could a nurse take to demonstrate that she is actively listening to a patient?

REFERENCES

Agency for Healthcare Research and Quality. (2012). *Guide to patient and family engagement: Environmental scan report* (AHRQ Publication No. 12-0042-EF; prepared by Maurer, M., Dardess, P., Carman, K. L., Frazier, K., & Smeeding, L.). Rockville, MD: Author.

Aronson, P. L., Yau, J., Helfaer, M. A., & Morrison, W. (2009). Impact of family presence during pediatric intensive care unit rounds on the family and medical team. *Pediatrics, 124*(4), 1119–1125.

Barnsteiner, J. H., Disch, J., & Walton, M. (2014). *Person- and family-centered care.* Indianapolis, IN: Sigma Theta Tau International.

Berwick, D. (2009). What patient-centered care should mean: Confessions of an extremist. *Health Affairs, 28*(4), w555–w565.

Centers for Medicare and Medicaid Services. (2010). Changes to the hospital and critical access hospital conditions of participation to ensure visitation rights for all patients (75 Fed. Reg. 70,831). Retrieved from http://www.gpo.gov/fdsys/pkg/FR-2010-11-19/pdf/2010-29194.pdf

Charmel, P. A., & Frampton, S. B. (2008). Building the business case for patient-centered care. *Healthcare Financial Management, 62*(3), 80–85.

Charmel, P. A., Stone, S., & Otero, D. (2013). The patient-centered care value equation. In S. B. Frampton, P. A. Charmel, & S. Guastello (Eds.), *The putting patients first field guide: Global lessons in designing and implementing patient-centered care* (pp. 19–44). Hoboken, NJ: Wiley-Blackwell.

Cronenwett, L., Sherwood, G., Barnsteiner, J., Disch, J., Johnson, J., Mitchell, P., . . . Warren, J. (2007). Quality and safety education for nurses. *Nursing Outlook, 55*(3), 122–131.

Disch, J. (2014). The role of leaders in assuring person- and family-centered care. In J. H. Barnsteiner, J. Disch, & M. Walton (Eds.), *Person- and family-centered care.* Indianapolis, IN: Sigma Theta Tau International.

Gerteis, M., Edgman-Levitan, S., Daley, J., & Delbanco, T. L. (1993). Introduction: Medicine and health from the patient's perspective. In M. Gerteis, S. Edgman-Levitan, J. Daley, & T. L. Delbanco (Eds.), *Through the patient's eyes: Understanding and promoting patient-centered care* (pp. 1–18). San Francisco, CA: Jossey-Bass.

Hibbard, J. H., Mahoney, E. R., Stockard, J., & Tusler, M. (2005). Development and testing of a short form of the Patient Activation Measure. *Health Services Research, 40*(6), 1918–1930.

Institute of Medicine. (2001). *Crossing the quality chasm: A new health system for the 21st century.* Washington, DC: National Academies Press.

Institute of Medicine. (2011). *The future of nursing: Leading change, advancing health.* Washington, DC: National Academies Press.

Institute of Medicine. (2014). *Partnering with patients to drive shared decisions, better value, and care improvement: Workshop proceedings.* Washington, DC: National Academies Press.

Jarousse, K. (2011). Putting patients first. *Trustee, 64*(10), 26.

Koloroutis, M., & Trout, M. (2014). Cultivating mindful and compassionate connections. In J. Barnsteiner, J. Disch, & M. K. Walton (Eds.), *Person- and family-centered care* (pp. 113–128). Indianapolis, IN: Sigma Theta Tau International.

National Patient Safety Foundation. (2015). *Free from harm: Accelerating patient safety improvement 15 years after To Err is Human.* Boston, MA: Author.

Schenck, D., & Churchill, L. (2012). *Healers: Extraordinary clinicians at work.* New York, NY: Oxford University Press.

The Joint Commission. (2009). *Leadership in healthcare organizations: A guide to Joint Commission leadership standards.* San Diego, CA: The Governance Institute.

CHAPTER 14

THE PATIENT EMPATHY PROJECT: A STUDY OF PATIENT FEARS

COLLEEN E. SWEENEY

LEARNING OBJECTIVES

- Understand the importance of patient fears.
- Experience an empathic connection with the experience of patients.
- Understand how to create an organizational culture for improving the personal experience of care.

KEY TERMS

Clinicaphobia

Empathy

HCAHPS metrics

Patient Empathy Project

Patient satisfaction

I have always loved hospitals. To me, they are like cities—fast-paced institutions that rely on interconnectedness and teamwork in order to survive. (No task, even volunteering, is too small.) And from the time I began working in them, at age 18, as a nursing student, I also thought of them as safe havens, where anxiety went *poof* in the mere presence of uniformed professionals.

But, it turns out, hospitals are not the least bit comforting to most people. I awoke to this reality in 2007, when I was the customer service director of a hospital in the Midwest. One day, as I was greeting patients and visitors at the entrance, I noticed a wheelchair-bound woman in the lobby whose hands were shaking uncontrollably, as if in fright. I approached her carefully, and asked her what was wrong. Without hesitation, she answered, "The last three times I visited a patient here in your hospital, they died. I'm worried that the same thing will happen to me." In an instant, my rosy outlook on our hospital dulled to gray. As far as this patient was concerned, she was not in a comfort zone, but on death row—even though, I later discovered, she was there due to a non–life-threatening condition.

Right after she was admitted, I marched back to my office and asked two fellow employees (both were nonclinicians) if they had a gripping fear about hospitals or health care in general.

They responded without missing a beat, as if they had been waiting to be questioned on the subject. I realized, immediately, that we are all prisoners of our past experiences (the negative ones, that is), and began to wonder about their impact on the *patient* experience. I personally had never had a traumatic episode at a hospital, but obviously while I could not speak for everyone, I could *empathize* with everyone's experience and started to ask a series of very important questions. Did most people have some sort of fear regarding health care? What would happen if clinicians were aware of a patient's fear before he or she came in, or at least as soon as he or she arrived? Would his or her hospital stay go more smoothly? And, just as important, would clinicians perform differently by having that extra bit of information?

> Empathy is, at its most basic, our own internal awareness of the feelings and emotions of other people. It is a key element of our relationships with each other because it is how we understand what others are experiencing as if we were feeling it ourselves.

Feeling part advocate, part researcher—and determined as ever—I made a personal commitment to get the answers as soon as I could.

The first step, of course, was to uncover what people feared about health care settings. It boiled down to a simple question—so simple that I could not believe that no one had bothered to ask it before (or at least not on the wide scale I was prepared to cover). Early one morning, I wrote it on the first line of a spiral-bound notebook: "If you were a patient in a hospital, what would your greatest fear be?" Later that day, at the hospital, I began to ask random adults this question, filling as many lines of the notebook as I could. Their reactions ranged from impassioned to heartbreaking to completely surprising, and many were unforgettable.

> "If you were a patient in a hospital, what would your greatest fear be?"

One gentleman I questioned, who happened to be an ex-professional basketball player, seemed to have it all figured out. "That's easy," he said. "I usually cancel my annual checkup several times before finally working up the nerve to keep the appointment!" When I asked him why, he took on the look of a frightened child and said, "It's all about what they are writing. I don't know what they're writing about me, and I always think they know more about my mortality than I know about myself, and aren't telling." I assured him that his caregivers had been recording their observations of his physical condition, as well as his responses to the standard questions. Suddenly relieved, he confessed that he had always been too afraid to ask. As an RN who had scribbled notes for decades, I was a bit embarrassed that I had never given this one bit of thought. Part of me wanted to apologize to him.

My quest for answers showed no signs of stopping. A few months later, I interviewed a cabbie who told me that his greatest fear was extended hospitalization due to staff incompetence. He explained that he often drove discharged patients home from the hospital, and that, more times than he could count, he'd had to turn the cab around and return them because their IV port had not been removed. If a nurse cannot remember to remove the IV, he wondered aloud, what else are they forgetting? His fear made me realize that some people are prisoners of witnessed experiences (in addition to, of course, their own). It also made me admit, tacitly, that after four decades in the health care industry, I had not seen and heard it all.

I continued to interview people for the next 3.5 years, sticking to the same question and seeking trends in their responses. By study's end, I had interviewed 1,080 adults between the ages of 18 and 90. I found that 96% of the subjects had some sort of fear about hospitals or health care, and that many of the subjects responded similarly. Here are the top 11 health care fears as determined by the study.

1. Infection
2. Incompetence
3. Death
4. Cost
5. Medical mix-up
6. Needles
7. Rude doctors and nurses
8. Germs
9. Diagnosis/prognosis
10. Communication issues
11. Loneliness

> I found that 96% of the subjects had some sort of fear about hospitals or health care, and that many of the subjects responded similarly.

Fear surrounding health care was, so far as I could tell, pervasive, and I could not help but give it a name: "clinicaphobia." I figured that if adopted, the word, despite its invented nature, could eventually help to destigmatize worries that caregivers either ignored or were unaware of.

If clinicaphobia were this widespread among potential patients, I wondered, how common would it be among existing patients? Would fears vary by department and subspecialty? Would they differ from the 11 most-common ones I'd found? It was time to ask patients, directly, what their fear was, and preferably in a specific unit of the hospital.

ON-SITE APPLICATION

In talking with the director of obstetrics (OB), and, later, the information technology (IT) nursing administrator, I realized that OB would be the perfect place to question actual patients about their fear: their concerns would probably be specific, and addressing them would, I hypothesized, better the patient experience and eventually reflect in the unit's satisfaction scores.

I proposed a simple 1-year pilot plan for OB: the question "What is your greatest fear or concern about your hospitalization?" was to be asked of every patient—not only during intake, but also at 12-hour intervals throughout his or her visit. I knew, as a mother of three, that asking the question consistently would be crucial, as the heady circumstances of childbirth tend to pose a certain set of anxieties. The OB director approved the plan enthusiastically, so I began to work on the logistics.

To fuel the brainstorming process, I asked clinicians why they did not explicitly question patients about their fear. Most said that time was a factor: asking the question (and, of course, addressing the response) would eat at the time they needed to deliver care not only to the patient at hand, but also to everyone else. Some said they were unaware of the full scope of resources available to patients, and that addressing a fear inadequately, or incompletely, could make them appear inept. And a few mentioned that usually a patient's fear was obvious and did not require questioning. Others, however, blithely admitted that they did not care enough to ask. The clinicians' answers, troubling as most of them were, proved invaluable as I outlined a plan for the OB unit. Revising the template of the patients' electronic medical records (EMRs), with help from the IT nursing administrator, was the centerpiece of the plan. I added the question, "What is your greatest fear or concern about your hospitalization?," strategically placing it late in the assessment to assure that the relationship had been established and each patient was trusting enough to answer. Below the question, I listed the top 11 fears from my survey study, and provided blank fields to capture additional responses. (The future contents of those fields, I figured, would eventually help me accurately determine what the unit-specific fears were.) Next to each fear, I placed a small box that, when clicked, would record an instance of that fear and provide pop-up text guides for the clinician. The guides explained how clinicians should immediately address a particular fear and, in quite a few cases, directed them to a specific hospital resource that could help to fully alleviate it. If, for example, the box next to "Cost" were to be clicked because the patient had financial concerns, a prepared script would appear for the clinician, along with a message field allowing him or her to schedule a meeting between a financial counselor and the patient. The electronic messaging eliminated the need for a phone call to the finance department. I refer to the entire process as the Patient Empathy Project.

Two months later, the new EMR template went live, and the plan was put into place. By all accounts, it was easy to follow and thus well received. A handful of clinicians said they altered the wording to fit their signature bedside manner or, when dealing with a particularly fragile patient, to avoid worsening her emotional state. Six months after the plan launched, the OB director and I were able to determine the most common fears and concerns among the unit's patients: the health of their baby (49%), pain during childbirth (42%), and a possible C-section (7.5%, see Figure 14.1). (The fears in OB were, in fact, markedly different from the top fears found by my survey study; the blank fields on the new EMR had done their job.) Though identifying the most prevalent concerns among OB patients satisfied my curiosity (and, of course, prompted me to rework the list of clickable fears), that was not the point. Knowing them helped me prioritize on my search for the best hospital resources available for fear-stricken patients, which, thanks

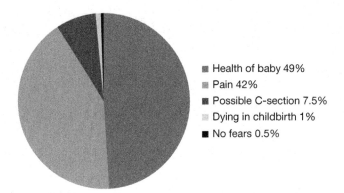

FIGURE 14.1 – Most prevalent concerns among OB patients.

to the EMR, I was able to put at the fingertips of every clinician in OB. Instructing the clinicians on where to direct patients with fears that could be alleviated only by certain departments made those patients feel cared about as a whole—not simply cared for, in the clinical sense.

OUTCOMES AND IMPACT

Some of the best outcomes are sometimes the least expected. Within 6 months of instituting the Patient Empathy Project, we had accurately identified the specialty-specific fears of both laboring and postpartum mothers. This information allowed nurses to fully anticipate the needs of expectant mothers and to better care for their physical and emotional needs. Knowing the most common fears and concerns of their patients gave the nurses a better understanding of the resources available to alleviate them.

The intended consequences of improving the patient experience became evident almost immediately, when we received our next round of Hospital Consumer Assessment of Healthcare Providers and Systems (HCAHPS) metrics. Within a month of the pilot's inception, in April 2011, the unit's hospital experience rating had increased by 10 points. Also, anecdotal accounts from team members revealed that unexpected changes in morale had occurred, with several nurses reporting that they had "reconnected to my purpose" and "remembered why I went into nursing in the first place." One year after the start of the Patient Empathy Project, the unit's employee engagement scores were in the 99th percentile, a significant increase from the year before.

> HCAHPS is a patient satisfaction survey required by the Centers for Medicare and Medicaid Services (CMS) for all hospitals in the United States. The survey is for adult inpatients, excluding psychiatric patients.

In health care, fear is a powerful driver of decision making. Knowing exactly what patients fear and marketing to their specific concerns can help quell their anxiety, effectively making them realize that we understand the complexities of their ordeal.

STEPS FOR IMPROVING THE PERSONAL EXPERIENCE OF CARE

Organizations have become frantic in their efforts to improve the patients' experience, as well as their scores; the move from volume to value, after all, has been one of the toughest challenges that health care has faced in many years. We try lots of things. Some succeed; some do not. But the truth is that campaigns, initiatives, and programs are not successful or sustainable on their own; it is organizations that make them work.

What patient experience efforts often lack is the infrastructure to support them. I have the honor of working with many health care organizations, and one of the things I find fascinating is that identical efforts to improve the patient experience can succeed in one organization but fall flat in another. Even more interesting: an improvement effort by one organization can succeed and become sustainable in one department but not in another.

The organizations that have enjoyed the most success share some common practices when it comes to their patient experience improvement efforts. Let me share just 10 I have found.

Start With a Team

High-performing organizations have a concrete infrastructure to support their improvement efforts; it is not one person who drives the efforts, but an entire team that includes both clinical and nonclinical members. The organizations that operate most efficiently have approximately 10 members on their team. When there are more than 10, things can get a little crazy; a larger committee can contribute to a lack of accountability on the part of the participants. Such a team may be titled the Patient Improvement Team, Patient Satisfaction Team, or Service Leader Team. It does not matter what you call it—just let your improvements be team driven.

Be Inclusive and Diverse

Think *big* when it comes to diversity on your patient-experience improvement team, making sure to include a wide range of people who will get you where you aim to be. Those who must be on the team are the chief nursing officer, managers (a good sample of them), frontline nurses, and personnel from human resources, nutritional services, and environmental services. Be creative when picking the rest, though I would suggest you include the directors of volunteers, parking services, and any very visible and fluid departments in the organization. Also include at least one out-of-the-box thinker who is perhaps new to health care. (New eyes are invaluable!)

Make It a Priority

Meet regularly and make every meeting a priority. Meet at the same times and on the same days every month so that everyone in the organization will know not to schedule any conflicting meetings. (As a member of a patient-experience improvement team, you must make your priorities clear.) Meeting just once a month is a suggestion for organizations whose efforts are well underway.

Cover It *All*!

Create subcommittees that are responsible for more specialized endeavors, such as a pain task force headed up by the pharmacy, or a discharge-phone-call team run by a nurse call center. Form committees around each domain, with representation from each modality. All of these subcommittees should report to the larger committee; a portion of every meeting should be dedicated to this.

Create a Common Language

Make sure that all team members speak the same language, one that is specific to your culture of patient experience. Reinforce the language in every way imaginable, using newsletters, banners, messaging in elevators and staff restrooms, buttons, screensavers, and signage in employee parking garages. Cast the vision for your organization by using a common language over and over again.

Start With Your Mission

Begin every meeting, assembly, or get-together by sharing your organization's mission. Have the marketing department create a slide that will be used first in *every* presentation. The slide may even be given to outside presenters so that they can incorporate it into their PowerPoint presentations. If there is no visible presentation, whoever opens the meeting should begin by reciting the organization's mission statement. How do you expect the members of an organization to move in the same direction and to live their promise to the community (your brand) if they are not all operating by the same mission statement? It cannot be done.

Train, Train, Train

If your goal is to change behaviors, team members need to be equipped with a new set of skills. However, this does not happen overnight, so someone has to be dedicated to the training and monitoring of team members. As an observer, I often see, for instance, extreme differences between bedside reporting and leader rounding, which are done in as many ways as there are nurses. We wonder why things do not stick but fail to think of the resources that often do not accompany the rollout of a new initiative. Skimping on resources when equipping team members with new skills will only cost you in the end.

Get Out!

I have worked in hospitals where there were a fair share of team members who had never worked in another organization. (In some cases, they had been born in that particular hospital, or their mother or father had worked there!) There is something to say about getting out and gaining some perspective, though it is hard to tell people to aim for something they have never seen. Scores are transparent nowadays. Find an organization that is doing well in an area that yours is weak in and request to visit, then ask as many questions as you can. I am always blown away when I discover that one organization is a mere car ride away from another but won't visit to find out what the latter is doing better; people love to show off what they do well. We really are good sharers—you just have to ask!

Focus!

We want to be good at everything immediately, but it does not work that way. I have gotten into a habit of asking organizations that I consult with to tell me one thing that they do *well* (with respect to a specific domain), even though it is a really hard question. Those who are honest say, "we do it all . . . but we're not sure if we've perfected any of it." So true! Choose one thing and be the very, very best at it!

Take Down the Kingpin!

No one has enough energy, time, or resources to go after every initiative that has proved to be a best practice. So, the question is: What do you pay attention to? I advise going after the initiatives that will have the biggest impact and the most influence on the patient's perception of his or her care. Right now, improving communication—communication between nurses, in particular—is what you should concentrate on. If we get this right, it will influence other, related domains; almost everything touches on communicating effectively. Be relentless when it comes to perfecting techniques related to bedside-shift reports. If these are done well, they are pretty much the kingpin when it comes to knocking down all the domains! Go for it!

CONCLUSION

The results of the Patient Empathy Project showed one overarching result: Patients fear us. Really fear us. The statistics were worse than I could have imagined. Ninety-six percent of people share one commonality—suffering from a fear of hospitals, health care, or doctors. It is unfortunate that in such a diverse world where people are so unique, the fear of health care is a common bond. More than anything, the results of this study show that recognizing patient fears is long overdue. We owe it to our patients to learn more about their fears so we can gain a better understanding of their perspective. My hope is that this book will help nudge our industry in the right direction.

> The results of the Patient Empathy Project showed one overarching result: Patients fear us. Really fear us.

It will take a total mind shift on the part of the health care professional to fully improve the personal experience of care. We have always had a mantra of "We deliver patient-centered care," but the reality is that we do not. It has truly been "us-centered care." It is why we do labs at 4 a.m. and 5 a.m.; it is why we discharge patients late in the afternoon. It really has not been about the patient, it has been about our processes. I think it will take a total mind shift for us to get inside the head of the patients and realize what is most important to them and what will work for them, and then tailor care and our systems around that. I do not believe we are there yet.

CASE STUDY

Tom is an 18-year-old young man who is just about to receive anesthesia in preparation for ACL reconstruction surgery. He lives with his mother, is starting college, has a job, and leads a very active life. While he is waiting to be taken to the operating room (OR), an anesthesiologist comes into his room to take Tom's history and discuss the anesthetic plan. In response, Tom refuses to talk and tears start to form in his eyes. A nurse sits down next to Tom, takes his blood pressure (BP), and finds that it is significantly elevated. After consultation with the anesthesiologist, the decision is made that Tom's high BP is temporary and is due to excessive anxiety about being in a medical environment (called "white coat syndrome").

After further discussion, the anesthesiologist and nurse agree that they should leave Tom alone for a while so he can calm down before starting the operation. They both return in about 30 minutes but still find Tom mute, upset, and with elevated BP.

At this point, the anesthesiologist notes that many patients are hypertensive when first admitted to a hospital due to anxiety, so the anesthesiologist administers an antihypertensive medication to Tom.

Administration of the antihypertensive medication continues as Tom is wheeled into the OR.

After 2 hours in the OR and 2 more hours in the recovery room, Tom is wheeled back into his room after a successful operation with all vital signs reading normal.

Issues to Consider

1. Was Tom afraid? If so, what role did fear play in Tom's experience in the hospital?

2. Is the use of an antihypertensive medication usually the best solution to "white coat syndrome?"

3. How might a greater show of empathy by the anesthesiologist and nurse affect Tom's experience?

4. What could have Tom done to improve his experience?

5. What could the hospital do in the future to better address situations like Tom's?

RESOURCE

Materials supporting this chapter are available through Sweeney Healthcare Enterprise at http://sweeneyhealthcareenterprises.com

CHAPTER 15

AVOIDING DIAGNOSTIC FIXATION ERRORS: A PERSON-FOCUSED APPROACH TO HUMAN FACTORS ANALYSIS

ELLEN GRADY VENDITTI

- Understand how human factors cause medical errors.
- Discover the different types of heuristics and learn how they cause misdiagnosis.
- Learn why encouraging and socializing a "reflective diagnostic practice" helps benefit patients.
- Learn how to conceptualize a curriculum for human factors engineering designed to avoid medical errors that includes input from patients and their families.

KEY TERMS

Active failures	Insurance captive
Cognitive bias	Latent failures
Cognitive shortcuts	Mental models
Diagnostic fixation error	Misdiagnosis
Error rate	Root cause analysis
Heuristics	Sentinel event
Human factors	Systems approach
Human factors analysis	

This chapter touches upon the enormity of preventable medical errors that cause injury or death and one root cause associated with those errors called "human factors." Human factors is a "catch all" term that refers to human behaviors, including how we think and communicate. Human factors have been identified as a root cause of medical errors, particularly diagnostic errors. Although human factors have been cited as a cause of error, human factors engineering is viewed as a solution to the problem of errors. The engineering or reengineering of human factors in a clinical setting is a process whereby protocols are designed to support human strengths and mitigate human weaknesses (The Joint Commission [TJC], 2015). This process is used to enhance the decision-making process in any setting where people are making a judgment call—such as a medical diagnosis.

The science of psychology and physiology tells us that the human mind works very rapidly, which raises the risk of making a judgment error. In a clinical setting, a physician can easily rush to judgment or perceive circumstances incorrectly due to dynamics operating within the subconscious mind. A specific example would be a "fixation error," which is known to occur during a medical diagnosis due to cognitive weaknesses in the subconscious mind of the physician. A fixation error occurs when a physician makes a wrong diagnosis; when the physician is presented with evidence of another diagnosis, he or she clings to his or her conclusion. Why would a physician engage in such conduct? What impairs his or her ability to redirect and reconsider the diagnosis?

This chapter explores some answers to those questions by introducing the reader to how fixation errors and heuristics (reasoning shortcuts) play a role in a misdiagnosis. A short literature review of studies across multiple health conditions is provided, which is intended to be a starting point for further research by the learner. Human factors reengineering is discussed as a much-needed mechanism to address fixation errors and decrease diagnostic errors.

> The question posed in this chapter is: How can patients and families be integrated into the human factors engineering solution to help decrease the number of medical errors, such as misdiagnosis?

HOW PREVALENT ARE MEDICAL ERRORS?

In 1999, the Institute of Medicine (IOM) published a book titled *To Err Is Human*, which explained that up to 98,000 people a year die due to preventable mistakes made in a hospital setting (IOM, 1999). In 2010, the Office of Inspector General for the U.S. Department of Health and Human Services cited 180,000 Medicare recipient deaths, over a 1-year time period, due to poor hospital care (U.S. Department of Health and Human Services, 2010). In 2013, the *Journal of Patient Safety* reported that between 210,000 and 440,000 patients die each year from preventable medical mistakes (James, 2013). This statistic makes medical errors the third leading cause of death for that time period (Advisory Board, 2013).

There are several different types of medical errors that can lead to injury or death. Some of the most common errors pertain to medical treatment, technical issues, medication, equipment failure, wrong site surgery, and misdiagnosis (La

Pietra, Calligaris, Molendini, Quattrin, & Brusaferro, 2005). When a medical error is classified as a sentinel event by TJC, the provider must conduct a root cause analysis and report findings to The Joint Commission (TJC, 2016a).

"A sentinel event is a Patient Safety Event that reaches a patient and results in any of the following:

- Death, permanent harm
- Severe temporary harm
- Intervention required to sustain life.

An event can also be considered a sentinel event even if the outcome was not death, permanent harm, severe temporary harm and intervention required to sustain life" (TJC, 2016b; reproduced by permission of The Joint Commission).

It is well studied that human factors is a common reason for medical errors, and sentinel events in particular. Human factors are defined by TJC as: "Staffing levels, staffing skill mix, staff orientation, in service education, competency assessment, staff supervision, resident supervision, medical staff credentialing/privileging, medical staff peer review, other (e.g., rushing, fatigue, distraction, complacency, bias)." In essence, human factors are in most cases the primary root cause of a medical error and in almost all cases in the top three root causes.

TJC cites the root causes of all reported sentinel events, including human factors.

As can be imagined, a diagnostic error is frequently caused by human factors. Human factors can be addressed by changing human behaviors. Misdiagnosis is prevalent and the result can mean preventable death for some patients.

WHAT IS THE ERROR RATE OF DIAGNOSTIC ERRORS IN HEALTH CARE?

Misdiagnosis is much too common in health care. The literature indicates that 10% to 15% of all diagnoses are estimated to be erroneous. These percentages are higher in clinical specialties than in perceptual specialties (Berner & Graber, 2008).

Several studies have been conducted regarding the measured rate of diagnostic errors across multiple specialties and specific diseases. In general, the error rate was consistently disappointingly high (see Table 15.1). The best studies involve data derived from autopsies where the error rate for misdiagnosis has been found to be as high as 10%. Although the accuracy of an autopsy is quite reliable, the population of people is smaller due to the number of people who actually undergo the procedure.

TABLE 15.1 – Results From Select Studies of Diagnostic Errors Across Specific Conditions

Procedure Utilized	Error Rate (%)	Findings
Autopsy—TB	50	Not diagnosed pre-mortem
Autopsy—Fatal PE	55	Not diagnosed pre-mortem
Mammogram reviews	21	Breast cancer missed
Retroactive chart review lab evidence of diabetes	18	Not mentioned in records
Chest x-ray in the emergency department re-read by radiologist	33	Error rate found

PE, pulmonary embolism; TB, tuberculosis.
Source: Berner and Graber (2008).

One study focused on misdiagnosis across multiple medical specialties using statistics derived from telemedicine cases found an error rate of 5% (Berner & Graber, 2008). Other studies have utilized actors as patients focused primarily on standardized cases and the error rate was found to be 13% (Berner & Graber, 2008). An examination of these studies reveals that diagnostic errors are largely due to fixation errors where a diagnosis was made too fast and contrary evidence was presented and ignored.

WHAT IS A FIXATION DIAGNOSTIC ERROR?

A diagnostic fixation error is a phenomenon of clinging to a single presumed diagnosis despite mounting evidence that one is on the wrong track (CRICO, n.d.). This is not surprising to human factors experts because errors are common, causes of errors are unknown, and most errors are a result of cognitive weakness.

Mental functioning is automatic, rapid, and effortless. We develop mental schemata or mental models that are preprogrammed instructions to ourselves. Mental models influence how humans think (see Table 15.2). Mental models are preprogrammed in our brains and operate automatically when triggered by some stimulus-making functioning after initial stimulation. If we are asked to confront a problem or a schema fails, our brain switches to conscious thought, which is slow, sequential, effortful, and usually difficult to sustain.

In general, humans want to find the easiest way to solve a problem. When a problem presents, we need to switch to the rule or knowledge based on thought. Humans prefer pattern recognition to calculation. We subconsciously search and search again for a pattern or rule before we switch to knowledge-based functioning. The more experienced we are, the less often we have to resort to knowledge-based functioning or reasoning. This is a problem at times because overreliance on weak aspects of cognition will lead to error, particularly when we rely on our memory and attention. Memory involves cognitive bias and pattern-mapping errors. Our attention span can be overtaken by tunnel vision and/or other factors, such as distraction, fatigue, and the like.

Cognitive errors occur subconsciously during a diagnosis. The physician integrates medical knowledge with a patient's history and findings. The thinking process is automatic. When some physicians are asked to describe how they

TABLE 15.2 – Characteristics of Heuristic Types	
Heuristic Type	**Characteristics of Heuristic Type**
Availability	People judge likelihood by how easily examples spring to mind
Anchoring	People stick with initial impressions
Blind obedience	People stop thinking when confronted with authority
Premature closure	Several alternatives are not pursued
Framing effects	People make different decisions depending on how information is presented

arrived on a certain conclusion, they cannot articulate the process. This is partially because as they analyze a patient's condition, a variety of heuristics, or reasoning shortcuts, come into play (Agency for Healthcare Research and Quality [AHRQ], 2014; Redelmeier, 2005).

A reduction in the prevalence of diagnostic errors, diagnostic fixation, and the role of heuristics requires changing physician behaviors. Such a reduction also includes implementation of a systems approach where protocols are changed across an enterprise. It is important to continue to actively increase awareness of these errors and how they occur by encouraging physicians to engage in a "reflective diagnostic practice." That is, once there is a working diagnosis, it should be examined carefully and consciously—the opposite diagnosis should be examined, key assumptions should be revisited, and other diagnoses that cannot afford to be missed should be considered. On a systems level, diagnostic decision supports must be available, such as protocols, cued documentation, checklists, and the like. Many of the cognitive functions that set up fixation errors also facilitate consistently accurate diagnoses. Remember, these are cognitive errors, not arrogance. So, do not demonize the shortcuts and do recognize the hazards. To effectively prevent error in any setting including health care, systems principles such as human factors reengineering must be implemented in all clinical settings.

HOW CAN HUMAN FACTORS REENGINEERING DECREASE MISDIAGNOSIS MADE BY PHYSICIANS?

Research shows that human failures cause 80% to 90% of errors in general (Reason, 2000). The most common root causes of sentinel events according to TJC are human failures (TJC, 2016b).

To avoid medical errors such as misdiagnosis, it is vital to understand how human factors engineering can effectively impact the ubiquitous nature of such errors. Human factors engineering systems are rooted in engineering disciplines from World War II when psychologists explored cognitive aspects of error systems including the analysis of human factors. Systems engineers looked at "man in his environment" and studied errors in order to understand their causation. As a result of those studies, effective strategies to prevent errors from occurring emerged. These strategies acknowledged that many errors are caused by activities that rely on weak aspects of cognition, such as memory and attention span. These strategies also honed in on useful cognitive functions by decreasing dependence on weak cognitive functions.

In general, human errors can be categorized into three topic areas (Reason, 1990).

1. Knowledge-based
2. Rule-based
3. Skill-based

James Reason has pointed out in his work that humans have known limitations; they are not perfect; "we cannot change the human condition but we can change the conditions in which humans work" (Reason, 2000, p. 769). In the medical environment, both active and latent failures come into play. The active failure is an unsafe act committed by frontline staff at the point of care (Reason, 2000).

Under human factors principles, mistakes are knowledge-based errors. A wrong rule is chosen—one may be selected that is frequently used, but proves to be wrong for a particular situation. Or, there may be a lack of knowledge or the wrong "pattern" is selected. We have a biased memory—that is, we see what we know or what we expect to see. The fact is that error is inevitable mostly due to human limitations. We have limited attention and memory capacity. Limits are imposed by stressors, fatigue, and other physical factors. Also, cultural effects influence how and when errors occur; flawed teamwork where members are not on the same page is another mental mode that causes errors.

In high-risk situations, the quality of human interaction is critical to the minimization of human errors. Patients are most vulnerable to communication failures during a change of shift, change of responsibility, and during handoffs when the margin of safety creates a zone of danger for patients. How can communication in a clinical setting be improved so that errors can be avoided?

- Standardize the process
- Assess and improve clinicians' communication skills
- Make clinical information available in real time to providers, patients, and families
- Avoid overrelying on patient and family—consider them as members of the care team, not exclusively responsible for shared communication
- Back up providers' memory with a less fallible system

HOW CAN PATIENTS AND THEIR FAMILIES BE INTEGRATED INTO A HUMAN FACTORS ENGINEERING SOLUTION?

The application of human factors engineering can and should include data from patients and their families so as to capture the most optimal solutions. Methods and tools that are being used to engage patients and their families are being studied and their outcomes are being measured because that data is valuable and necessary.

Patients are more equipped and enabled to engage due mostly to advances in technology. Culture is changing rapidly in the medical community. More than ever, clinicians are turning to patients as true partners not only to avoid medical errors but also to make medical decisions in general.

CONCLUSION

Acknowledging our humanness and interdependence on one another is key when it comes to human factors reengineering. Clinical staff need to be committed to becoming more self-aware and to active listening.

CASE STUDY

At the time of the patient's admission, the primary care provider (PCP) is not available to the emergency department (ED) or admitting team. There is difficulty determining an accurate medication list, allergies, and problem list. The health history includes "on chemo," but the nurse is not able to determine the medications involved at the time of admission. The family brought bottles of medication. The pharmacist entered information with a stop date on the electronic medication administration record 5 days on 28 days off. However, the pharmacist did not transfer information to the physician profile page.

The physician and pharmacist both agree that a root cause analysis should be done to discover why this happened and how it can be avoided in the future. They want to use the approach endorsed by TJC for sentinel events.

Issues to Consider

1. Should the medication error be self-reported to TJC?

2. Can you conceptualize five reasons as to "why" this happened, similar to how a root cause analysis would be conducted?

3. What would a corrective action plan include to avoid this happening in the future?

4. What are the best practices that are offered by the Institute for Healthcare Improvement for protocols relative to self-reporting? Which ones do you recommend and why?

5. How might the principle of person-focused care be used to minimize the risk of medication errors?

REFERENCES

Advisory Board. (2013). Medical errors may be the country's third-leading cause of death. Retrieved from https://www.advisory.com/daily-briefing/2013/09/24/medical-errors-may-be-the-country-third-leading-cause-of-death

Agency for Healthcare Research and Quality. (2014). Diagnostic errors. Retrieved from https://psnet.ahrq.gov/primers/primer/12/diagnostic-errors

Berner, E., & Graber, M. (2008). Overconfidence as a cause of diagnostic error in medicine. *The American Journal of Medicine, 121*(Suppl. 5), S2–S23.

CRICO. (n.d.). Strategies for patient safety. Retrieved from https://www.rmf.harvard.edu

Institute of Medicine. (1999). *To err is human: Building a safer health system.* Washington, DC: National Academies Press. Retrieved from https://www.nationalacad

emies.org/hmd/~/media/Files/Report%20Files/1999/To-Err-is-Human/ To%20Err%20is%20Human%201999%20%20report%20brief.pdf

James, J. T. (2013). A new, evidence-based estimate of patient harms associated with hospital care. *Journal of Patient Safety, 9*(3), 122–128.

La Pietra, L., Calligaris, L., Molendini, L., Quattrin, R., & Brusaferro, S. (2005). Medical errors and clinical risk management: State of the art. *Acta Otorhinolaryngologica Italica, 25*(6), 339–346.

Reason, J. (1990). *Human error.* New York, NY: Cambridge University Press.

Reason, J. (2000). Human error: Models and management. *British Medical Journal, 320*(7237), 768–770.

Redelmeier, D. (2005). The cognitive psychology of missed diagnosis. *Annals of Internal Medicine, 142*(2), 115–120.

The Joint Commission. (2015). Human factors analysis in patient safety systems. *The Source, 13*(4). Retrieved from http://www.jointcommission.org/assets/1/6/HumanFactorsThe_Source.pdf

The Joint Commission. (2016a). Patient safety systems chapter, sentinel event policy and RCA2. Retrieved from http://www.jointcommission.org/sentinel_event.aspx

The Joint Commission. (2016b). Sentinel event policy and procedures. Retrieved from http://www.jointcommission.org/sentinel_event_policy_and_procedures

U.S. Department of Health and Human Services. (2010). Adverse events in hospitals: National incidence among Medicare beneficiaries. Retrieved from http://oig.hhs.gov/oei/reports/oei-06-09-00090.pdf

CHAPTER 16

THE PATIENT'S ROLE IN CARE: HOW FAR HAVE WE COME?

SHERRIE H. KAPLAN AND SHELDON GREENFIELD

LEARNING OBJECTIVES

- Understand the background and conceptual basis for involving patients in care.
- Quantify the effects of interventions designed to improve patients' active involvement in care relative to their various roles—as recipients, implementers, evaluators, and researchers.
- Discover and study the myths and barriers to effective patient collaboration in care.
- Review and analyze data that supports how patienthood leads to better health outcomes.

KEY TERMS

Comparative effectiveness research

Health insurance literacy

Health outcomes

Patienthood

Randomized controlled trial

The U.S. health care system is arguably the most complex in the world. Technologies that enhance and support health care are advancing at an unprecedented pace. Consumers or "patients" are being regularly bombarded with new and often conflicting health care information. Pharmaceutical companies market medications directly to the public. Most major network newscasts have a health care segment; news "magazine" shows often have a staff physician brought in to brief the public on the results of the most recent scientific studies, controversies in disease management, efficacy of new drug therapies or technologies, issues related to health insurance and organization of health care delivery, and so on, often on the same day they appear in the scientific media. Sophisticated search engines put vast amounts of health care information at the fingertips of motivated individuals. Comparisons of health insurance plans appear with increasing frequency in the popular press. Even quality of care profiles are publicly reported for hospitals, health plans, and individual physicians.

And yet we currently have no national policy for training the present or future health care–consuming public in how to use information to be effective, efficient patients. In fact, we lack training programs for preparing patients in the fundamental skills they need to participate effectively in any of their current roles— not only as users of health care, but also as implementers of treatment plans, as evaluators of health care quality, and, more recently, as researchers into their own health problems. It should come as no great surprise, therefore, that the average patient asks fewer than five lexical questions during a 15-minute office visit (R. Brown, Butow, Boyer, & Tattersall, 1999; R. F. Brown, Butow, Dunn, & Tattersall, 2001; Bruera et al., 2003; Butow, Brown, Cogar, Tattersall, & Dunn, 2002; Cegala, McClure, Marinelli, & Post, 2000; Galliher et al., 2010; Kindler, Szirt, Sommer, Häusler, & Langewitz, 2005; Sleath, Roter, Chewning, & Svarstad, 1999; Tai-Seale, Foo, & Stults, 2013), that a substantial proportion of patients do not actively participate in the decision-making process during treatment (Brom et al., 2014; Burton, Blundell, Jones, Fraser, & Elwyn, 2010; Guadagnoli & Ward, 1998; Kaplan, Billimek, Sorkin, Ngo-Metzger, & Greenfield, 2013; Levinson, Kao, Kuby, & Thisted, 2005; Mansell, Poses, Kazis, & Duefield, 2000; S. G. Smith, Pandit, Rush, Wolf, & Simon, 2016; Thompson & Miller, 2014), and that truly "informed consent" is rarely that (Falagas, Korbila, Giannopoulou, Kondilis, & Peppas, 2009).

The consequences of this lack of training are costly not only for the individual patient but also for the health care system more broadly. Patients arrive at outpatient visits frequently unprepared to be optimal "reporters" of and participants in their health, patients and families are unsure how to advocate for or participate in safety initiatives while in the hospital (e.g., to ensure hand washing by providers, avoid medication errors, and so forth), and, after discharge, patients are frequently unprepared to implement discharge plans effectively and resume the management of their health care. Among the major contributors to poor participation in care are poor "health system literacy" (knowing how to use the health care system effectively), poor risk literacy (Gigerenzer, Gaissmaier, Kurz-Milcke, Schwartz, & Woloshin, 2007), and missing links between access to disease-specific and personal health information and training in how to use that information during interactions with providers. Estimates of the costs of low health literacy range from $106 billion to $238 billion annually (Vernon, Trujillo, Rosenbaum, & DeBuono, 2007).

A substantial body of evidence has now accumulated documenting the beneficial effects of effective patient participation in care on patients' health care and health outcomes (Clayman, Bylund, Chewning, & Makoul, 2016; Greene, Hibbard, Sacks, Overton, & Parrotta, 2015; Guadagnoli & Ward, 1998; Vlemmix et al., 2013), but this practice is still far from routine. Why? This chapter reviews the background and conceptual basis for involving patients in care, the effects of interventions designed to improve patients' active involvement in care in their various roles (recipients, implementers, evaluators, and researchers), myths and barriers to effective patient collaboration in care, and recommendations for training in "advanced patienthood."

BACKGROUND

Most of us, if we have been lucky, have not had much practice being patients. We learn the skills of "patienthood"—how to evaluate health insurance plans and coverage; our rights and obligations as patients; how to choose or change physicians; how to participate effectively with our physicians in treatment decisions and weigh risks and benefits of treatment against our personal preferences; how to be "health media savvy," including understanding health advertising messages; how to influence the quality and safety of care we receive; and even determine how and when to refuse care—through a haphazard, trial-and-error process, if we learn at all. There is currently no central, trusted resource to which patients can turn to get the kind of comprehensive training that would convert them from passive recipients of health care from a system organized by and for providers, to one in which their participation was an integral feature of the design, use, evaluation, and revision of all components of health care, not simply an "empty ritual" (Arnstein, 1969; Wicks et al., 2015).

Clearly the notion of including patients in all facets of health care, from the macroenvironment, for example, the design of new modes of health care delivery (Johnson et al., 2008), the design of health insurance benefits (Goold, Biddle, Klipp, Hall, & Danis, 2005), or development of new medications (Wicks et al., 2015), to the microenvironment of the doctor–patient relationship where specific treatment decisions are made, is evolving. Three reports of the Institute of Medicine (IOM) called for greater involvement of patients in care as a quality improvement strategy (IOM, 2000, 2001, 2008). The Joint Commission for Accreditation of Health Care Organizations' 2008 National Patient Safety Goal # 13 was to "Encourage patients' active involvement in their own care as a patient safety strategy." The WHO recently called for patient participation in programs to improve safety (World Health Organization, 2013).

The Affordable Care Act (ACA) of 2010 provided for the Patient-Centered Outcomes Research Institute to ensure that the comparative effectiveness research underpinning evidence-based medicine reflected patient engagement through all phases of research from design to dissemination. The ACA also provided that patients' ratings of and reports about the quality of their physicians' care, part of an incentive program for providers under the Physician Quality Reporting System, be publicly reported (e.g., Physician Compare: www.medicare.gov/physiciancompare). Furthermore, the advent of social media, the diffusion of smartphones, and patient portals in many electronic medical records (EMRs) put health information (often of varying quality), potentially health-enhancing materials and apps, in the hands of a much broader range of patients and offer much faster diffusion of research results.

So is it just a matter of time before current trends achieve the aspirational goal of a well-trained, fully informed, and optimally participating population of U.S. patients who will use the health care system to their best advantage? Almost certainly not. Although we increasingly ask patients to assume more responsibility for financing their care, and most patients indicate they want to be active participants in their care (Brom et al., 2014; Chewning et al., 2012; Müller-Engelmann et al., 2013; S. G. Smith et al., 2016), we have yet to provide patients with systematic training in the skills they need to successfully accomplish the tasks of patienthood as routine practice. So is the problem a dearth of effective interventions to prepare patients for a more active role in care? Although some would argue that there is insufficient evidence from randomized controlled trials to support the spectrum of interventions developed to address specific patienthood skills (e.g., decision aids to promote effective participation in treatment decisions; Adsul et al., 2015; Clayman et al., 2016; de Jongh, Gurol-Urganci, Vodopivec-Jamsek, Car, & Atun, 2012; Gurol-Urganci, de Jongh, Vodopivec-Jamsek, Car, & Atun, 2012; Gustafson et al., 2001; Hamine, Gerth-Guyette, Faulx, Green, & Ginsburg, 2015; Marcano Belisario, Huckvale, Greenfield, Car, & Gunn, 2013; O'Connor et al., 1999; Vlemmix et al., 2013), the body of evidence now amassed over decades of empirical study suggests that there are feasible interventions that work (i.e., improve health and health care) and could be integrated into a multicomponent skills training program.

What then is the problem? It is probably *not* the paucity of interventions, the scarcity of evidence that they work, the lack of a conceptual basis for involving patients in care, nor is it likely to be the actual costs associated with intervening, since the costs associated with not implementing such a program appear to be so great. More likely are a set of prevailing myths and barriers to the effective inclusion of patients in health care delivery and evaluation, the persistence of a relatively maladaptive paternalistic culture of medicine, and a fundamental disparity in how the health care system and those it serves view patienthood.

The Tasks of Patienthood

What do we now ask individuals to do as "consumers" of health care services? A partial list of the tasks of patienthood is presented in Table 16.1, along with examples of current efforts to improve the skills related to those tasks. However, despite accelerating efforts to improve individuals' skills in each of these discrete areas (Bennett, Coleman, Parry, Bodenheimer, & Chen, 2010; Chan et al., 2014; Clayman et al., 2016; de Jongh et al., 2012; Gurol-Urganci et al., 2012; Harrington, Noble, & Newman, 2004; Marcano Belisario et al., 2013; Thom, Hessler, et al., 2015; Thom, Willard-Grace, et al., 2015; Turner et al., 2012; Vale, Jelinek, Best, et al., 2003; Willard-Grace et al., 2015), these efforts tend to be fragmented, limited to specific subgroups (e.g., self-management tasks for patients with specific health care problems), not widely implemented, of varying quality (i.e., not uniformly evaluated for effectiveness), and largely passively administered. That is, while some resources to address specific tasks may be available, patients must either find them themselves, use them without feedback, or synthesize (without assistance) common skills needed for related tasks. Furthermore, targeted interventions to improve some of the skills needed to accomplish the tasks listed earlier often suffer from timing problems and lack of availability close in time (e.g., immediately before an office visit) to when the target behaviors are occurring. Nevertheless, a body of evidence has now accrued linking patient involvement in care, either as a function of targeted interventions or some other learned process, to positive outcomes.

The Evidence for Improving Patient Participation in Care

Although the key words and their definitions vary—patient participation, patient involvement, patient activation, patient collaboration, shared decision making, participatory decision making—and the research designs vary (from randomized controlled trials of interventions to cross-sectional studies of associations), the body of evidence supporting the benefits of the overarching construct of patient involvement in care spans over 30 years, a broad array of health behaviors, health

TABLE 16.1 – The Tasks of Patienthood	
Tasks	**Interventions**
• Choosing/changing health plans	• Health insurance literacy training programs, e.g., Choosing Healthplans All Together (CHAT), Consumer Reports, Kaiser Family Foundation (Kim, Braun, & Williams, 2013)
• Choosing/changing providers	• Consumer Reports; archive.ahrq.gov/consumer/qnt/qntdr.htm; www.healthfinder.gov/HealthTopics/Category/doctor-visits/regular-check-ups/choosing-a-doctor-quick-tips; www.nia.nih.gov/health/publication/choosing-doctor
• Participating in care	• Health coaching (Bennett et al., 2010; Chan et al., 2014; Greenfield, Billimek, Sorkin, & Kaplan, 2014; Jelinek et al., 2009; Lindner, Menzies, Kelly, Taylor, & Shearer, 2003; Mbah et al., 2015; Thom et al., 2013; Thom, Hessler, et al., 2015; Thom, Willard-Grace, et al., 2015; Turner et al., 2012; Willard-Grace et al., 2013, 2015) • Decision aids (Adsul et al., 2015; Gustafson et al., 2001; Kuppermann et al., 2009; Légaré et al., 2010, 2014; O'Connor et al., 1999; Say, Robson, & Thomson, 2011; Stacey et al., 1996; Vlemmix et al., 2013) • Communicating with providers (Cegala & Post, 2009; Deen, Lu, Rothstein, Santana, & Gold, 2011; Greenfield, Kaplan, Ware, Yano, & Frank, 1988; Harrington et al., 2004; Jefferson, Bloor, Birks, Hewitt, & Bland, 2013; Kaplan, Greenfield, & Ware, 1989; Kaplan et al., 2013; Stewart, 1995) • Improving numeracy (Clement, Ibrahim, Crichton, Wolf, & Rowlands, 2009; Gigerenzer et al., 2007; Peters, Hibbard, Slovic, & Dieckmann, 2007; Tait, Voepel-Lewis, Brennan-Martinez, McGonegal, & Levine, 2012; Tait, Zikmund-Fisher, Fagerlin, & Voepel-Lewis, 2010; Woloshin, Schwartz, & Welch, 2007, 2008)
• Following through on care (also known as adherence)	• Computerized reminders (Tao, Xie, Wang, & Wang, 2015) • mHealth (Dayer, Heldenbrand, Anderson, Gubbins, & Martin, 2013; Free et al., 2013; Hamine et al., 2015; Klasnja & Pratt, 2012; Lin & Wu, 2014; Misono et al., 2010; Pop-Eleches et al., 2011) • Telemedicine (Gurol-Urganci et al., 2012)
• Self-management	• Condition-specific interventions (de Jongh et al., 2012; Glasgow & Toobert, 2000; Marcano Belisario et al., 2013; Ong et al., 2016)
• Accessing and navigating the health care system	• Patient navigators (Genoff et al., 2016; Kim et al., 2015; Luckett, Pena, Vitonis, Bernstein, & Feldman, 2015; Myers et al., 2013; Wang et al., 2015; Wells et al., 2012)

outcomes, patient experience, and quality of care measures (Guadagnoli & Ward, 1998). Examples of studies describing the effects of, or associations between, patient involvement in care and better health and health care are outlined in Table 16.2. As noted, patients who participate more effectively in their care are more likely to participate in preventive screening, have better health habits, are more effective in managing chronic diseases and mental health problems, have better quality of care for chronic diseases, have better cancer care, are more likely to follow through on treatment plans, are more likely to have safer care, have more positive experiences with care (including greater satisfaction with their providers), have better communication skills during office visits, are more likely to trust their physicians, are more likely to use quality of care data optimally, and are more likely to use the health care system more efficiently.

TABLE 16.2 – Relationships of Greater Patient Participation in Care to Health Behaviors, Outcomes, and Patient Experience

Outcome Measures	References
• More participation in preventive screening	Greene and Hibbard (2012)
• Better health habits (more exercise, less smoking, less obesity, less substance abuse)	Greene and Hibbard (2012); Salyers et al. (2009); Vale et al. (2003)
• More effective self-management	Heisler, Bouknight, Hayward, Smith, and Kerr (2002); Hibbard, Mahoney, Stock, and Tusler (2007); Lorig et al. (2001); Rask et al. (2009)
• Better quality of care for chronic diseases	Adams, Appleton, Wilson, and Ruffin (2005); Adams, Smith, and Ruffin (2001); Choi et al. (2015); Coulter and Ellins (2006); Greenfield, Kaplan, and Ware (1985); Greenfield et al. (1988); Kaplan et al. (1989); Mosen et al. (2007); Parchman, Zeber, and Palmer (2010); Rask et al. (2009); Schillinger et al. (2002); Weingart et al. (2011)
• Better adherence to treatment plans	Loh, Leonhart, Wills, Simon, and Härter (2007); Parchman et al. (2010)
• Better quality of care for mental health	Arora, Weaver, Clayman, Oakley-Girvan, and Potosky (2009); Clever et al. (2006); Gilbody, Bower, Fletcher, Richards, and Sutton (2006); Loh, Simon, et al. (2007)
• Better quality of care for cancer patients	Andersen et al. (2012); Andersen and Urban (1999); Arora et al. (2009); Hawley et al. (2007); Murray et al. (2001)
• Safer care	Berger, Flickinger, and Dy (2013); Longtin et al. (2010); McGuckin et al. (2001); Weingart et al. (2011)
• More positive experiences of care (greater satisfaction)	Hurwitz et al. (2015); Sleath et al. (2011); Xu (2004)
• Better preparation before visits, better questions during visits, awareness of treatment guidelines, openness in discussion of complementary and alternative medicine	Alegría, Sribney, Perez, Laderman, and Keefe (2009); Deen et al. (2011); Katz, Jacobson, Veledar, and Kripalani (2007); Sleath, Callahan, DeVellis, and Sloane (2005)
• Greater trust in physicians	Becker and Roblin (2008); Lee and Lin (2010)
• Use of quality of care data	Hibbard, Peters, Dixon, and Tusler (2007)
• Reduced hospital stays, use of emergency departments	Arterburn et al. (2012); Begum, Donald, Ozolins, and Dower (2011); Billimek (2016); Frosch, Rincon, Ochoa, and Mangione (2010); Greene and Hibbard (2012); Hibbard, Greene, and Tusler (2009); Kuppermann et al. (2014); Remmers et al. (2009); Shively et al. (2013); Veroff, Marr, and Wennberg (2013)

Recent comprehensive reviews have underscored the general need for more randomized controlled trials of interventions designed to increase patient participation in health care, including quality of care and safety initiatives (Clayman et al., 2016; Hall et al., 2010; Hibbard & Greene, 2013; Hibbard, Greene, Sacks, & Overton, 2015; Schwappach, 2010).

> What is a *randomized controlled trial*? As explained by MedicineNet.Com, a randomized controlled trial is a study in which people are allocated at random (by chance alone) to receive one of several clinical interventions. One of these interventions is the standard of comparison or control. The control may be a standard practice, a placebo, or no intervention at all. See www.medicinenet .com/script/main/art.asp?articlekey=39532

However, since the 1980s, a diverse range of interventions designed to increase patients' active involvement in care have been developed and tested, with the majority showing positive effects on patients' outcomes and/or experiences of care (Clayman et al., 2016; Guadagnoli & Ward, 1998; Sanders et al., 2013; Vlemmix et al., 2013). Although the evidence focuses on different patient skills and behaviors, the underlying premise this body of work shares in common is not the traditional paternalistic model of health care delivery, but a more egalitarian approach in which patients are not only encouraged to take a more active role in health care but also are given the assistance they need to support the development of appropriate skills to take on that role.

When Is a Person a Patient? The 5,000+ Hours

So given the accumulated evidence, why have we yet to implement a comprehensive training program to improve the skills of patienthood? Some of the difficulty involves the timeliness of intervention administration and mutually inconsistent views of the health care system and its users regarding when an individual is a "patient." Most reference sources define a patient as someone under care or treatment, or someone receiving health care services ("Definition of patient," n.d.; "patient," n.d.-a; "patient," n.d.-b). However, patienthood is a complex, dynamic concept that is not a dominant role in most people's lives. It varies in relevance and requirements, not just over the life cycle but even within short time periods as patients generally consider themselves "patients" only while they are at a health care facility or in the presence of a health care provider. Furthermore, for different subgroups or illnesses/conditions, an individual's interest in engaging in efforts to increase his or her involvement in health care may vary considerably (Brom et al., 2014).

It has been observed that even patients with chronic disease spend only a handful of hours in a year with health care providers, but 5,000 hours doing everything else, including following though (or not) on recommended treatment plans (Asch, Muller, & Volpp, 2012). And yet, since there is no comprehensive formal training program in the diffuse skills required to be an effective manager of a disease condition, making key elements of the program available to patients at the time they are making key health care decisions would enhance the usefulness, efficacy, and effectiveness of such a program. Also, finding "teachable moments" (Lawson & Flocke, 2009) when patients are active in management of their condition outside the health care system would be an important feature of a successful program. Reinforcing commitments to treatment goals and engaging in the broad array of patienthood skills needed to maximize an individual's health will almost certainly require some contact with patients in the 5,000+ hours, in order for those individuals to effectively engage in the critical and relatively intense interaction with providers when face-to-face and multiple tasks must be accomplished in that brief encounter (see Figure 16.1).

Since conventional approaches to increasing patients' involvement in care have been noted to be personnel intensive, some have called for "automated hovering" using health information technology to intervene to ensure adherence to treatment plans in the 5,000 hours space (Asch et al., 2012). A number of studies of mobile technology and social media to support disease self-management, reduce health risk behaviors, and improve adherence to treatment plans have been developed and tested in a broad array of patient populations (Hamine et al., 2015; Ong et al.,

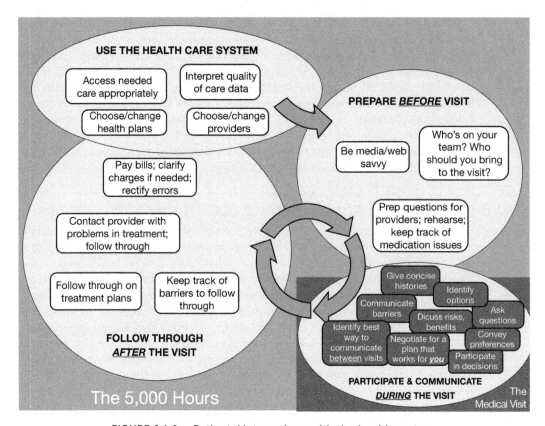

FIGURE 16.1 – Patients' interactions with the health system.

2016) with mixed results. Although the health care system and its personnel must play a pivotal role, technological outreach to patients during the 5,000+ hours when they are not "under care" must be considered as an important element for a more integrated "patienthood skills training" program to be successful.

Myths and Barriers to Patient Involvement in Care

The success of a comprehensive patienthood skills training program must overcome or at least address a number of prevailing and well-documented myths and barriers to patient participation in care. We have provided some relatively prevalent examples and some countervailing empirical evidence in Table 16.3. One prominent myth is that patients are too poorly educated to participate in care. Although a number of studies document an inverse relationship between patients' educational status and actual participation in care (Kaplan et al., 2013; Kaplan, Gandek, Greenfield, Rogers, & Ware, 1995; S. K. Smith, Dixon, Trevena, Nutbeam, & McCaffery, 2009; S. G. Smith et al., 2016), and interventions to address disparities in participation in care are not widespread (Kaplan et al., 2013), there is some evidence that, when successful, such interventions may have a more substantial impact on the health outcomes of less well-educated patients (Greenfield et al., 1985, 1988, 2014; Kaplan, Billimek, Sorkin, Ngo-Metzger, & Greenfield, 2010). Furthermore, patient behavior, such as bringing questions to office visits, may be more important to active participation in care than educational status or health literacy (Kaphingst et al., 2014).

Prevailing Myths	Reality
TABLE 16.3 – Prevailing Myths and Barriers to Patient Participation in Care	
• Patients are too poorly educated to participate in care	• While poor, less well-educated patients have been observed to participate less in care (Kaplan et al., 1995, 2013; S. K. Smith et al., 2009; S. G. Smith et al., 2016), efforts to improve participation often have more substantial impact in this group (Greenfield et al., 2014).
• Patients don't want to participate in care	• There is a substantial body of evidence that the majority of patients *do* want to participate (Chewning et al., 2012) and while some do not, the consequences of lack of participation for that subgroup may be suboptimal (Kaplan, Dukes, Sullivan, Tripp, & Greenfield, 1996; Kaplan et al., 2013).
• Patient participation in care will lengthen office visits	• Patient participation in care does require office visits of a certain length (e.g., 20 min; Burton et al., 2010; Dugdale, Epstein, & Pantilat, 1999; Jefferson et al., 2013; Kaplan et al., 1995). However, interventions to improve patient participation did not appear to lengthen office visits (Kaplan et al., 1995).
• Encouraging patients to participate in care will make them "difficult" patients	• There is no empirical support for this notion. Conversely, patients who felt poorly informed about their care were more likely to sue their providers (Huntington & Kuhn, 2003; Levinson, Roter, Mullooly, Dull, & Frankel, 1997).
• Training patients to participate in care is a new innovation that needs considerably more testing before being integrated into routine clinical practice	• The last 30+ years has seen a plethora of empirically tested intervention types to increase patients' involvement in various aspects of their care. There is historical evidence that we have been sharing guidelines for treatment with the public for millennia.

Another common rationale for not routinely involving all patients in care is that some patients prefer a passive role. There is a substantial body of evidence spanning a number of years, diseases and conditions, and patient populations, indicating that the majority of patients *do* want to participate in their care (Zikmund-Fisher et al., 2010). Although some patients do prefer a passive role (Arora & McHorney, 2000; Levinson et al., 2005) and individual patient preferences for an active role in care may vary over time, types of decisions and severity and types of illness or health problem or condition, to the extent that such passivity is associated with suboptimal health outcomes (Kaplan, Dukes, et al., 1996; Kaplan et al., 2013; Malik et al., 2013), it could be considered a risk factor for poor health, and, along with smoking, obesity, and lack of exercise, targeted for behavioral intervention.

A concern among providers, particularly in light of incentives to increase efficiency (and reduce the length) of outpatient visits, is that greater participation in care will require more time per patient. Some evidence suggests that office visits of less than 20 minutes in length are associated with less patient participation in care (Burton et al., 2010; Kaplan et al., 1995). However, interventions that increased patient involvement in care did not appear to lengthen office visits (Eckman et al., 1995). Another expressed concern is that promoting patient involvement in care will create "difficult patients" (Hull & Broquet, 2007; Mayer, 2008). There is no apparent empirical support for this relationship. However, there is evidence for a link between poorly informed patients (who did not actively participate in care) and lawsuits (Huntington & Kuhn, 2003; Levinson et al., 1997).

Finally, some resistance to including patients as active participants in their care is based on the notion that this role represents a relatively new concept that warrants considerably more testing before it becomes part of routine clinical practice. As noted earlier, the past three decades have produced a considerable body of work documenting the effects of an active role in their care across a range of outcomes, health care settings, diseases, and patient populations. Furthermore, there is historical evidence that guidelines for managing diseases have been shared with the public for centuries. Following is an excerpt from Leviticus 13:1–59, describing in detail what to expect for the management of leprosy. We have used the text to generate a branching flow diagram or algorithm for treatment (Figure 16.2). This same branching algorithm has served as the cornerstone of guideline development for sharing with patients to increase their participation in treatment decisions in a number of studies in chronic disease (Greenfield et al., 1985, 1988, 2014).

Leviticus Chapter 13 וַיִּקְרָא
א. וַיְדַבֵּר יְהוָה, אֶל-מֹשֶׁה וְאֶל-אַהֲרֹן לֵאמֹר.	**1** And the LORD spoke unto Moses and unto Aaron, saying:
ב אָדָם, כִּי-יִהְיֶה בְעוֹר-בְּשָׂרוֹ שְׂאֵת אוֹ-סַפַּחַת אוֹ בַהֶרֶת, וְהָיָה בְעוֹר-בְּשָׂרוֹ, לְנֶגַע צָרָעַת--וְהוּבָא אֶל-אַהֲרֹן הַכֹּהֵן, אוֹ אֶל-אַחַד מִבָּנָיו הַכֹּהֲנִים.	**2** When a man shall have in the skin of his flesh a rising, or a scab, or a bright spot, and it become in the skin of his flesh the plague of leprosy, then he shall be brought unto Aaron the priest, or unto one of his sons the priests.
ג וְרָאָה הַכֹּהֵן אֶת-הַנֶּגַע בְּעוֹר-הַבָּשָׂר וְשֵׂעָר בַּנֶּגַע הָפַךְ לָבָן, וּמַרְאֵה הַנֶּגַע עָמֹק מֵעוֹר בְּשָׂרוֹ--נֶגַע צָרַעַת, הוּא; וְרָאָהוּ הַכֹּהֵן, וְטִמֵּא אֹתוֹ.	**3** And the priest shall look upon the plague in the skin of the flesh; and if the hair in the plague be turned white, and the appearance of the plague be deeper than the skin of his flesh, it is the plague of leprosy; and the priest shall look on him, and pronounce him unclean.
ד וְאִם-בַּהֶרֶת לְבָנָה הִוא בְּעוֹר בְּשָׂרוֹ, וְעָמֹק אֵין-מַרְאֶהָ מִן-הָעוֹר, וּשְׂעָרָה, לֹא-הָפַךְ לָבָן--וְהִסְגִּיר הַכֹּהֵן אֶת-הַנֶּגַע, שִׁבְעַת יָמִים.	**4** And if the bright spot be white in the skin of his flesh, and the appearance thereof be not deeper than the skin, and the hair thereof be not turned white, then the priest shall shut up him that hath the plague seven days.
ה וְרָאָהוּ הַכֹּהֵן, בַּיּוֹם הַשְּׁבִיעִי, וְהִנֵּה הַנֶּגַע עָמַד בְּעֵינָיו, לֹא-פָשָׂה הַנֶּגַע בָּעוֹר--וְהִסְגִּירוֹ הַכֹּהֵן שִׁבְעַת יָמִים, שֵׁנִית.	**5** And the priest shall look on him the seventh day; and, behold, if the plague stay in its appearance, and the plague be not spread in the skin, then the priest shall shut him up seven days more.
ו וְרָאָה הַכֹּהֵן אֹתוֹ בַּיּוֹם הַשְּׁבִיעִי, שֵׁנִית, וְהִנֵּה כֵּהָה הַנֶּגַע, וְלֹא-פָשָׂה הַנֶּגַע בָּעוֹר--וְטִהֲרוֹ הַכֹּהֵן מִסְפַּחַת הִיא, וְכִבֶּס בְּגָדָיו וְטָהֵר.	**6** And the priest shall look on him again the seventh day; and, behold, if the plague be dim, and the plague be not spread in the skin, then the priest shall pronounce him clean: it is a scab; and he shall wash his clothes, and be clean.

There are a number of other barriers to the implementation of a comprehensive program to enhance patient involvement in care (see Table 16.4). Certainly, there are some patients—for example, older patients, men, the poor, and less well-educated—who may require additional resources to become more active participants in their care. Similarly, there are some physicians with fewer participatory decision-making styles (e.g., male physicians, specialists), who may also require training or preparation to encourage patient involvement in care. In fact, in order to successfully communicate risk–benefit information to patients, physicians may themselves require training to improve their "risk literacy." There also appears to be a misperception among physicians regarding patient preferences for involvement in treatment decisions, as noted earlier, along with the perception that

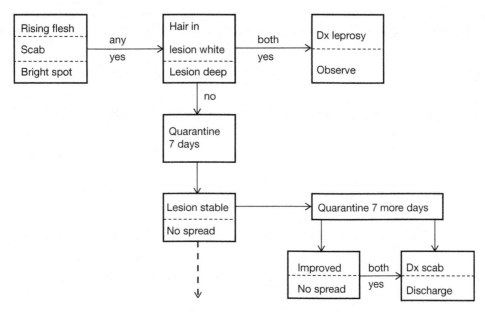

FIGURE 16.2 – An early algorithm.

TABLE 16.4 – Other Barriers to Patient Participation in Care

Barriers	References
• Patient demographics (older patients, men) associated with fewer participation in care	Arora et al. (2009); Kaplan et al. (1995); Ryan and Sysko (2007); S. G. Smith et al. (2016)
• Physician demographics (male providers, specialists) associated with fewer participatory styles	Kaplan, Greenfield, Gandek, Rogers, and Ware (1996); Roter and Hall (2004); Sandhu, Adams, Singleton, Clark-Carter, and Kidd (2009)
• Physician incentives (e.g., relative value limits) to increase outpatient efficiency (and reduce length of visits)	
• Physician perceptions (e.g., patient preferences for passive role; lack of patient preparation for participation; patient incapacity to participate)	Gigerenzer et al. (2007); Kaplan, Greenfield, et al. (1996); Mühlbacher and Juhnke (2013); Roter et al. (1995); Stalmeier et al. (2007); Tunzi (2001); Zikmund-Fisher et al. (2010)
• Lack of adequate physician preparation/training to encourage/stimulate patient involvement in care (e.g., poor risk–benefit understanding and communication skills)	Wegwarth, Schwartz, Woloshin, Gaissmaier, and Gigerenzer (2012)
• Lack of available evidence supporting treatment efficacy for subgroups of patients to tailor care appropriateness	Kreuter, Farrell, Olevitch, and Brennan (1999); Müller-Engelmann et al. (2013)
• Lack of trustworthy sources of health and health care information and how to use it for patients to make effective decisions	Hibbard, Slovic, Peters, and Finucane (2002); Madathil, Rivera-Rodriguez, Greenstein, and Gramopadhye (2015)
• Poor presentation of health and health care information (complex language, not available when needed, poor format)	Gigerenzer et al. (2007); Peters et al. (2007)

(continued)

TABLE 16.4 – Other Barriers to Patient Participation in Care (*continued*)	
Barriers	**References**
• Lack of adequate patient training in interrelated skills (e.g., numeracy, weighing of risks–benefits, being media savvy, recognizing decisions, effective communication with provider skills)	Cooper, Beach, and Clever (2005); Edwards et al. (2000); Edwards et al. (2008); Hibbard, Peters, et al. (2007); Higgins and Begoray (2013); Jolls and Wilson (2014); Kim et al. (2013); Kravitz et al. (2005); Reyna, Nelson, Han, and Dieckmann (2009); Schwartz and Woloshin (2011); Trevena et al. (2013); West et al. (2013)

patients do not have the capacity to participate effectively and that evaluating that capacity would require considerable effort, reducing practice efficiency (Tunzi, 2001). Certainly the lack of available evidence from studies of heterogeneity of treatment effects to support physicians' discussions with patients of the risks and benefits of specific treatments in order to tailor appropriate care is a considerable barrier to effective patient participation in care. However, some evidence suggests that it is when evidence is limited that physicians are more inclusive of patients' participation (Müller-Engelmann et al., 2013).

Other barriers to care are more systemic. The lack of trustworthy sources of health and health care information and how to use it effectively in health care decision making represents a significant problem. Even when information is available, the use of complex language, poor formatting, and barriers to timely access compromise the utility of such information to patients when making health care decisions. Finally, the current spectrum of interventions to improve patient participation in care is fragmented and does not adequately address the interrelated nature of the skills needed by patients across the array of tasks they must perform to be maximally effective users of health care. What is needed is a comprehensive, integrated training program, delivered by trusted sources, tailored to the individual patient's skills deficits, and delivered using innovative methods to support health care decisions in real time. We discuss the elements of that program in the next section.

A number of researchers have proposed conceptual models linking patient involvement in care and its potential outcomes, covariates, mediators, and moderators (Kaplan et al., 2013; Longtin et al., 2010; Shay & Lafata, 2014). The model we would propose linking the comprehensive patienthood skills training program with health outcomes, patient experience, and efficient use of health care is based on integration of the mastery model of health and illness (Roepke & Grant, 2011; Rotter, 1982; Seeman, 1991; Seeman & Seeman, 1983) on which we have based our previous work, along with related social psychological theories on the consequences of powerlessness, autonomy, and participation in decisions on decision-related follow-through (see Figure 16.3). Grounded in social learning theory (Rotter, 1982), the mastery model asserts that people will take action to improve outcomes they value, based on their perceptions of a contingent relationship between their actions and those outcomes. With this model, we have integrated social psychological theories positing that individuals will be more likely to follow through on the consequences of decisions in which they feel they have participated versus those dictated by some external source (Bacharach, 1980; Miserandino, 2000). That is, a more active role during visits with their physicians, coupled with a sense that they have participated in treatment decisions, and greater "risk and health system literacy" may increase patients' disease/condition

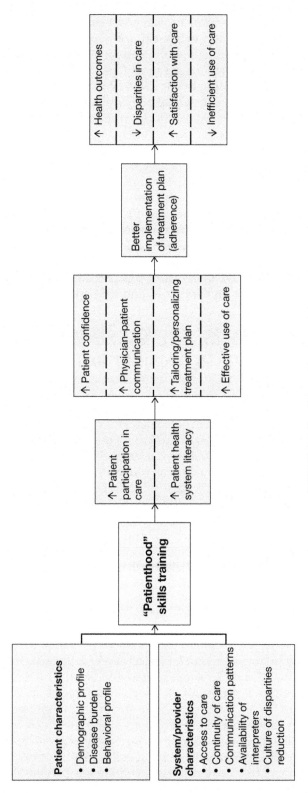

FIGURE 16.3 – Conceptual model.

management confidence, improve physician–patient communication, and improve the personalizing of the treatment plan and thereby maximize the effectiveness of care. These attitudes and behaviors are hypothesized to enhance patients' commitment to follow-through on the treatment plan and may combine to produce actual follow-through on treatment plans, together with other health-enhancing behaviors, leading to improved health outcomes.

In summary, there is a substantial body of literature suggesting that training patients in the various elements of effective patienthood as described earlier leads to improved health outcomes, better patient experience, and higher efficiencies in the use of health services. Much of the research, particularly on shared or participatory decision making, has focused on patients with chronic diseases (Balaban et al., 2015; Greenfield et al., 1988; Kaplan et al., 2013; Thom et al., 2013), since these patients tend to use more health care services, interact more frequently with health care providers, and are handicapped by quality of care gaps, all of which are well documented. There is some evidence that involvement of pregnant patients in decision making improves decision-making confidence (Vlemmix et al., 2013), active responsibility of personal and infant health (Harrison, Kushner, Benzies, Rempel, & Kimak, 2003), more rapid postpartum recovery (Green & Baston, 2003), and less postpartum depression and stress (Jomeen, 2004).

RECOMMENDATIONS: THE CASE FOR A COMPREHENSIVE PLANNED PATIENTHOOD PROGRAM

There is now an extensive body of evidence supporting the relationship of patient participation in care to positive outcomes. However, most intervention programs have targeted individual or small clusters of patienthood skills. We think it is now time to create, from the most effective elements of these programs, a comprehensive, multicomponent integrated intervention strategy to help patients improve their ability to be active participants in all of the tasks they must perform to be effective users and evaluators of the health care system, or "health care system literate." The components of such a program, which could be completed over time in different combinations as needed, include training in effective participation in care, effective communication, health insurance literacy, risk literacy/numeracy, media literacy, and quality of care data literacy. Specific skills associated with each component, based on the literature in each area, are summarized in Table 16.5.

Participation in Care

The elements of effective patient participation in treatment decisions have been well described (Elwyn et al., 2012; Fowler, Levin, & Sepucha, 2011; Garber, Abrahamson, Barzilay, Blonde, & Bloomgarden, 2015; Sakala & Corry, 2008; Transforming Maternity Care Symposium Steering Committee et al., 2010; Transforming Maternity Care Vision Team et al., 2010). Treatment algorithms or clinical guidelines, including multiple treatment options at key nodes to account for variations in patient preferences and conditions without compromising quality of care, could serve as the evidence base for specific treatment decisions. This could ensure tailoring of treatment plans to accommodate patients' life circumstances. Algorithms or treatment guidelines could be used to guide patient focus on

TABLE 16.5 – Overall "Health Systems Literacy": Planned Patienthood Skills Training Intervention Components

Concept	Specific Skills

Participation in care	• How to recognize decisions (e.g., to do or not to do):
	    ○ Lab tests, medications, procedures (e.g., ultrasounds)
	• How to elicit options for decisions (e.g.):
	    ○ What other tests might be done (or not done)?
	    ○ What other medications might be ordered?
	    ○ Are there behavioral options?
	• How to discuss pros/cons (or benefits/harms) of each option (e.g.):
	    ○ Risks associated with tests; why tests are needed
	    ○ Side effects of medications
	    ○ Risks associated with <u>not</u> having the test or procedure
	• Stating personal preferences:
	    ○ Include personal barriers to follow-through on any of the proposed options
	• Understanding provider preferences:
	    ○ Getting the provider rationale for proposed treatment
	• Negotiation if provider/patient preferences differ:
	    ○ Engaging providers in proposing short-term compromises with appropriated monitoring
	    ○ Understanding any value conflicts
	    ○ Reviewing outcome of negotiated compromise

Effective communication	• Asking specific, targeted questions:
	    ○ Avoiding vague language
	    ○ Direct questions vs. "I heard that . . ."
	    ○ Asking most important questions first:
	        □ Examples: What is the test for? How many times have you done this procedure? When will I get the results? Why do I need this treatment? Are there any alternatives? What are the possible complications? How do you spell the name of that drug? Are there any side effects? Will this medicine interact with medicines that I am already taking?
	• Giving concise history:
	    ○ Summarizing problems, progress/changes since last visit
	    ○ Advance preparation, rehearsal
	    ○ Recording questions, issues, concerns in real time

Health insurance literacy	• How to evaluate health plan benefits/coverage and compare • How to evaluate and compare premiums • How to understand "out-of-pocket" costs (copays, deductibles, annual caps) • Understanding formularies, provider networks, covered services • Negotiating/appealing health insurance claims

Risk communication/ numeracy literacy	• Understanding numbers, statistics:
	    ○ Basics (percentages, proportions, ratios, etc.)
	    ○ Credible sources for health statistics for consumers
	• Understanding basic concepts of risk:
	    ○ Absolute vs. relative risks, risk reduction; applying risks to specific groups
	• Understanding basic concepts of benefits/harms:
	    ○ Size/importance of benefits of different treatment options
	    ○ Evaluating harms (e.g., side effects, severity); weighing benefits vs. harms

Media literacy	• Media literacy in health care concepts (Higgins & Begoray, 2013; Jolls & Wilson, 2014):
	    ○ Authorship: Who created the message?
	    ○ Format: What creative techniques are used to attract attention?
	    ○ Audience: How to tell if you are the target audience; how might different people understand the message differently?
	    ○ Content: What points of view are represented in or omitted from the message?
	    ○ Purpose: Why is the message being sent? What is being marketed?
	• "Spinning" results to the public; credibility of the message:
	    ○ Use of unrepresentative anecdotes
	    ○ Exaggerating what is good (benefits), while minimizing what is bad

Quality of care data literacy	• Understand where to find quality report card data • Understand how to read and interpret report card data • Understand how to compare different providers and health plans

decisions likely to arise on specific office visits and prepare them in advance of visits to think about questions, treatment options, risk–benefit tradeoffs, and personal preferences related to life circumstances that would guide a more effective discussion with their doctors during those visits.

Effective Doctor–Patient Communication

A systematic review of risk communication and decision-making interventions highlighted the importance of "co-interventions" as equally if not more important than informational or educational components alone (Edwards et al., 2008). Helping patients effectively communicate any "life context barriers" to optimal implementation of treatment plans would be another key intervention component (Billimek, Guzman, & Angulo, 2015). Another key component of effective communication would require patients to identify and prepare questions to be asked for upcoming encounters with providers, training in effective question asking (including repeating the question if the response by the provider was unclear or inadequate), and techniques for overcoming barriers to communication (including embarrassment, interruptions, and so forth) and barriers to effective implementation of the treatment plan (including costs of medications).

Health Insurance Literacy

In a recent expert roundtable of the Consumers Union and academic partners, health insurance literacy was defined as individuals having the "knowledge, ability, and confidence to find and evaluate information about health plans, select the best plan for his or her family for their own or their family's financial and health circumstances, and use the plan once enrolled" (Consumers Union, 2012).

> Current programs aimed at improving individuals' understanding of health insurance coverage include Choosing Healthplans All Together (CHAT), a program that has been widely tested nationally and internationally (Goold et al., 2005) and modified for use in computer-based (Danis, Ginsburg, & Goold, 2010) and web-based exercises (www.usechat.org), along with websites to support patient choice of plans.

Systematic training provided by trusted sources in how to use health plans, how to challenge disallowed reimbursements, and so forth, is not widely available (Cox & Slepian, 2013; Hibbard et al., 2002; Kim et al., 2013), but should be developed as a key element of the comprehensive patienthood skills training program.

Risk Literacy/Numeracy

In a recent article, it was noted about health literacy that "when demands exceed the requisite skills, patients may feel overwhelmed and retreat into silence or stop actively participating in their own care" (Yeh, 2014, p. 1413). As noted earlier, low health literacy has been associated with poorer medical decision making, poorer health outcomes, and less efficient use of the health care system in systematic reviews (Berkman, Sheridan, Donahue, Halpern, & Crotty, 2011; Reyna et al., 2009). A number of recommendations have been made for the improvement of risk literacy and numeracy (Gigerenzer et al., 2007; Gigerenzer & Gray, 2013; Paling, 2006;

Trevena et al., 2013). Some interventions are currently available. For example, Drs. Woloshin and Schwartz have developed a resource primer, *Know Your Chances* (Woloshin et al., 2008), that has been used in a variety of settings and in librarian-facilitating book clubs. In two trials, adults with high or low socioeconomic status (SES) subjects were randomly assigned to receive a primer about understanding risk or a general health booklet. In both SES groups, adults receiving the primer more often passed a medical data interpretation test than did those receiving the general health booklet. They also expressed greater interest in medical statistics but not greater confidence in interpreting statistics, and most rated the primer helpful or very helpful (Woloshin et al., 2007). A risk literacy/numeracy training module would be another key and interrelated component of the planned patienthood program.

Media Literacy

The core concepts of media literacy have been well articulated (Higgins & Begoray, 2013; Jolls & Wilson, 2014; Potter, 2004) and include the ability to identify authorship of a message and the format of the message (creative techniques used), identify the target audience, identify the content being represented, and identify the purpose of the message. These skills should be reflected in a media literacy training module and were key elements of Dr. Kravitz and colleagues' randomized controlled trials of direct-to-consumer advertising of antidepressant medications and of a tailored interactive multimedia computer program (IMCP) to improve care for depressed patients (Kravitz et al., 2005, 2013).

Quality of Care Data Literacy

Randomized trials of varying formats for the presentation of quality of care data underscore the importance of format and presentation to ensure informed, active choices between health care providers (Elbel, Gillespie, & Raven, 2014; Fasolo, Reutskaja, Dixon, & Boyce, 2010; Hibbard, Greene, & Daniel, 2010; Hibbard et al., 2002), particularly for vulnerable subgroups of the population. Using the best presentation principles identified from the literature (Hibbard & Peters, 2003), training in the understanding and use of quality data for identifying and choosing the best available care for specific health problems, diseases, or conditions as a key skills training module should be integrated with other skills training modules into the comprehensive planned patienthood skills training program.

CONSOLIDATING THE MULTICOMPONENT PLANNED PATIENTHOOD PROGRAM: TRAINING IN HEALTH SYSTEM LITERACY

In order to be maximally effective, these training modules must be tailored to individual patient needs and circumstances, administered in a timely way, maintained and vetted by trusted sources, and presented in a way that allows rapid understanding and uptake by individuals—a tall order. But not impossible. And especially not if we use existing innovations in messaging, game strategy, animation, risk communication, and so forth, used in advertising other industries and adapted for health care, or create innovative content and new delivery methods specific to the needs of the patienthood skills training program.

Patients almost certainly do not need access to all components of the program at all times. For example, individuals do not change health plans frequently; most commonly they do so when they move, or when employer offerings or personal circumstances change, and then during annual open enrollment periods. A rational approach to tailoring the administration of the components of the program would include an initial comprehensive evaluation of "skills deficits" along with patient priorities for appropriate training modules, along with a more abbreviated, regularly updated skills assessment, both to evaluate progress and to revise patient priorities for training.

Patients who have regular contact with the health care system may be ideal first targets of an integrated training program, outlined in the following section ("Sustainability"), because they will have numerous opportunities to practice the patienthood skills they learn. Pregnant women face a number of treatment decisions during prenatal care, for which they could repeatedly practice and rehearse learned patienthood skills. They also face often serious decisions during the rapidly changing labor and delivery period for which they need to be prepared. Furthermore, after delivery, they must interact successfully with the health care system as caregiver for their infants. Such patients, along with those who have chronic diseases, could be the early focus of the consolidated program.

SUSTAINABILITY

Practically, to be implemented as national policy and routine practice, this training program would need a number of parallel initiatives to succeed. First, as noted earlier, physicians are not systematically and adequately trained themselves in many skills (e.g., risk communication/numeracy, distilling evidence, negotiating with patients, and so forth; Gigerenzer et al., 2007). Corresponding training for physicians in this area is the need for them to be an effective partner for patients in providing tailored, optimally effective care. Second, better data are needed on subgroups of patients who could differentially benefit from new or existing treatments. The Patient-Centered Outcomes Research Institute, with its emphasis on designing research to investigate heterogeneity of treatment effects, may help to propagate comparative effectiveness data to expand the evidence base in this area. Third, payers need to play an active role in supporting the effective and comprehensive training of patients in the skills outlined earlier. The efficiencies gained by more active patient participation in care that have been documented to date (Greene & Hibbard, 2012; Greenfield et al., 1988; Polsky, Keating, Weeks, & Schulman, 2002) could be enhanced by an even more comprehensive program. Those efficiencies could offset the costs associated with implementing the program and ensure its sustainability by such mechanisms as premium reductions and the like. Finally, as suggested in part by Fowler et al. (2011), making the presence of such a program part of a routine, health care system-wide quality assessment, with associated reimbursement incentives, is another potential mechanism for making sure that the program is implemented and maintained.

THE FUTURE

Where to from here? It is always easy to call for more research, a basic tenet of academia. But while studying improvements in care has now been endorsed as part of the learning health care system (M. Smith et al., 2013), we have now amassed more than 30 years of evidence that supports patients' involvement in care for multiple health conditions, for multiple patient populations, in multiple treatment settings, in more multiple aspects of health care delivery, and more recently in quality and safety programs. And we still do not have a national policy supporting such a program (Fowler et al., 2011). It is much more difficult to make major innovations, often radical departures from current practice, and watch what happens. Restructuring the health care system to involve patients from the design of health care delivery (including telemedicine, "virtual" practice, simulations not only to teach physicians but also to teach patients) to the design of new medications (Wicks et al., 2015), the design of health benefits, and the design of new measures to evaluate the effectiveness of health care, will require a concerted and committed effort in order to change patient-centered medicine from a slogan or "empty ritual" (Arnstein, 1969) to routine practice (Elwyn et al., 2012; Fowler et al., 2011; O'Connor et al., 2007).

CONCLUSION

We have reviewed the barriers to implementing interventions to support the inclusion of patients in their care. They are daunting and resilient. To make the transformation from a health care system designed by and for providers, to one made with and for patients, will require a culture change, or, more realistically, a seismic paradigm shift. To fully integrate patients in their care from how it is delivered and by whom, to how it is used and evaluated, we will have to redefine what it means to be a patient—not only the rights but also the responsibilities associated with effective patienthood. In a fully participatory health care system, for example, there should be sharing of responsibility for the outcomes of care, both good and bad. We will have to address whose care is being evaluated with patients who are full participants. Also, what happens with "e-Care," telemedicine, and "facility-free" health care environments?

It is now possible to reach patients in the 5,000 hours using advances in technology and innovations in the delivery of interventions (e.g., videogames, creative apps, and so forth), to model new health care behaviors, and to generate new evidence rapidly capturing data from a variety of different sources (Berger, Mamdani, Atkins, & Johnson, 2009; D'Avolio, Farwell, & Fiore, 2010; Ohmann & Kuchinke, 2009; Sarkar, 2010; Sox & Greenfield, 2009). Some think we have reached the "tipping point" for the creation of an informed, actively participating patient population (O'Connor et al., 2007). We should create a comprehensive program for optimizing patient training in the skills they need to be effective partners and participants in their care. We should start the training in childhood (Bond, 2009; Kaplan, 1999; Levin-Zamir, Lemish, & Gofin, 2011; Primack et al., 2012). And we should start it now.

CASE STUDY

Provide one example of each outcome measure listed in Table 16.6. Consider the prevailing myths set forth in Table 16.7. Why are they considered myths? What realities does the research show to rebut the myth?

(continued)

CASE STUDY (*continued*)

TABLE 16.6 – Relationships of Greater Patient Participation in Care to Health Behaviors, Outcomes, and Patient Experience

Outcome Measures

- More participation in preventive screening
- Better health habits (more exercise, less smoking, less obesity, less substance abuse)
- More effective self-management
- Better quality of care for chronic diseases
- Better adherence to treatment plans
- Better quality of care for mental health
- Better quality of care for cancer patients
- Safer care
- More positive experiences of care (greater satisfaction)
- Better preparation before visits, better questions during visits, awareness of treatment guidelines, openness in discussion of complementary and alternative medicine
- Greater trust in physicians
- Use of quality of care data
- Reduced hospital stays, use of emergency departments

TABLE 16.7 – Prevailing Myths and Barriers to Patient Participation in Care

Prevailing Myths

- Patients are too poorly educated to participate in care.
- Patients don't want to participate in care.
- Patient participation in care will lengthen office visits.
- Encouraging patients to participate in care will make them "difficult" patients.
- Training patients to participate in care is a new innovation that needs considerably more testing before it is integrated into routine clinical practice.

REFERENCES

Adams, D. R. J., Appleton, S., Wilson, D. H., & Ruffin, R. E. (2005). Participatory decision making, asthma action plans, and use of asthma medication: A population survey. *Journal of Asthma, 42*(8), 673–678. http://dx.doi.org/10.1080/02770900500265041

Adams, R. J., Smith, B. J., & Ruffin, R. E. (2001). Impact of the physician's participatory style in asthma outcomes and patient satisfaction. *Annals of Allergy, Asthma & Immunology: Official Publication of the American College of Allergy, Asthma, & Immunology, 86*(3), 263–271. http://dx.doi.org/10.1016/S1081-1206(10)63296–6

Adsul, P., Wray, R., Spradling, K., Darwish, O., Weaver, N., & Siddiqui, S. (2015). Systematic review of decision aids for newly diagnosed patients with prostate cancer making treatment decisions. *The Journal of Urology, 194*(5), 1247–1252. http://dx.doi.org/10.1016/j.juro.2015.05.093

Alegría, M., Sribney, W., Perez, D., Laderman, M., & Keefe, K. (2009). The role of patient activation on patient–provider communication and quality of care for US and foreign born Latino patients. *Journal of General Internal Medicine, 24*(Suppl. 3), 534–541. http://dx.doi.org/10.1007/s11606-009-1074-x

Andersen, M. R., Sweet, E., Lowe, K. A., Standish, L. J., Drescher, C. W., & Goff, B. A. (2012). Involvement in decision-making about treatment and ovarian cancer survivor quality of life. *Gynecologic Oncology, 124*(3), 465–470. http://dx.doi.org/10.1016/j.ygyno.2011.10.029

Andersen, M. R., & Urban, N. (1999). Involvement in decision-making and breast cancer survivor quality of life. *Annals of Behavioral Medicine: A Publication of the Society of Behavioral Medicine, 21*(3), 201–209.

Arnstein, S. R. (1969). A ladder of citizen participation. *Journal of the American Institute of Planners, 35*(4), 216–224. http://dx.doi.org/10.1080/01944366908977225

Arora, N. K., & McHorney, C. A. (2000). Patient preferences for medical decision making: Who really wants to participate? *Medical Care, 38*(3), 335–341.

Arora, N. K., Weaver, K. E., Clayman, M. L., Oakley-Girvan, I., & Potosky, A. L. (2009). Physicians' decision-making style and psychosocial outcomes among cancer survivors. *Patient Education and Counseling, 77*(3), 404–412. http://dx.doi.org/10.1016/j.pec.2009.10.004

Arterburn, D., Wellman, R., Westbrook, E., Rutter, C., Ross, T., McCulloch, D., . . . Jung, C. (2012). Introducing decision aids at group health was linked to sharply lower hip and knee surgery rates and costs. *Health Affairs, 31*(9), 2094–2104. http://dx.doi.org/10.1377/hlthaff.2011.0686

Asch, D. A., Muller, R. W., & Volpp, K. G. (2012). Automated hovering in health care—watching over the 5000 hours. *The New England Journal of Medicine, 367*(1), 1–3. http://dx.doi.org/10.1056/NEJMp1203869

Bacharach, S. B. (1980). *Power and politics in organizations: The social psychology of conflict, coalitions, and bargaining* (1st ed.). San Francisco, CA: Jossey-Bass.

Balaban, R. B., Galbraith, A. A., Burns, M. E., Vialle-Valentin, C. E., Larochelle, M. R., & Ross-Degnan, D. (2015). A patient navigator intervention to reduce hospital readmissions among high-risk safety-net patients: A randomized controlled trial. *Journal of General Internal Medicine, 30*(7), 907–915. http://dx.doi.org/10.1007/s11606-015-3185-x

Becker, E. R., & Roblin, D. W. (2008). Translating primary care practice climate into patient activation: The role of patient trust in physician. *Medical Care, 46*(8), 795–805. http://dx.doi.org/10.1097/MLR.0b013e31817919c0

Begum, N., Donald, M., Ozolins, I. Z., & Dower, J. (2011). Hospital admissions, emergency department utilisation and patient activation for self-management among people with diabetes. *Diabetes Research and Clinical Practice, 93*(2), 260–267. http://dx.doi.org/10.1016/j.diabres.2011.05.031

Bennett, H. D., Coleman, E. A., Parry, C., Bodenheimer, T., & Chen, E. H. (2010). Health coaching for patients with chronic illness. *Family Practice Management, 17*(5), 24–29.

Berger, M. L., Mamdani, M., Atkins, D., & Johnson, M. L. (2009). Good research practices for comparative effectiveness research: Defining, reporting and interpreting nonrandomized studies of treatment effects using secondary data sources: The ISPOR Good Research Practices for Retrospective Database Analysis Task Force Report—Part I. *Value in Health: The Journal of the International Society for Pharmacoeconomics and Outcomes Research, 12*(8), 1044–1052. http://dx.doi.org/10.1111/j.1524-4733.2009.00600.x

Berger, Z., Flickinger, T., & Dy, S. (2013). Promoting engagement by patients and families to reduce adverse events. In P. Shekelle, R. Wachter, P. Pronovost, K. Schoelles, K. McDonald, S. Dy, . . . B. Winters (Eds.), *Making health care safer II: An updated critical analysis of the evidence for patient safety practices* (pp. 351–361). Rockville, MD: Agency for Healthcare Research and Quality.

Berkman, N. D., Sheridan, S. L., Donahue, K. E., Halpern, D. J., & Crotty, K. (2011). Low health literacy and health outcomes: An updated systematic review. *Annals of Internal Medicine, 155*(2), 97–107. http://dx.doi.org/10.7326/0003-4819-155-2-201107190-00005

Billimek, J. (2016, June). *Food insecurity, housing instability and material deprivation: The epidemiology of unmet basic needs in diabetes.* Paper presented at the 76th Scientific Sessions of the American Diabetes Association, New Orleans, LA.

Billimek, J., Guzman, H., & Angulo, M. A. (2015). Effectiveness and feasibility of a software tool to help patients communicate with doctors about problems they face with their medication regimen (EMPATHy): Study protocol for a randomized controlled trial. *Trials, 16.* http://dx.doi.org/10.1186/s13063-015-0672-7

Bond, M. (2009). Decision-making: Risk school. *Nature News, 461*(7268), 1189–1192. http://dx.doi.org/10.1038/4611189a

Brom, L., Hopmans, W., Pasman, H. R. W., Timmermans, D. R., Widdershoven, G. A., & Onwuteaka-Philipsen, B. D. (2014). Congruence between patients' preferred and perceived participation in medical decision-making: A review of the literature. *BMC Medical Informatics and Decision Making, 14,* 25. http://dx.doi.org/10.1186/1472-6947-14-25

Brown, R., Butow, P. N., Boyer, M. J., & Tattersall, M. H. (1999). Promoting patient participation in the cancer consultation: Evaluation of a prompt sheet and coaching in question-asking. *British Journal of Cancer, 80*(1–2), 242–248. http://dx.doi.org/10.1038/sj.bjc.6690346

Brown, R. F., Butow, P. N., Dunn, S. M., & Tattersall, M. H. (2001). Promoting patient participation and shortening cancer consultations: A randomised trial. *British Journal of Cancer, 85*(9), 1273–1279. http://dx.doi.org/10.1054/bjoc.2001.2073

Bruera, E., Sweeney, C., Willey, J., Palmer, J. L., Tolley, S., Rosales, M., & Ripamonti, C. (2003). Breast cancer patient perception of the helpfulness of a prompt sheet versus a general information sheet during outpatient consultation: A randomized, controlled trial. *Journal of Pain and Symptom Management, 25*(5), 412–419.

Burton, D., Blundell, N., Jones, M., Fraser, A., & Elwyn, G. (2010). Shared decision-making in cardiology: Do patients want it and do doctors provide it? *Patient Education and Counseling, 80*(2), 173–179. http://dx.doi.org/10.1016/j.pec.2009.10.013

Butow, P. N., Brown, R. F., Cogar, S., Tattersall, M. H. N., & Dunn, S. M. (2002). Oncologists' reactions to cancer patients' verbal cues. *Psycho-oncology, 11*(1), 47–58.

Cegala, D. J., McClure, L., Marinelli, T. M., & Post, D. M. (2000). The effects of communication skills training on patients' participation during medical interviews. *Patient Education and Counseling, 41*(2), 209–222.

Cegala, D. J., & Post, D. M. (2009). The impact of patients' participation on physicians' patient-centered communication. *Patient Education and Counseling, 77*(2), 202–208. http://dx.doi.org/10.1016/j.pec.2009.03.025

Chan, J. C. N., Ozaki, R., Luk, A., Kong, A. P. S., Ma, R. C. W., Chow, F. C. C., . . . JADE Collaborative Study Group. (2014). Delivery of integrated diabetes care using logistics and information technology—the Joint Asia Diabetes Evaluation (JADE) program. *Diabetes Research and Clinical Practice, 106*(Suppl. 2), S295–S304. http://dx.doi.org/10.1016/S0168-8227(14)70733-8

Chewning, B., Bylund, C. L., Shah, B., Arora, N. K., Gueguen, J. A., & Makoul, G. (2012). Patient preferences for shared decisions: A systematic review. *Patient Education and Counseling, 86*(1), 9–18. http://dx.doi.org/10.1016/j.pec.2011.02.004

Choi, S. E., Ngo-Metzger, Q., Billimek, J., Greenfield, S., Kaplan, S. H., & Sorkin, D. H. (2015). Contributors to patients' ratings of quality of care among ethnically diverse patients with type 2 diabetes. *Journal of Immigrant and Minority Health/Center for Minority Public Health, 18*(2), 382–389. http://dx.doi.org/10.1007/s10903-015-0173-5

Clayman, M. L., Bylund, C. L., Chewning, B., & Makoul, G. (2016). The impact of patient participation in health decisions within medical encounters: A systematic review. *Medical Decision Making, 36*(4), 427–452. http://dx.doi.org/10.1177/0272989X15613530

Clement, S., Ibrahim, S., Crichton, N., Wolf, M., & Rowlands, G. (2009). Complex interventions to improve the health of people with limited literacy: A systematic review. *Patient Education and Counseling, 75*(3), 340–351. http://dx.doi.org/10.1016/j.pec.2009.01.008

Clever, S. L., Ford, D. E., Rubenstein, L. V., Rost, K. M., Meredith, L. S., Sherbourne, C. D., . . . Cooper, L. A. (2006). Primary care patients' involvement in decision-making is associated with improvement in depression. *Medical Care, 44*(5), 398–405. http://dx.doi.org/10.1097/01.mlr.0000208117.15531.da

Consumers Union. (2012). Measuring health insurance literacy: A call to action. Retrieved from http://consumersunion.org/wp-content/uploads/2013/03/Health_Insurance_Literacy_Roundtable_rpt.pdf

Cooper, L., Beach, M., & Clever, S. (2005). Participatory decision-making in the medical encounter and its relationship to patient literacy. In J. Schwartzberg, J. VanGeest, & C. Wang (Eds.), *Understanding health literacy: Implications for medicine and public health* (pp. 141–154). Chicago, IL: AMA Press.

Coulter, A., & Ellins, J. (2006). *Patient-focused interventions: A review of the evidence.* London, UK: The Health Foundation.

Cox, J. B., & Slepian, M. (2013, August 27). Half of U.S. adults fail "Health Insurance 101." Retrieved from http://www.aicpa.org/press/pressreleases/2013/pages/us-adults-fail-health-insurance-101-aicpa-survey.aspx

Danis, M., Ginsburg, M., & Goold, S. (2010). Experience in the United States with public deliberation about health insurance benefits using the small group decision exercise, CHAT. *The Journal of Ambulatory Care Management, 33*(3), 205–214. http://dx.doi.org/10.1097/JAC.0b013e3181e56340

D'Avolio, L. W., Farwell, W. R., & Fiore, L. D. (2010). Comparative effectiveness research and medical informatics. *American Journal of Medicine, 123*(12), e32–e37. http://dx.doi.org/10.1016/j.amjmed.2010.10.006

Dayer, L., Heldenbrand, S., Anderson, P., Gubbins, P. O., & Martin, B. C. (2013). Smartphone medication adherence apps: Potential benefits to patients and providers. *Journal of the American Pharmacists Association, 53*(2), 172–181.

Deen, D., Lu, W.-H., Rothstein, D., Santana, L., & Gold, M. R. (2011). Asking questions: The effect of a brief intervention in community health centers on patient activation. *Patient Education and Counseling, 84*(2), 257–260. http://dx.doi.org/10.1016/j.pec.2010.07.026

Definition of patient. (n.d.). Retrieved from http://www.medicinenet.com/script/main/art.asp?articlekey=39154

de Jongh, T., Gurol-Urganci, I., Vodopivec-Jamsek, V., Car, J., & Atun, R. (2012). Mobile phone messaging for facilitating self-management of long-term illnesses. *Cochrane Database of Systematic Reviews, 12*, CD007459. http://dx.doi.org/10.1002/14651858.CD007459.pub2

Dugdale, D. C., Epstein, R., & Pantilat, S. Z. (1999). Time and the patient-physician relationship. *Journal of General Internal Medicine, 14*(Suppl. 1), S34–S40.

Eckman, M. H., Greenfield, S., Mackey, W. C., Wong, J. B., Kaplan, S., Sullivan, L., . . . Pauker, S. G. (1995). Foot infections in diabetic patients. Decision and cost-effectiveness analyses. *Journal of the American Medical Association, 273*(9), 712–720.

Edwards, A., Gray, J., Clarke, A., Dundon, J., Elwyn, G., Gaff, C., . . . Thornton, H. (2008). Interventions to improve risk communication in clinical genetics: Systematic review. *Patient Education and Counseling, 71*(1), 4–25. http://dx.doi.org/10.1016/j.pec.2007.11.026

Edwards, A., Hood, K., Matthews, E., Russell, D., Russell, I., Barker, J., . . . Stott, N. (2000). The effectiveness of one-to-one risk communication interventions in health care: A systematic review. *Medical Decision Making: An International Journal of the Society for Medical Decision Making, 20*(3), 290–297.

Elbel, B., Gillespie, C., & Raven, M. C. (2014). Presenting quality data to vulnerable groups: Charts, summaries or behavioral economic nudges? *Journal of Health Services Research & Policy, 19*(3), 161–168. http://dx.doi.org/10.1177/1355819614524186

Elwyn, G., Frosch, D., Thomson, R., Joseph-Williams, N., Lloyd, A., Kinnersley, P., . . . Barry, M. (2012). Shared decision making: A model for clinical practice. *Journal of General Internal Medicine, 27*(10), 1361–1367. http://dx.doi.org/10.1007/s11606-012-2077-6

Falagas, M. E., Korbila, I. P., Giannopoulou, K. P., Kondilis, B. K., & Peppas, G. (2009). Informed consent: How much and what do patients understand? *American Journal of Surgery, 198*(3), 420–435. http://dx.doi.org/10.1016/j.amjsurg.2009.02.010

Fasolo, B., Reutskaja, E., Dixon, A., & Boyce, T. (2010). Helping patients choose: How to improve the design of comparative scorecards of hospital quality. *Patient Education and Counseling, 78*(3), 344–349. http://dx.doi.org/10.1016/j.pec.2010.01.009

Fowler, F. J., Levin, C. A., & Sepucha, K. R. (2011). Informing and involving patients to improve the quality of medical decisions. *Health Affairs, 30*(4), 699–706. http://dx.doi.org/10.1377/hlthaff.2011.0003

Free, C., Phillips, G., Galli, L., Watson, L., Felix, L., Edwards, P., . . . Haines, A. (2013). The effectiveness of mobile-health technology-based health behaviour change or disease management interventions for health care consumers: A systematic review. *PLOS Medicine, 10*(1), e1001362. http://dx.doi.org/10.1371/journal.pmed.1001362

Frosch, D. L., Rincon, D., Ochoa, S., & Mangione, C. M. (2010). Activating seniors to improve chronic disease care: Results from a pilot intervention study. *Journal of the American Geriatrics Society, 58*(8), 1496–1503. http://dx.doi.org/10.1111/j.1532-5415.2010.02980.x

Galliher, J. M., Post, D. M., Weiss, B. D., Dickinson, L. M., Manning, B. K., Staton, E. W., . . . Pace, W. D. (2010). Patients' question-asking behavior during primary care visits: A report from the AAFP National Research Network. *Annals of Family Medicine, 8*(2), 151–159. http://dx.doi.org/10.1370/afm.1055

Garber, A. J., Abrahamson, M. J., Barzilay, J. I., Blonde, L., & Bloomgarden, Z. T. (2015). AACE/ACE comprehensive diabetes management algorithm. *Endocrinology Practice,* (21), 438–447.

Genoff, M. C., Zaballa, A., Gany, F., Gonzalez, J., Ramirez, J., Jewell, S. T., & Diamond, L. C. (2016). Navigating language barriers: A systematic review of patient navigators' impact on cancer screening for limited English proficient patients. *Journal of General Internal Medicine, 31*(4), 426–434. http://dx.doi.org/10.1007/s11606-015-3572-3

Gigerenzer, G., Gaissmaier, W., Kurz-Milcke, E., Schwartz, L. M., & Woloshin, S. (2007). Helping doctors and patients make sense of health statistics. *Psychological Science in the Public Interest: A Journal of the American Psychological Society, 8*(2), 53–96. http://dx.doi.org/10.1111/j.1539-6053.2008.00033.x

Gigerenzer, G., & Gray, J. A. M. (2013). Launching the century of the patient. In G. Gigerenzer & J. A. M. Gray (Eds.), *Better doctors, better patients, better decisions: Envisioning health care 2020* (1st ed., Vol. 6). Cambridge, MA: The MIT Press.

Gilbody, S., Bower, P., Fletcher, J., Richards, D., & Sutton, A. J. (2006). Collaborative care for depression: A cumulative meta-analysis and review of longer-term outcomes. *Archives of Internal Medicine, 166*(21), 2314–2321. http://dx.doi.org/10.1001/archinte.166.21.2314

Glasgow, R. E., & Toobert, D. J. (2000). Brief, computer-assisted diabetes dietary self-management counseling: Effects on behavior, physiologic outcomes, and quality of life. *Medical Care, 38*(11), 1062–1073.

Goold, S. D., Biddle, A. K., Klipp, G., Hall, C. N., & Danis, M. (2005). Choosing healthplans all together: A deliberative exercise for allocating limited health care resources. *Journal of Health Politics, Policy and Law, 30*(4), 563–601.

Green, J. M., & Baston, H. A. (2003). Feeling in control during labor: Concepts, correlates, and consequences. *Birth, 30*(4), 235–247.

Greene, J., & Hibbard, J. H. (2012). Why does patient activation matter? An examination of the relationships between patient activation and health-related outcomes. *Journal of General Internal Medicine, 27*(5), 520–526. http://dx.doi.org/10.1007/s11606-011-1931-2

Greene, J., Hibbard, J. H., Sacks, R., Overton, V., & Parrotta, C. D. (2015). When patient activation levels change, health outcomes and costs change, too. *Health Affairs, 34*(3), 431–437. http://dx.doi.org/10.1377/hlthaff.2014.0452

Greenfield, S., Billimek, J., Sorkin, D. H., & Kaplan, S. H. (2014, June). *Comparative effectiveness of patient participation training vs diabetes education in low socioeconomic status patients with type 2 diabetes: A pragmatic randomized trial of coached care.* Poster presented at the 74th Scientific Sessions of the American Diabetes Association, San Fransisco, CA.

Greenfield, S., Kaplan, S., & Ware, J. E. (1985). Expanding patient involvement in care. Effects on patient outcomes. *Annals of Internal Medicine, 102*(4), 520–528.

Greenfield, S., Kaplan, S. H., Ware, J. E., Yano, E. M., & Frank, H. J. (1988). Patients' participation in medical care: Effects on blood sugar control and quality of life in diabetes. *Journal of General Internal Medicine, 3*(5), 448–457.

Guadagnoli, E., & Ward, P. (1998). Patient participation in decision-making. *Social Science & Medicine (1982), 47*(3), 329–339.

Gurol-Urganci, I., de Jongh, T., Vodopivec-Jamsek, V., Car, J., & Atun, R. (2012). Mobile phone messaging for communicating results of medical investigations. *Cochrane Database of Systematic Reviews, 6*, CD007456. http://dx.doi.org/10.1002/14651858.CD007456.pub2

Gustafson, D. H., Hawkins, R., Pingree, S., McTavish, F., Arora, N. K., Mendenhall, J., . . . Salner, A. (2001). Effect of computer support on younger women with breast cancer. *Journal of General Internal Medicine, 16*(7), 435–445.

Hall, J., Peat, M., Birks, Y., Golder, S., PIPS Group, Entwistle, V., . . . Wright, J. (2010). Effectiveness of interventions designed to promote patient involvement to enhance safety: A systematic review. *Quality & Safety in Health Care, 19*(5), e10. http://dx.doi.org/10.1136/qshc.2009.032748

Hamine, S., Gerth-Guyette, E., Faulx, D., Green, B. B., & Ginsburg, A. S. (2015). Impact of mHealth chronic disease management on treatment adherence and patient outcomes: A systematic review. *Journal of Medical Internet Research, 17*(2), e52. http://dx.doi.org/10.2196/jmir.3951

Harrington, J., Noble, L. M., & Newman, S. P. (2004). Improving patients' communication with doctors: A systematic review of intervention studies. *Patient Education and Counseling, 52*(1), 7–16. http://dx.doi.org/10.1016/S0738-3991(03)00017-X

Harrison, M. J., Kushner, K. E., Benzies, K., Rempel, G., & Kimak, C. (2003). Women's satisfaction with their involvement in health care decisions during a high-risk pregnancy. *Birth, 30*(2), 109–115.

Hawley, S. T., Lantz, P. M., Janz, N. K., Salem, B., Morrow, M., Schwartz, K., . . . Katz, S. J. (2007). Factors associated with patient involvement in surgical treatment decision making for breast cancer. *Patient Education and Counseling, 65*(3), 387–395. http://dx.doi.org/10.1016/j.pec.2006.09.010

Heisler, M., Bouknight, R. R., Hayward, R. A., Smith, D. M., & Kerr, E. A. (2002). The relative importance of physician communication, participatory decision making, and patient understanding in diabetes self-management. *Journal of General Internal Medicine, 17*(4), 243–252.

Hibbard, J. H., & Greene, J. (2013). What the evidence shows about patient activation: Better health outcomes and care experiences; fewer data on costs. *Health Affairs, 32*(2), 207–214. http://dx.doi.org/10.1377/hlthaff.2012.1061

Hibbard, J. H., Greene, J., & Daniel, D. (2010). What is quality anyway? Performance reports that clearly communicate to consumers the meaning of quality of care. *Medical Care Research and Review, 67*(3), 275–293. http://dx.doi.org/10.1177/1077558709356300

Hibbard, J. H., Greene, J., Sacks, R., & Overton, V. (2015). Does compensating primary care providers to produce higher quality make them more or less patient centric? *Medical Care Research and Review, 72*(4), 481–495. http://dx.doi.org/10.1177/1077558715586291

Hibbard, J. H., Greene, J., & Tusler, M. (2009). Improving the outcomes of disease management by tailoring care to the patient's level of activation. *American Journal of Managed Care, 15*(6), 353–360.

Hibbard, J. H., Mahoney, E. R., Stock, R., & Tusler, M. (2007). Do increases in patient activation result in improved self-management behaviors? *Health Services Research, 42*(4), 1443–1463. http://dx.doi.org/10.1111/j.1475-6773.2006.00669.x

Hibbard, J. H., & Peters, E. (2003). Supporting informed consumer health care decisions: Data presentation approaches that facilitate the use of information in choice. *Annual Review of Public Health, 24*, 413–433. http://dx.doi.org/10.1146/annurev.publhealth.24.100901.141005

Hibbard, J. H., Peters, E., Dixon, A., & Tusler, M. (2007). Consumer competencies and the use of comparative quality information: It isn't just about literacy. *Medical Care Research and Review, 64*(4), 379–394. http://dx.doi.org/10.1177/1077558707301630

Hibbard, J. H., Slovic, P., Peters, E., & Finucane, M. L. (2002). Strategies for reporting health plan performance information to consumers: Evidence from controlled studies. *Health Services Research, 37*(2), 291–313.

Higgins, J., & Begoray, D. (2013). Exploring the borderlands between media and health: Conceptualizing "critical media health literacy." *Journal of Media Literacy Education, 4*(2). Retrieved from http://digitalcommons.uri.edu/jmle/vol4/iss2/4

Hull, S. K., & Broquet, K. (2007). How to manage difficult patient encounters. *Family Practice Management, 14*(6), 30–34.

Huntington, B., & Kuhn, N. (2003). Communication gaffes: A root cause of malpractice claims. *Proceedings (Baylor University Medical Center), 16*(2), 157–161.

Hurwitz, L. M., Cullen, J., Elsamanoudi, S., Kim, D. J., Hudak, J., Colston, M., . . . Rosner, I. L. (2016). A prospective cohort study of treatment decision-making for prostate cancer following participation in a multidisciplinary clinic. *Urologic Oncology, 34*(5), 233.e17–233.e25. http://dx.doi.org/10.1016/j.urolonc.2015.11.014

Institute of Medicine. (2000). *To err is human: Building a safer health system.* Washington, DC: National Academies Press.

Institute of Medicine. (2001). *Crossing the quality chasm: A new health system for the 21st century.* Washington, DC: National Academies Press.

Institute of Medicine. (2008). *Cancer care for the whole patient: Meeting psychosocial health needs.* Washington, DC: National Academies Press.

Jefferson, L., Bloor, K., Birks, Y., Hewitt, C., & Bland, M. (2013). Effect of physicians' gender on communication and consultation length: A systematic review and meta-analysis. *Journal of Health Services Research & Policy, 18*(4), 242–248. http://dx.doi.org/10.1177/1355819613486465

Jelinek, M., Vale, M. J., Liew, D., Grigg, L., Dart, A., Hare, D. L., & Best, J. D. (2009). The COACH program produces sustained improvements in cardiovascular risk factors and adherence to recommended medications-two years follow-up. *Heart, Lung & Circulation, 18*(6), 388–392. http://dx.doi.org/10.1016/j.hlc.2009.06.001

Johnson, B., Abraham, M., Conway, J., Simmons, L., Edgman-Levitan, S., Sodomka, P., . . . Ford, D. (2008, April). Partnering with patients and families to design a patient- and family-centered health care system: Recommendations and promising practices. Institute for Patient- and Family-Centered Care and Institute for Healthcare Improvement. Retrieved from http://www.ipfcc.org/pdf/PartneringwithPatientsandFamilies.pdf

Jolls, T., & Wilson, C. (2014). The core concepts: Fundamental to media literacy yesterday, today and tomorrow. *Journal of Media Literacy Education, 6*(2), 68–78.

Jomeen, J. (2004). The importance of assessing psychological status during pregnancy, childbirth and the postnatal period as a multidimensional construct: A literature review. *Clinical Effectiveness in Nursing, 8*(3–4), 143–155. http://dx.doi.org/10.1016/j.cein.2005.02.001

Kaphingst, K. A., Weaver, N. L., Wray, R. J., Brown, M. L. R., Buskirk, T., & Kreuter, M. W. (2014). Effects of patient health literacy, patient engagement and a system-level health literacy attribute on patient-reported outcomes: A representative statewide survey. *BMC Health Services Research, 14*, 475. http://dx.doi.org/10.1186/1472-6963-14-475

Kaplan, S. H. (1999). Coaching children to participate in healthcare decision making. *The Quality Letter for Healthcare Leaders, 11*(1), 11–14.

Kaplan, S. H., Billimek, J., Sorkin, D. H., Ngo-Metzger, Q., & Greenfield, S. (2010). Who can respond to treatment? Identifying patient characteristics related to heterogeneity of treatment effects. *Medical Care, 48*(Suppl. 6), S9–S16. http://dx.doi.org/10.1097/MLR.0b013e3181d99161

Kaplan, S. H., Billimek, J., Sorkin, D. H., Ngo-Metzger, Q., & Greenfield, S. (2013). Reducing racial/ethnic disparities in diabetes: The Coached Care (R2D2C2) Project. *Journal of General Internal Medicine, 28*(10), 1340–1349. http://dx.doi.org/10.1007/s11606-013-2452-y

Kaplan, S. H., Dukes, K. A., Sullivan, L. M., Tripp, T. J., & Greenfield, S. (1996). Is passivity a risk factor for poor health outcomes? *Journal of General Internal Medicine, 11*(Suppl. 1), 76.

Kaplan, S. H., Gandek, B., Greenfield, S., Rogers, W., & Ware, J. E. (1995). Patient and visit characteristics related to physicians' participatory decision-making style: Results from the medical outcomes study. *Medical Care, 33*(12), 1176–1187.

Kaplan, S. H., Greenfield, S., Gandek, B., Rogers, W. H., & Ware, J. E. (1996). Characteristics of physicians with participatory decision-making styles. *Annals of Internal Medicine, 124*(5), 497–504.

Kaplan, S. H., Greenfield, S., & Ware, J. E. (1989). Assessing the effects of physician-patient interactions on the outcomes of chronic disease. *Medical Care, 27*(Suppl. 3), S110–S127.

Katz, M. G., Jacobson, T. A., Veledar, E., & Kripalani, S. (2007). Patient literacy and question-asking behavior during the medical encounter: A mixed-methods analysis. *Journal of General Internal Medicine, 22*(6), 782–786. http://dx.doi.org/10.1007/s11606-007-0184-6

Kim, J., Braun, B., & Williams, A. D. (2013). Understanding health insurance literacy: A literature review. *Family and Consumer Sciences Research Journal, 42*(1), 3–13. http://dx.doi.org/10.1111/fcsr.12034

Kim, S., Molina, Y., Glassgow, A. E., Berrios, N., Guadamuz, J., & Calhoun, E. (2015). The effects of navigation and types of neighborhoods on timely follow-up of abnormal mammogram among Black women. *Medical Research Archives, 2*(3), 1–17.

Kindler, C. H., Szirt, L., Sommer, D., Häusler, R., & Langewitz, W. (2005). A quantitative analysis of anaesthetist-patient communication during the pre-operative visit. *Anaesthesia, 60*(1), 53–59. http://dx.doi.org/10.1111/j.1365-2044.2004.03995.x

Klasnja, P., & Pratt, W. (2012). Healthcare in the pocket: Mapping the space of mobile-phone health interventions. *Journal of Biomedical Informatics, 45*(1), 184–198. http://dx.doi.org/10.1016/j.jbi.2011.08.017

Kravitz, R. L., Epstein, R. M., Feldman, M. D., Franz, C. E., Azari, R., Wilkes, M. S., . . . Franks, P. (2005). Influence of patients' requests for direct-to-consumer advertised antidepressants: A randomized controlled trial. *Journal of the American Medical Association, 293*(16), 1995–2002. http://dx.doi.org/10.1001/jama.293.16.1995

Kravitz, R. L., Franks, P., Feldman, M. D., Tancredi, D. J., Slee, C. A., Epstein, R. M., . . . Jerant, A. (2013). Patient engagement programs for recognition and initial treatment of depression in primary care: A randomized trial. *Journal of the American Medical Association, 310*(17), 1818–1828. http://dx.doi.org/10.1001/jama.2013.280038

Kreuter, M. W., Farrell, D. W., Olevitch, L. R., & Brennan, L. K. (1999). *Tailoring health messages: Customizing communication with computer technology.* Mahwah, NJ: Routledge.

Kuppermann, M., Norton, M. E., Gates, E., Gregorich, S. E., Learman, L. A., Nakagawa, S., . . . Nease, R. F. (2009). Computerized prenatal genetic testing decision-assisting tool: A randomized controlled trial. *Obstetrics and Gynecology, 113*(1), 53–63. http://dx.doi.org/10.1097/AOG.0b013e31818e7ec4

Kuppermann, M., Pena, S., Bishop, J. T., Nakagawa, S., Gregorich, S. E., Sit, A., . . . Norton, M. E. (2014). Effect of enhanced information, values clarification, and removal of financial barriers on use of prenatal genetic testing: A randomized clinical trial. *Journal of the American Medical Association, 312*(12), 1210–1217. http://dx.doi.org/10.1001/jama.2014.11479

Lawson, P. J., & Flocke, S. A. (2009). Teachable moments for health behavior change: A concept analysis. *Patient Education and Counseling, 76*(1), 25–30. http://dx.doi.org/10.1016/j.pec.2008.11.002

Lee, Y.-Y., & Lin, J. L. (2010). Do patient autonomy preferences matter? Linking patient-centered care to patient-physician relationships and health outcomes. *Social Science & Medicine (1982), 71*(10), 1811–1818. http://dx.doi.org/10.1016/j.socscimed.2010.08.008

Légaré, F., Ratté, S., Stacey, D., Kryworuchko, J., Gravel, K., Graham, I. D., & Turcotte, S. (2010). Interventions for improving the adoption of shared decision making by healthcare professionals. *Cochrane Database of Systematic Reviews,* (5), CD006732. http://dx.doi.org/10.1002/14651858.CD006732.pub2

Légaré, F., Stacey, D., Turcotte, S., Cossi, M.-J., Kryworuchko, J., Graham, I. D., . . . Donner-Banzhoff, N. (2014). Interventions for improving the adoption of shared decision making by healthcare professionals. *Cochrane Database of Systematic Reviews,* Issue No. 9, CD006732. http://dx.doi.org/10.1002/14651858.CD006732.pub3

Levinson, W., Kao, A., Kuby, A., & Thisted, R. A. (2005). Not all patients want to participate in decision making. *Journal of General Internal Medicine, 20*(6), 531–535. http://dx.doi.org/10.1111/j.1525-1497.2005.04101.x

Levinson, W., Roter, D. L., Mullooly, J. P., Dull, V. T., & Frankel, R. M. (1997). Physician-patient communication: The relationship with malpractice claims among primary care physicians and surgeons. *Journal of the American Medical Association, 277*(7), 553–559. http://dx.doi.org/10.1001/jama.1997.03540310051034

Levin-Zamir, D., Lemish, D., & Gofin, R. (2011). Media health literacy (MHL): Development and measurement of the concept among adolescents. *Health Education Research, 26*(2), 323–335. http://dx.doi.org/10.1093/her/cyr007

Lin, H., & Wu, X. (2014). Intervention strategies for improving patient adherence to follow-up in the era of mobile information technology: A systematic review and meta-analysis. *PLOS ONE, 9*(8), e104266. http://dx.doi.org/10.1371/journal.pone.0104266

Lindner, H., Menzies, D., Kelly, J., Taylor, S., & Shearer, M. (2003). Coaching for behaviour change in chronic disease: A review of the literature and the implications for coaching as a self-management intervention. *Australian Journal of Primary Health, 9*(3), 177–185.

Loh, A., Leonhart, R., Wills, C. E., Simon, D., & Härter, M. (2007). The impact of patient participation on adherence and clinical outcome in primary care of depression. *Patient Education and Counseling, 65*(1), 69–78. http://dx.doi.org/10.1016/j.pec.2006.05.007

Loh, A., Simon, D., Wills, C. E., Kriston, L., Niebling, W., & Härter, M. (2007). The effects of a shared decision-making intervention in primary care of depression: A cluster-randomized controlled trial. *Patient Education and Counseling, 67*(3), 324–332. http://dx.doi.org/10.1016/j.pec.2007.03.023

Longtin, Y., Sax, H., Leape, L. L., Sheridan, S. E., Donaldson, L., & Pittet, D. (2010). Patient participation: Current knowledge and applicability to patient safety. *Mayo Clinic Proceedings, 85*(1), 53–62. http://dx.doi.org/10.4065/mcp.2009.0248

Lorig, K. R., Ritter, P., Stewart, A. L., Sobel, D. S., Brown, B. W., Bandura, A., . . . Holman, H. R. (2001). Chronic disease self-management program: 2-year health status and health care utilization outcomes. *Medical Care, 39*(11), 1217–1223.

Luckett, R., Pena, N., Vitonis, A., Bernstein, M. R., & Feldman, S. (2015). Effect of patient navigator program on no-show rates at an academic referral colposcopy clinic. *Journal of Women's Health, 24*(7), 608–615. http://dx.doi.org/10.1089/jwh.2014.5111

Madathil, K. C., Rivera-Rodriguez, A. J., Greenstein, J. S., & Gramopadhye, A. K. (2015). Healthcare information on YouTube: A systematic review. *Health Informatics Journal, 21*(3), 173–194. http://dx.doi.org/10.1177/1460458213512220

Malik, S., Billimek, J., Greenfield, S., Sorkin, D. H., Ngo-Metzger, Q., & Kaplan, S. H. (2013). Patient complexity and risk factor control among multimorbid patients with type 2 diabetes: Results from the R2D2C2 study. *Medical Care, 51*(2), 180–185. http://dx.doi.org/10.1097/MLR.0b013e318273119b

Mansell, D., Poses, R. M., Kazis, L., & Duefield, C. A. (2000). Clinical factors that influence patients' desire for participation in decisions about illness. *Archives of Internal Medicine, 160*(19), 2991–2996. http://dx.doi.org/10.1001/archinte.160.19.2991

Marcano Belisario, J. S., Huckvale, K., Greenfield, G., Car, J., & Gunn, L. H. (2013). Smartphone and tablet self management apps for asthma. *Cochrane Database of Systematic Reviews, 11*, CD010013. http://dx.doi.org/10.1002/14651858.CD010013.pub2

Mayer, M. L. (2008). On being a "difficult" patient. *Health Affairs, 27*(5), 1416–1421. http://dx.doi.org/10.1377/hlthaff.27.5.1416

Mbah, O., Ford, J. G., Qiu, M., Wenzel, J., Bone, L., Bowie, J., . . . Dobs, A. S. (2015). Mobilizing social support networks to improve cancer screening: The COACH randomized controlled trial study design. *BMC Cancer, 15*, 907. http://dx.doi.org/10.1186/s12885-015-1920-7

McGuckin, M., Waterman, R., Storr, I. J., Bowler, I. C., Ashby, M., Topley, K., & Porten, L. (2001). Evaluation of a patient-empowering hand hygiene programme in the UK. *The Journal of Hospital Infection, 48*(3), 222–227. http://dx.doi.org/10.1053/jhin.2001.0983

Miserandino, M. (2000). *Insights into social psychology, 2003 edition.* Boston, MA: Pearson Custom.

Misono, A. S., Cutrona, S. L., Choudhry, N. K., Fischer, M. A., Stedman, M. R., Liberman, J. N., . . . Shrank, W. H. (2010). Healthcare information technology interventions to improve cardiovascular and diabetes medication adherence. *American Journal of Managed Care, 16*(Suppl. 12), SP82–92.

Mosen, D. M., Schmittdiel, J., Hibbard, J., Sobel, D., Remmers, C., & Bellows, J. (2007). Is patient activation associated with outcomes of care for adults with chronic conditions? *The Journal of Ambulatory Care Management, 30*(1), 21–29.

Mühlbacher, A. C., & Juhnke, C. (2013). Patient preferences versus physicians' judgement: Does it make a difference in healthcare decision making? *Applied Health Economics and Health Policy, 11*(3), 163–180. http://dx.doi.org/10.1007/s40258-013-0023-3

Müller-Engelmann, M., Donner-Banzhoff, N., Keller, H., Rosinger, L., Sauer, C., Rehfeldt, K., & Krones, T. (2013). When decisions should be shared: A study of social norms in medical decision making using a factorial survey approach. *Medical Decision Making: An International Journal of the Society for Medical Decision Making, 33*(1), 37–47. http://dx.doi.org/10.1177/0272989X12458159

Murray, E., Davis, H., Tai, S. S., Coulter, A., Gray, A., & Haines, A. (2001). Randomised controlled trial of an interactive multimedia decision aid on hormone replacement therapy in primary care. *British Medical Journal, 323*(7311), 490–493.

Myers, R. E., Bittner-Fagan, H., Daskalakis, C., Sifri, R., Vernon, S. W., Cocroft, J., . . . Andrel, J. (2013). A randomized controlled trial of a tailored navigation and a standard intervention in colorectal cancer screening. *Cancer Epidemiology, Biomarkers & Prevention: A Publication of the American Association for Cancer Research, Cosponsored by the American Society of Preventive Oncology, 22*(1), 109–117. http://dx.doi.org/10.1158/1055-9965.EPI-12-0701

O'Connor, A. M., Bennett, C., Stacey, D., Barry, M. J., Col, N. F., Eden, K. B., . . . Rovner, D. R. (2007). Do patient decision aids meet effectiveness criteria of the international patient decision aid standards collaboration? A systematic review and meta-analysis. *Medical Decision Making: An International Journal of the Society for Medical Decision Making, 27*(5), 554–574. http://dx.doi.org/10.1177/0272989X07307319

O'Connor, A. M., Rostom, A., Fiset, V., Tetroe, J., Entwistle, V., Llewellyn-Thomas, H., . . . Jones, J. (1999). Decision aids for patients facing health treatment or screening decisions: Systematic review. *British Medical Journal, 319*(7212), 731–734. http://dx.doi.org/10.1136/bmj.319.7212.731

Ohmann, C., & Kuchinke, W. (2009). Future developments of medical informatics from the viewpoint of networked clinical research. Interoperability and integration. *Methods of Information in Medicine, 48*(1), 45–54.

Ong, S. W., Jassal, S. V., Miller, J. A., Porter, E. C., Cafazzo, J. A., Seto, E., . . . Logan, A. G. (2016). Integrating a smartphone-based self-management system into usual care of advanced CKD. *Clinical Journal of the American Society of Nephrology, 11*(6), 1054–1062. http://dx.doi.org/10.2215/CJN.10681015

Paling, J. (2006). *Helping patients understand risks: 7 simple strategies for successful communication* (2nd ed.). Gainesville, FL: The Risk Communication Institute.

Parchman, M. L., Zeber, J. E., & Palmer, R. F. (2010). Participatory decision making, patient activation, medication adherence, and intermediate clinical outcomes in type 2 diabetes: A STARNet study. *Annals of Family Medicine, 8*(5), 410–417. http://dx.doi.org/10.1370/afm.1161

Patient. (n.d.-a). Retrieved from http://www.merriam-webster.com/dictionary/patient

Patient. (n.d.-b). Retrieved from http://www.oxforddictionaries.com/us/definition/american_english/patient

Peters, E., Hibbard, J., Slovic, P., & Dieckmann, N. (2007). Numeracy skill and the communication, comprehension, and use of risk-benefit information. *Health Affairs, 26*(3), 741–748. http://dx.doi.org/10.1377/hlthaff.26.3.741

Polsky, D., Keating, N. L., Weeks, J. C., & Schulman, K. A. (2002). Patient choice of breast cancer treatment: Impact on health state preferences. *Medical Care, 40*(11), 1068–1079. http://dx.doi.org/10.1097/01.MLR.0000032188.93444.20

Pop-Eleches, C., Thirumurthy, H., Habyarimana, J. P., Zivin, J. G., Goldstein, M. P., de Walque, D., . . . Bangsberg, D. R. (2011). Mobile phone technologies improve adherence to antiretroviral treatment in a resource-limited setting: A randomized controlled trial of text message reminders. *AIDS, 25*(6), 825–834. http://dx.doi.org/10.1097/QAD.0b013e32834380c1

Potter, W. J. (2004). *Theory of media literacy: A cognitive approach*. Thousand Oaks, CA: Sage.

Primack, B. A., Carroll, M. V., McNamara, M., Klem, M. L., King, B., Rich, M., . . . Nayak, S. (2012). Role of video games in improving health-related outcomes: A systematic review. *American Journal of Preventive Medicine, 42*(6), 630–638. http://dx.doi.org/10.1016/j.amepre.2012.02.023

Rask, K. J., Ziemer, D. C., Kohler, S. A., Hawley, J. N., Arinde, F. J., & Barnes, C. S. (2009). Patient activation is associated with healthy behaviors and ease in managing diabetes in an indigent population. *The Diabetes Educator, 35*(4), 622–630. http://dx.doi.org/10.1177/0145721709335004

Remmers, C., Hibbard, J., Mosen, D. M., Wagenfield, M., Hoye, R. E., & Jones, C. (2009). Is patient activation associated with future health outcomes and health-care utilization among patients with diabetes? *The Journal of Ambulatory Care Management, 32*(4), 320–327. http://dx.doi.org/10.1097/JAC.0b013e3181ba6e77

Reyna, V. F., Nelson, W. L., Han, P. K., & Dieckmann, N. F. (2009). How numeracy influences risk comprehension and medical decision making. *Psychological Bulletin, 135*(6), 943–973. http://dx.doi.org/10.1037/a0017327

Roepke, S. K., & Grant, I. (2011). Toward a more complete understanding of the effects of personal mastery on cardiometabolic health. *Health Psychology: Official Journal of the Division of Health Psychology, American Psychological Association, 30*(5), 615–632. http://dx.doi.org/10.1037/a0023480

Roter, D. L., & Hall, J. A. (2004). Physician gender and patient-centered communication: A critical review of empirical research. *Annual Review of Public Health, 25*, 497–519. http://dx.doi.org/10.1146/annurev.publhealth.25.101802.123134

Roter, D. L., Hall, J. A., Kern, D. E., Barker, L. R., Cole, K. A., & Roca, R. P. (1995). Improving physicians' interviewing skills and reducing patients' emotional distress: A randomized clinical trial. *Archives of Internal Medicine, 155*(17), 1877–1884.

Rotter, J. B. (1982). *The development and applications of social learning theory: Selected papers*. New York, NY: Praeger.

Ryan, J., & Sysko, J. (2007). The contingency of patient preferences for involvement in health decision making. *Health Care Management Review, 32*(1), 30–36.

Sakala, C., & Corry, M. P. (2008). *Evidence-based maternity care: What it is and what it can achieve* (Print). New York, NY: Millbank Memorial Fund. Retrieved from http://www.milbank.org/wp-content/files/documents/0809Maternity Care/0809MaternityCare.html

Salyers, M. P., Matthias, M. S., Spann, C. L., Lydick, J. M., Rollins, A. L., & Frankel, R. M. (2009). The role of patient activation in psychiatric visits. *Psychiatric Services, 60*(11), 1535–1539. http://dx.doi.org/10.1176/appi.ps.60.11.1535

Sanders, A. R. J., van Weeghel, I., Vogelaar, M., Verheul, W., Pieters, R. H. M., de Wit, N. J., & Bensing, J. M. (2013). Effects of improved patient participation in primary care on health-related outcomes: A systematic review. *Family Practice, 30*(4), 365–378. http://dx.doi.org/10.1093/fampra/cmt014

Sandhu, H., Adams, A., Singleton, L., Clark-Carter, D., & Kidd, J. (2009). The impact of gender dyads on doctor–patient communication: A systematic review. *Patient Education and Counseling, 76*(3), 348–355. http://dx.doi.org/10.1016/j.pec.2009 .07.010

Sarkar, I. N. (2010). Biomedical informatics and translational medicine. *Journal of Translational Medicine, 8*, 22. http://dx.doi.org/10.1186/1479-5876-8-22

Say, R., Robson, S., & Thomson, R. (2011). Helping pregnant women make better decisions: A systematic review of the benefits of patient decision aids in obstetrics. *British Medical Journal Open, 1*(2), e000261. http://dx.doi.org/10.1136/ bmjopen-2011-000261

Schillinger, D., Grumbach, K., Piette, J., Wang, F., Osmond, D., Daher, C., . . . Bindman, A. B. (2002). Association of health literacy with diabetes outcomes. *Journal of the American Medical Association, 288*(4), 475–482.

Schwappach, D. L. B. (2010). Review: Engaging patients as vigilant partners in safety: A systematic review. *Medical Care Research and Review, 67*(2), 119–148. http://dx.doi.org/10.1177/1077558709342254

Schwartz, L. M., & Woloshin, S. (2011). Communicating uncertainties about prescription drugs to the public: A national randomized trial. *Archives of Internal Medicine, 171*(16), 1463–1468. http://dx.doi.org/10.1001/archinternmed.2011.396

Seeman, M., & Seeman, T. E. (1983). Health behavior and personal autonomy: A longitudinal study of the sense of control in illness. *Journal of Health and Social Behavior, 24*(2), 144–160.

Seeman, T. E. (1991). Personal control and coronary artery disease: How generalized expectancies about control may influence disease risk. *Journal of Psychosomatic Research, 35*(6), 661–669.

Shay, L. A., & Lafata, J. E. (2014). Understanding patient perceptions of shared decision making. *Patient Education and Counseling, 96*(3), 295–301. http://dx .doi.org/10.1016/j.pec.2014.07.017

Shively, M. J., Gardetto, N. J., Kodiath, M. F., Kelly, A., Smith, T. L., Stepnowsky, C., . . . Larson, C. B. (2013). Effect of patient activation on self-management in patients with heart failure. *Journal of Cardiovascular Nursing, 28*(1), 20–34. http://dx.doi .org/10.1097/JCN.0b013e318239f9f9

Sleath, B., Ayala, G. X., Washington, D., Davis, S., Williams, D., Tudor, G., . . . Gillette, C. (2011). Caregiver rating of provider participatory decision-making style and caregiver and child satisfaction with pediatric asthma visits. *Patient Education and Counseling, 85*(2), 286–289. http://dx.doi.org/10.1016/j.pec.2010.09.016

Sleath, B., Callahan, L., DeVellis, R. F., & Sloane, P. D. (2005). Patients' perceptions of primary care physicians' participatory decision-making style and communication about complementary and alternative medicine for arthritis. *Journal of Alternative and Complementary Medicine, 11*(3), 449–453. http://dx.doi .org/10.1089/acm.2005.11.449

Sleath, B., Roter, D., Chewning, B., & Svarstad, B. (1999). Asking questions about medication: Analysis of physician-patient interactions and physician perceptions. *Medical Care, 37*(11), 1169–1173.

Smith, S. G., Pandit, A., Rush, S. R., Wolf, M. S., & Simon, C. J. (2016). The role of patient activation in preferences for shared decision making: Results from a national survey of U.S. adults. *Journal of Health Communication, 21*(1), 67–75. http://dx.doi.org/10.1080/10810730.2015.1033115

Smith, S. K., Dixon, A., Trevena, L., Nutbeam, D., & McCaffery, K. J. (2009). Exploring patient involvement in healthcare decision making across different education and functional health literacy groups. *Social Science & Medicine (1982), 69*(12), 1805–1812. http://dx.doi.org/10.1016/j.socscimed.2009.09.056

Smith, M., Saunders, R., Stuckhardt, L., McGinnis, J. M., Committee on the Learning Health Care System in America & Institute of Medicine. (2013). *Best care at lower cost: The path to continuously learning health care in America.* Washington, DC: National Academies Press. Retrieved from http://nap.edu/13444

Sox, H. C., & Greenfield, S. (2009). Comparative effectiveness research: A report from the Institute of Medicine. *Annals of Internal Medicine, 151*(3), 203–205.

Stacey, D., Légaré, F., Col, N. F., Bennett, C. L., Barry, M. J., Eden, K. B., . . . Wu, J. H. (2014). Decision aids for people facing health treatment or screening decisions. *Cochrane Database of Systematic Reviews.* Retrieved from http://onlinelibrary.wiley.com/doi/10.1002/14651858.CD001431.pub4/abstract

Stalmeier, P. F. M., van Tol-Geerdink, J. J., van Lin, E. N. J. T., Schimmel, E., Huizenga, H., van Daal, W. A. J., & Leer, J.-W. (2007). Doctors' and patients' preferences for participation and treatment in curative prostate cancer radiotherapy. *Journal of Clinical Oncology: Official Journal of the American Society of Clinical Oncology, 25*(21), 3096–3100. http://dx.doi.org/10.1200/JCO.2006.07.4955

Stewart, M. A. (1995). Effective physician-patient communication and health outcomes: A review. *Canadian Medical Association Journal, 152*(9), 1423–1433.

Tai-Seale, M., Foo, P. K., & Stults, C. D. (2013). Patients with mental health needs are engaged in asking questions, but physicians' responses vary. *Health Affairs, 32*(2), 259–267. http://dx.doi.org/10.1377/hlthaff.2012.0962

Tait, A. R., Voepel-Lewis, T., Brennan-Martinez, C., McGonegal, M., & Levine, R. (2012). Using animated computer-generated text and graphics to depict the risks and benefits of medical treatment. *American Journal of Medicine, 125*(11), 1103–1110. http://dx.doi.org/10.1016/j.amjmed.2012.04.040

Tait, A. R., Zikmund-Fisher, B. J., Fagerlin, A., & Voepel-Lewis, T. (2010). Effect of various risk/benefit trade-offs on parents' understanding of a pediatric research study. *Pediatrics, 125*, e1475–82. http://dx.doi.org/10.1542/peds.2009-1796

Tao, D., Xie, L., Wang, T., & Wang, T. (2015). A meta-analysis of the use of electronic reminders for patient adherence to medication in chronic disease care. *Journal of Telemedicine and Telecare, 21*(1), 3–13. http://dx.doi.org/10.1177/1357633X14541041

Thom, D. H., Ghorob, A., Hessler, D., Vore, D. D., Chen, E., & Bodenheimer, T. A. (2013). Impact of peer health coaching on glycemic control in low-income patients with diabetes: A randomized controlled trial. *Annals of Family Medicine, 11*(2), 137–144. http://dx.doi.org/10.1370/afm.1443

Thom, D. H., Hessler, D., Willard-Grace, R., DeVore, D., Prado, C., Bodenheimer, T., & Chen, E. H. (2015). Health coaching by medical assistants improves patients' chronic care experience. *American Journal of Managed Care, 21*(10), 685–691.

Thom, D. H., Willard-Grace, R., Hessler, D., DeVore, D., Prado, C., Bodenheimer, T., & Chen, E. (2015). The impact of health coaching on medication adherence in patients with poorly controlled diabetes, hypertension, and/or hyperlipidemia:

A randomized controlled trial. *Journal of the American Board of Family Medicine, 28*(1), 38–45. http://dx.doi.org/10.3122/jabfm.2015.01.140123

Thompson, R., & Miller, Y. D. (2014). Birth control: To what extent do women report being informed and involved in decisions about pregnancy and birth procedures? *BMC Pregnancy and Childbirth, 14,* 62. http://dx.doi.org/10.1186/1471 -2393-14-62

Transforming Maternity Care Symposium Steering Committee, Angood, P. B., Armstrong, E. M., Ashton, D., Burstin, H., Corry, M. P., . . . Salganicoff, A. (2010). Blueprint for action: Steps toward a high-quality, high-value maternity care system. *Women's Health Issues: Official Publication of the Jacobs Institute of Women's Health, 20*(Suppl. 1), S18–S49. http://dx.doi.org/10.1016/j.whi.2009.11.007

Transforming Maternity Care Vision Team, Carter, M. C., Corry, M., Delbanco, S., Foster, T. C.-S., Friedland, R., . . . Simpson, K. R. (2010). 2020 vision for a high-quality, high-value maternity care system. *Women's Health Issues: Official Publication of the Jacobs Institute of Women's Health, 20*(Suppl. 1), S7–S17. http://dx.doi .org/10.1016/j.whi.2009.11.006

Trevena, L. J., Zikmund-Fisher, B. J., Edwards, A., Gaissmaier, W., Galesic, M., Han, P. K. J., . . . Woloshin, S. (2013). Presenting quantitative information about decision outcomes: A risk communication primer for patient decision aid developers. *BMC Medical Informatics and Decision Making, 13*(Suppl. 2), S7. http://dx .doi.org/10.1186/1472-6947-13-S2-S7

Tunzi, M. (2001). Can the patient decide? Evaluating patient capacity in practice. *American Family Physician, 64*(2), 299–306.

Turner, B. J., Hollenbeak, C. S., Liang, Y., Pandit, K., Joseph, S., & Weiner, M. G. (2012). A randomized trial of peer coach and office staff support to reduce coronary heart disease risk in African-Americans with uncontrolled hypertension. *Journal of General Internal Medicine, 27*(10), 1258–1264. http://dx.doi .org/10.1007/s11606-012-2095-4

Vale, M. J., Jelinek, M. V., Best, J. D., Dart, A. M., Grigg, L. E., Hare, D. L., . . . McNeil, J. J. (2003). Coaching patients on achieving cardiovascular health (coach): A multicenter randomized trial in patients with coronary heart disease. *Archives of Internal Medicine, 163*(22), 2775–2783. http://dx.doi.org/10.1001/ archinte.163.22.2775

Vernon, J., Trujillo, A., Rosenbaum, S., & DeBuono, B. (2007). *Low health literacy: Implications for national health policy.* Washington, DC: Department of Health Policy, School of Public Health and Health Services, The George Washington University. Retrieved from http://hsrc.himmelfarb.gwu.edu/sphhs_policy _facpubs/172

Veroff, D., Marr, A., & Wennberg, D. E. (2013). Enhanced support for shared decision making reduced costs of care for patients with preference-sensitive conditions. *Health Affairs, 32*(2), 285–293. http://dx.doi.org/10.1377/hlthaff.2011.0941

Vlemmix, F., Warendorf, J. K., Rosman, A. N., Kok, M., Mol, B. W. J., Morris, J. M., & Nassar, N. (2013). Decision aids to improve informed decision-making in pregnancy care: A systematic review. *British Journal of Obstetrics and Gynaecology: An International Journal of Obstetrics and Gynaecology, 120*(3), 257–266. http:// dx.doi.org/10.1111/1471-0528.12060

Wang, M. L., Gallivan, L., Lemon, S. C., Borg, A., Ramirez, J., Figueroa, B., . . . Rosal, M. C. (2015). Navigating to health: Evaluation of a community health center patient navigation program. *Preventive Medicine Reports, 2,* 664–668. http://dx.doi.org/10.1016/j.pmedr.2015.08.002

Wegwarth, O., Schwartz, L. M., Woloshin, S., Gaissmaier, W., & Gigerenzer, G. (2012). Do physicians understand cancer screening statistics? A national survey of primary care physicians in the United States. *Annals of Internal Medicine, 156*(5), 340–349. http://dx.doi.org/10.7326/0003-4819-156-5-201203060-00005

Weingart, S. N., Zhu, J., Chiappetta, L., Stuver, S. O., Schneider, E. C., Epstein, A. M., . . . Weissman, J. S. (2011). Hospitalized patients' participation and its impact on quality of care and patient safety. *International Journal for Quality in Health Care, 23*(3), 269–277. http://dx.doi.org/10.1093/intqhc/mzr002

Wells, K. J., Lee, J.-H., Calcano, E. R., Meade, C. D., Rivera, M., Fulp, W. J., & Roetzheim, R. G. (2012). A cluster randomized trial evaluating the efficacy of patient navigation in improving quality of diagnostic care for patients with breast or colorectal cancer abnormalities. *Cancer Epidemiology, Biomarkers & Prevention: A Publication of the American Association for Cancer Research, Cosponsored by the American Society of Preventive Oncology, 21*(10), 1664–1672. http://dx.doi.org/10.1158/1055-9965.EPI-12-0448

West, S. L., Squiers, L. B., McCormack, L., Southwell, B. G., Brouwer, E. S., Ashok, M., . . . Sullivan, H. W. (2013). Communicating quantitative risks and benefits in promotional prescription drug labeling or print advertising. *Pharmacoepidemiology and Drug Safety, 22*(5), 447–458. http://dx.doi.org/10.1002/pds.3416

Wicks, P., Lowe, M., Gabriel, S., Sikirica, S., Sasane, R., & Arcona, S. (2015). Increasing patient participation in drug development. *Nature Biotechnology, 33*(2), 134–135. http://dx.doi.org/10.1038/nbt.3145

Willard-Grace, R., Chen, E. H., Hessler, D., DeVore, D., Prado, C., Bodenheimer, T., & Thom, D. H. (2015). Health coaching by medical assistants to improve control of diabetes, hypertension, and hyperlipidemia in low-income patients: A randomized controlled trial. *Annals of Family Medicine, 13*(2), 130–138. http://dx.doi.org/10.1370/afm.1768

Willard-Grace, R., DeVore, D., Chen, E. H., Hessler, D., Bodenheimer, T., & Thom, D. H. (2013). The effectiveness of medical assistant health coaching for low-income patients with uncontrolled diabetes, hypertension, and hyperlipidemia: Protocol for a randomized controlled trial and baseline characteristics of the study population. *BMC Family Practice, 14,* 27. http://dx.doi.org/10.1186/1471-2296-14-27

Woloshin, S., Schwartz, L. M., & Welch, H. G. (2007). The effectiveness of a primer to help people understand risk: Two randomized trials in distinct populations. *Annals of Internal Medicine, 146*(4), 256–265. http://dx.doi.org/10.7326/0003-4819-146-4-200702200-00004

Woloshin, S., Schwartz, L. M., & Welch, H. G. (2008). *Know your chances: Understanding health statistics.* Berkeley: University of California Press. Retrieved from http://www.ncbi.nlm.nih.gov/books/NBK115435

World Health Organization. (2013). Exploring patient participation in reducing health-care-related safety risks. Retrieved from http://www.euro.who.int/__data/assets/pdf_file/0010/185779/e96814.pdf

Xu, K. T. (2004). The combined effects of participatory styles of elderly patients and their physicians on satisfaction. *Health Services Research, 39*(2), 377–392. http://dx.doi.org/10.1111/j.1475-6773.2004.00233.x

Yeh, J. (2014). Improving evidence-based practices through health literacy. *Journal of the American Medical Association Internal Medicine, 174*(8), 1413. http://dx.doi.org/10.1001/jamainternmed.2014.847

Zikmund-Fisher, B. J., Couper, M. P., Singer, E., Ubel, P. A., Ziniel, S., Fowler, F. J., . . . Fagerlin, A. (2010). Deficits and variations in patients' experience with making 9 common medical decisions: The DECISIONS survey. *Medical Decision Making: An International Journal of the Society for Medical Decision Making, 30*(Suppl. 5), 85S–95S. http://dx.doi.org/10.1177/0272989X10380466

CONCLUSION

CHAPTER  17

SUMMARY AND CONCLUSION

DENISE G. OSBORN-HARRISON

Each chapter has offered observations, ideas, reflections, and recommendations that, when considered in the aggregate, provide a rich venue for a more person-focused approach to health care management.

Although at a technical level, a person-focused approach offers much to still discuss, in the first chapter the basic model of person-focused care was developed inductively out of the direct experience of a terrible episode in an intensive care unit (ICU). This experience provided a clear example of why it is important to look through the abstract and reified role of the typical patient in order to better see the actual needs of the real person who is living inside that role.

This example then led to the identification of four core principles designed to escalate the lived experience of each person receiving care into a management priority for all health care professionals. These core principles were not proposed as part of a definitive theory or doctrine, but rather as the starting point for further development of a more person-aware approach to health care management. The four core principles are presented, each with a question to help with further thinking:

> **Principle One: The patient is not a person:** Do you demonstrate through words and behavior that every patient is a unique person who has fears, values, and preferences that directly impact the way in which he or she should receive medical care?

> **Principle Two: "Caring about" is a prerequisite to managing the "caring for" patients:** Do you understand how to move beyond a rote application of medical protocols so that patients feel like you care about them while you are caring for them?

> **Principle Three: Quality of care is more than just a clinical outcome:** As a health care professional, do you measure quality of medical care only by clinical outcomes or are you also looking at ways to address the millions of little personal tragedies experienced by people all over the country (and the world) caused by a lack of access to needed health care services?

> **Principle Four: Every health care professional has an impact on the personal experience of care:** Do you actively support and help to create an organizational culture that expects every health care professional to have a positive impact on the personal experience of care?

These four underlying principles of person-focused care were then used to frame a general and very basic question for the contributing experts to answer through their respective chapters:

How might health care services be better managed so that the people being treated as patients fare better than they currently do?

In Section I, clinicians and other health care experts examined how to incorporate a more person-focused approach into care with a variety of medical settings. While aligning *medical protocols* with best practices is nonnegotiable for the practice of medicine, adhering to those protocols in a way that shows you *care for and care about a patient* need not take more time. Through language and behavior, the health care professional can achieve a connection with the patient that will generate patient satisfaction data. Correlations between that data and clinical outcomes can then be explored. Success stories and best practices should be communicated to staff on an ongoing basis to achieve optimal process improvement. This requires both enhanced interaction between medical staff and patients, and support for targeted data tracking. The manager is responsible for socializing these practices and proving their intrinsic value.

Some key questions for further thought and development include:

- In your position as a health care manager, do you measure and correlate provider perceptions with patient satisfaction to improve processes?
- What evidence can you gather that reflects that your team supports a movement away from a physician-centric approach to the delivery of health care to a person-focused approach?
- Do you as a leader exhibit empathy for others, including patients, families of patients, clinicians, and staff? How do you teach others to effectively communicate empathy?
- How can physicians assist with transforming the ICU into a venue where ongoing positive interaction between patients and their families leads to measurable health outcomes?
- Does your organization track and mitigate cases of post–intensive care syndrome? If so, how do they use the data to improve postdischarge outcomes?
- Has your organization created a family support zone in the ICU?
- Do health care professionals in your organization receive ongoing training to improve their communication skills? How do you measure improvement and avoid problem situations between patients and clinicians?

Section II shifted the perspective from clinical settings to a system-level management perspective. Overall, this section provided evidence that everyone within a given system of care, regardless of position, has an impact of the personal experience of care provided through that system. Chapters examined how such areas as payment and reimbursement, legal and regulatory compliance, policy, informatics, supply chain management, and quality improvement can all be better managed to improve the personal experience of patients. These chapters are of particular importance to those who view such roles in a health care system as a purely technical, business-oriented function. Each of these chapters makes the case, in theory and in practice, that every management decision made within a system of care, regardless of its location within the organization, can have a direct impact on the personal experience of a patient. As reflected by the Seven Pillars approach, such a shift to a more person-focused perspective can provide a platform for a powerful tool for reducing medical errors.

The following questions can help further this type of thinking for making systems of care more person focused:

- How do payment policies affect the personal experience of care?
- How can person-focused care improve the bottom line on an enterprise level?
- Do laws and regulations preclude a person-focused care environment from reaching full potential?
- Can regulatory compliance mandates be implemented to better support a positive personal experience of care?
- What kind of data should be collected to fully reflect patient thoughts, feelings, and concerns in a way that can impact future internal and large external public policy debates?
- How can supplies and other materials needed to provide health care services be best managed to improve the patient's personal experience?
- How can quality improvement strategies designed to improve clinical patient outcomes be modified to expand the focus on the personal experience within and outside a system of care?

Section III moved the discussion from the concerns of clinicians and system managers to the direct personal experiences of the patient. Given the emotional component of many health care situations, it is sometimes odd that health care professionals may need to be reminded to include family and other supporting people into the patients' experience of their care. The need to bring family into the patient equation is underscored by the development of empathy and understanding among all clinical and nonclinical staff.

Although this section started off with a call for health care professionals to improve their understanding of the "emotional" side of patient care, the next chapter made a powerful case that doing so is not just about "feelings," it is also about reducing the frequency of unnecessary and, many times, fatal medical errors.

This section ended with a history of the patient's role through the last decade. Although many aspects of this role have changed and morphed over time, the unaddressed fears and dread experienced by some patients have remained constant through it all. Addressing such worries should be central to the teaching of health care professionals, to their organizations, and to all who care about others.

Some questions for further thought include:

- Why are family advisory councils effective in enhancing the patient experience? How can I implement one in a way that aligns with best practices?

- Why is it necessary to assist patients with understanding their various roles and to master "patienthood?"
- How does greater patient participation lead to better health behaviors, health outcomes, and a heightened patient experience?
- How do I further develop my ability to practice empathy?
- What sort of protocols should be in place to systematically incorporate the personal experience of care into new systems that reduce medical errors?
- Can I recognize fear when it is being communicated through behaviors and words by patients?

Overall, a health care culture that empowers every staff member to *positively impact person-focused care* says that everyone matters. It also spreads the responsibility to ensure that patients feel cared about across and beyond the entire enterprise. At a minimum, this means that no one individual, such as the physician, for example, is tasked with ensuring an optimal patient experience. For the health care manager, it is not enough to simply communicate support for a culture of coordinated collaboration across an organization. Rather, the manager as an influencer of change must understand how to inspire the staff and mobilize them to achieve a common goal of improving care through actively caring about all the people who are in need of care.

CONCLUSION

A person-focused approach to health care management asks the health care professional to remember the importance of caring about the real people living inside the patient being treated. In the current context of new technologies, data systems, funding limitations, political debates, and global challenges, it can be easy to lose sight of people.

Becoming a more person-focused health care professional is not an easy path. This perspective demands that the manager watch more carefully, listen harder, and continuously question and affirm that he or she is truly treating the person and not just the patient.

A commitment to a person-focused approach means that a manager must find an entry point in his or her organization to create an opportunity for leading changes in the way people are being treated as patients. Such changes may be small, medium, or large, but the need for change remains an urgent priority to those who will suffer through a lack of personal attention to their care.

CASE STUDY

Sometime in the future, unanimous national legislation is signed into law by the president to reinvent the entire U.S. health care system. You are appointed to serve on a high-level, national task force charged with designing the new system. At the first meeting of the task force, the goals of the legislation are discussed and four goals for the new system are outlined. The goals of the new system are:

(continued)

CASE STUDY (continued)

Goal 1: It must be based on the principles of person-focused care.

Goal 2: It must be cost-efficient, improve clinical quality, and be easily accessible.

Goal 3: It must be designed to be compatible with best medical practices.

Goal 4: It must be able to quickly adapt to and support ongoing technological innovations.

Issues to Consider

Using these four goals as your guide, how would you answer the following questions?

1. How can the principles of person-focused care be built into the way health care services are routinely provided?

2. How would a system that would ensure maximum cost-efficiency, better clinical quality, and improved access to health care services be best organized and financed?

3. How can a person focus to care be fully integrated into best medical practices?

4. How can the personal experience of all those in need remain paramount in a context of rapid technological innovation?

5. What is the role of health care managers in leading efforts to improve the personal experience of all people in need of care and treatment?

INDEX